STUDENT STUDY GUIDE
TO ACCOMPANY

MODERN AUDITING

SIXTH EDITION

WILLIAM C. BOYNTON
California Polytechnic State University at San Luis Obispo

WALTER G. KELL
University of Michigan

PREPARED BY

STEPHEN W. WHEELER
University of the Pacific

John Wiley & Sons, Inc.
New York · Chichester · Brisbane · Toronto · Singapore

ISBN 0-471-59690-6

Printed in the United States of America

10 9 8 7 6 5 4 3 2 1

To The Student

This study guide is provided to facilitate your study of *Modern Auditing* by William C. Boynton and Walter G. Kell. It is important to recognize that the guide is a supplement to and not a substitute for *Modern Auditing*.

The guide contains the following materials for each chapter in the textbook: (a) a chapter outline, (b) chapter highlights, (c) 25 true or false statements, (d) 15 completion statements, and (e) 20 multiple-choice questions. Many of the multiple choice questions have been taken from professional examinations; others have been prepared by the authors. At the end of each chapter, solutions are provided to allow you to assess immediately your comprehension of the material.

There are a number of ways in which this guide may be used with the textbook. Our suggested approach is as follows:

1. Read the chapter outline in the study guide to get an overview of the text chapter contents.
2. Carefully read and study the text chapter.
3. Read the chapter highlights in the study guide.
4. Answer the statements and questions in the study guide for the chapter and then compare your solutions with the solutions provided. For any incorrect answers, refer back to the textbook for a discussion of the point you have missed.
5. Answer the end-of-chapter questions in the textbook that have been assigned by your professor.

When used as suggested above, this study guide should significantly enhance and reinforce your understanding of *Modern Auditing*.

The study guide should be helpful in preparing for examinations in your auditing course. It should also be useful in preparing for the Auditing section of the Uniform CPA Examination, the Financial Accounting and Reporting and Decision Analysis and Information Systems parts of the Certified Management Accountant Examination, and the Theory and Practice sections of the Certified Internal Auditor Examination.

Stephen W. Wheeler
William C. Boynton
Walter G. Kell

CONTENTS

Chapter 1

Auditing and the Public Accounting Profession

A. CHAPTER OUTLINE

I. Introduction to Contemporary Auditing

  A. Auditing Defined

  B. Types of Audits

   1. Financial Statement Audit

   2. Compliance Audit

   3. Operational Audit

  C. Types of Auditors

   1. Independent Auditors

   2. Internal Auditors

   3. Government Auditors

II. The Public Accounting Profession: An Historical Perspective

  A. The Roots of Auditing

  B. Rise of the U.S. Profession

III. Services Performed by CPA Firms

  A. Attest Services

   1. Audit

   2. Examination

   3. Review

   4. Agreed-upon Procedures

  B. Nonattest Services

   1. Accounting

   2. Tax

        3. Consulting

  IV.   Organizations Associated with the Public Accounting Profession

     A. Private Sector Organizations

        1. American Institute of Certified Public Accountants (AICPA)

        2. State Societies of Certified Public Accountants

        3. Practice Units (CPA Firms)

        4. Accounting Standard Setting Bodies (FASB, GASB)

     B. Public Sector Organizations

        1. State Boards of Accountancy

        2. Securities and Exchange Commission (SEC)

        3. U.S. General Accounting Office (GAO)

        4. Internal Revenue Service (IRS)

        5. State and Federal Courts

        6. U.S. Congress

  V.   Regulatory Framework for Ensuring Quality Services

     A. Standard Setting

        1. Quality Control Standards

     B. Firm Regulation

     C. Self-Regulation (Peer Review)

        1. Division for CPA Firms

        2. Quality Review Division

     D. Government Regulation (SEC, Courts)

  VI.   Summary

B. CHAPTER HIGHLIGHTS

1. **Auditing** may be defined as a systematic process of objectively obtaining and evaluating evidence regarding assertions about economic actions and events to ascertain the degree of correspondence between those assertions and established criteria and communicating the results to interested users.

2. Audits are generally classified into three categories:
    a. A **financial statement audit** involves obtaining and evaluating evidence about an entity's statements for the purpose of expressing an opinion on whether they are presented fairly in conformity with established criteria--usually GAAP.
    b. A **compliance audit** involves obtaining and evaluating evidence to determine whether certain financial or operating activities of an entity conform to specified conditions, rules, or regulations.
    c. An **operational audit** involves obtaining and evaluating evidence about an organization's operating activities in relation to specified objectives.

3. Individuals who are engaged to audit economic actions and events are generally classified into three groups: independent auditors, internal auditors, and government auditors.
    a. **Independent auditors** are qualified to perform financial statement audits, compliance audits, and operational audits for clients. Two distinguishing characteristics of independent auditors are:
        • They are independent of the client with respect to the audit and in reporting the results.
        • They are generally licensed to practice as certified public accountants (CPAs).
    b. **Internal auditors** are employees of the company that they audit. They are involved in an independent appraisal activity called internal auditing, which is designed to assist the management of the organization in the effective discharge of its responsibilities.
    c. **Government auditors** are employed by various local, state, and federal governmental agencies.

4. The **focus of early audits** was on finding errors in balance sheet accounts stemming from fraud, professional managers, and absentee owners.

5. During the early 1900's, following the 1929 stock market crash, the **Securities Acts of 1933 and 1934** required audits for publicly-traded companies.

6. The services CPAs may perform are classified as either attest or nonattest services.
    a. An attest service occurs when a CPA firm issues a written communication that expresses a conclusion about the reliability of a written assertion that is the responsibility of another party. There are four types of attest services: **audit, examination, review,** and **agreed-upon procedures.**
    b. A **nonattest service** occurs when a CPA firm does not issue any conclusion about the reliability of a written assertion made by another party. This type of service consists of **accounting, tax,** and **consulting services.**

7. The public accounting profession consists of entities that function within the profession itself and other entities that have a direct influence on the profession.

8. The entities within the profession are as follows:
   a. The **American Institute of Certified Public Accountants (AICPA)** is the public accounting profession's national professional organization. The AICPA operates through a number of divisions including the following that pertain to auditing: Auditing Standards, CPA Firms, Quality Review, and Professional Ethics.
   b. **State societies of certified public accountants** function through small full-time staffs and committees composed of their members. State societies have their own code of professional ethics and they cooperate with the AICPA in areas of mutual interest, such as continuing professional education and ethics.
   c. **State boards of accountancy** set forth the conditions for licensing of CPAs, codes of professional ethics, and mandatory continuing education requirements. Their primary functions are issuing licenses to practice as CPAs, renewing licenses, and suspending or revoking licenses to practice.
   d. **Practice units** are CPA firms that may be organized as a proprietorship, a partnership, or a professional corporation. CPA firms are classified as international, national, regional, or local.

9. The entities that have a direct influence on the profession are as follows:
   a. The **Financial Accounting Standards Board (FASB)** is an independent private body whose primary function is the development of GAAP for the private sector.
   b. The **Governmental Accounting Standards Board (GASB)** is the standard-setting body for the government sector.
   c. The **Securities and Exchange Commission (SEC)** is a federal government agency that exerts considerable influence over auditing and the public accounting profession.
   d. The **U.S. General Accounting Office (GAO)** is a federal agency that issues government auditing standards that CPAs must follow in performing audits of governmental entities.
   e. The **Internal Revenue Service (IRS)** is the division of the U.S. Treasury Department that is responsible for the administration and enforcement of federal tax laws. CPAs who perform tax services must follow IRS rules.

10. The AICPA has established **nine elements of quality control** for CPA firms: (a) independence, (b) assigning personnel to engagements, (c) consultation, (d) supervision, (e) hiring, (f) professional development, (g) advancement, (h) acceptance and continuance of clients, and (i) inspection.

11. To help ensure quality services in the public accounting profession, a **multilevel regulatory framework** has been developed. The levels are as follows:
    a. **Standard setting** by private sector bodies such as the FASB, GASB and the AICPA. The AICPA's **Quality Control Standards** mandates that a CPA firm shall have a system of quality control in effect.
    b. **Firm regulation** is the internal implementation of a quality control system.
    c. **Self (Peer) Regulation** relates to monitoring of quality control by organizations outside the firm, such as the AICPA's **Division for Firms**. The Division for Firms consists of the **SEC Practice Section** for firms that audit SEC-registered companies, and the **Private Companies Practice Section** for those firms that do not.
    d. Firms enrolled in the SEC Practice Section must report to the section's **Quality Control Inquiry Committee (QCIC)** should litigation against the firm arise.
    e. The autonomous **Public Oversight Board** oversees all peer reviews and QCIC inquiries.

C. TRUE OR FALSE STATEMENTS

Indicate in the space provided whether each of the following statements is true or false.

_____ 1. The public accounting profession consists of entities and governmental agencies that function within the profession.

_____ 2. The authority for licensing an individual as a CPA rests with the American Institute of Certified Public Accountants (AICPA).

_____ 3. Practice units (CPA firms) are classified as either international, national, regional, or local.

_____ 4. In an attest service a CPA firm issues a written communication that expresses a conclusion about the reliability of a written assertion that is the responsibility of another party.

_____ 5. The scope of work in performing agreed-upon procedures is less than in an audit but more than in an examination.

_____ 6. The three types of nonattest services are tax, accounting and consulting service.

_____ 7. Auditing is a systematic process of subjectively obtaining and evaluating evidence regarding assertions about economic actions and events.

_____ 8. The three types of audits are (a) financial statement, (b) compliance, and (c) operational.

_____ 9. The focus of early audits was on errors stemming primarily from fraud.

_____ 10. The requirement for audits of publicly-traded companies arose primarily as a result of the 1929 stock market crash.

_____ 11. The Governmental organization that oversees the trading of stock on the public stock exchanges is the Federal Trade Commission.

_____ 12. The major accounting standard setting body for the governmental sector is the Internal Revenue Service.

_____ 13. The primary focus of an operational audit is the fairness of the financial statements.

_____ 14. In a nonattest engagement, no conclusion about the reliability of another party's written assertion is made.

_____ 15. State Societies of CPAs have the authority to rescind a CPA's licence to practice in that state.

_____ 16. The purpose of a peer review is to determine whether a CPA firm has effectively implemented a system of quality control in its practice.

_____ 17. The purpose of the Public Oversight Board is to oversee inquiries made concerning the peer review and quality control monitoring process.

_____ 18. CPAs who audit publicly-traded companies must join the AICPA's SEC Practice Section of the Division for Firms.

_____ 19. For an individual to maintain his/her membership in the AICPA when he/she is active in performing audit engagements, he/she must be associated with a firm that subjects itself to quality control review.

_____ 20. An "unqualified" peer review letter from another CPA firm ensures that the reviewed firm is conducting effective audits.

_____ 21. CPA firms enrolled in the SEC Practice Section of the AICPA's Division for Firms must report any litigation asserting audit deficiencies to the Quality Control Inquiry Committee (QCIC).

_____ 22. CPA firms who do not audit publicly-traded companies cannot belong to the Division for Firms.

_____ 23. The SEC has considerable indirect influence over audit standard setting.

_____ 24. An audit designed to determine whether a company supplying parts to the military has followed all regulations of the Department of Defense would be classified as an operational audit.

_____ 25. An engagement to perform certain agreed-upon procedures is a nonattest engagement.

D. COMPLETION STATEMENTS

Fill in the blanks with the word or words that correctly complete the following statements.

1. The divisions of the American Institute of Certified Public Accountants that affect the audit function are _____, _____, _____, and _____.

2. The regulations of the SEC contain qualifications for determining the _____ of the accountant and standards of_____.

3. In addition to an audit, attest services consist of an _____, a _____, and performing_____.

4. The three types of nonattest services are _____, _____, and _____.

5. Auditing may be defined as a systematic process to ascertain the_____ between assertions and _____and communicating the results to interested parties.

6. The major division of the AICPA that monitors quality control is the _____ for _____, which consists of two sections: the _____ Section and the _____ Section.

7. The two organizations that deal with accounting and auditing standards for the governmental sector are the _____ and the _____.

8. In most cases, professional licensing of accountants involves two requirements: _____ and _____.

9. The independent auditor is responsible in a financial statement audit for _____ management's financial statements and _____ on their fairness.

10. Operational audits would most likely be performed by _____auditors.

11. Compliance audits would most likely be performed by _____auditors.

12. CPA licences are issued and monitored by _____.

13. The two major pieces of governmental legislation that require audits for publicly-traded companies are the_____ and the_____.

14. An attest engagement can be defined as a _____ about a _____ _____ that is the responsibility of a _____ _____.

15. The two organizations primarily concerned with the oversight into alleged audit deficiencies are the _____ and the _____.

E. MULTIPLE CHOICE

Choose the best answer for each of the following questions and enter the identifying letter in the space provided.

_____ 1. Which of the following are the established criteria against which management's assertions are judged in an audit?
   a. Generally Accepted Accounting Principles.
   b. Generally Accepted Auditing Standards.
   c. Consistently Reported Accounting Procedures.
   d. Fairness in application of accounting principles.

_____ 2. Which of the following criteria is unique to the auditor's attest function?
   a. General competence.
   b. Familiarity with the particular industry of which the client is part.
   c. Due professional care.
   d. Independence.

_____ 3. The auditor's judgment concerning the overall fairness of the presentation of financial position, results of operations, and cash flows is applied within the framework of
   a. Quality control.
   b. Generally accepted auditing standards which include the concept of materiality.
   c. The auditor's evaluation of the audited company's internal control.
   d. Generally accepted accounting principles.

_____ 4. Independent auditing can best be described as
   a. A branch of accounting.
   b. A discipline which attests to the results of accounting and other functional operations and data.
   c. A professional activity that measures and communicates financial and business data.
   d. A regulatory function that prevents the issuance of improper financial information.

_____ 5. The essence of the audit function is to
   a. Detect fraud.
   b. Examine individual transactions so that the auditor may certify as to their validity.
   c. Determine whether the client's financial statements are fairly stated.
   d. Assure the consistent application of correct accounting procedures.

_____ 6. A CPA, while performing an audit, strives to achieve independence in appearance in order to
   a. Reduce risk and liability.
   b. Maintain public confidence in the profession.
   c. Become independent in fact.
   d. Comply with the generally accepted standards of fieldwork.

_____ 7. Which of the following is not an attest engagement?
   a. Tax return preparation
   b. Examination
   c. Review
   d. Audit

_____ 8. Which of the following types of auditors would most likely perform a financial statement audit?
   a. Internal auditor
   b. Government auditor
   c. Independent auditor
   d. Compliance auditor

_____ 9. If a CPA is found to be grossly negligent in the conduct of an audit, what is the greatest sanction that can be imposed by the AICPA on the CPA?
   a. Revoke the CPA's license to practice
   b. Revoke the CPA's membership in the AICPA
   c. Require minimum continuing education courses
   d. Invoke monetary penalties

_____ 10. If a CPA is found to be grossly negligent in the conduct of an audit, what is the greatest sanction that can be imposed by the State Board of Accountancy on the CPA?
   a. Revoke the CPA's license to practice
   b. Revoke the CPA's membership in the State Society
   c. Require minimum continuing education courses
   d. Invoke monetary penalties

_____ 11. CPA firms who audit publicly-traded companies must join
   a. The Division for Firms
   b. The Private Company Practice Section
   c. The SEC Practice Section
   d. The Division for Firms and the SEC Practice Section

_____ 12. The primary consequences to the CPA firm when it joins the AICPA's Division for Firms are:
   a. Mandatory minimum number of staff and mandatory individual membership for all professional staff in the AICPA
   b. Mandatory quality control monitoring and mandatory individual membership for all professional staff in the AICPA
   c. Mandatory minimum continuing professional education requirements and mandatory quality control monitoring
   d. Mandatory minimum number of staff and mandatory quality control monitoring

_____ 13. If a CPA who is a member of the AICPA is sued by an publicly-traded audit client for negligence, the CPA may be subject to scrutiny from
   a. The Public Oversight Board
   b. The Quality Control Inquiry Committee
   c. The SEC
   d. all of the above

_____ 14. A CPA may not organize under which of the following organizational structures?
   a. a Partnership
   b. a Professional Corporation
   c. a Limited Liability Partnership
   d. a Proprietorship
   e. all forms are acceptable organizational structures

_____ 15. Which of these is not a part of a multilevel regulatory framework to ensure quality services?
   a. Standard Setting
   b. Self Regulation
   c. Internal Firm Regulation
   d. all of these are levels of regulation for quality

_____ 16. Publicly-traded companies are required to submit an annual financial report (10K) to which regulatory agency?
   a. Public Company Practice Commission (PCPC)
   b. Federal Trade Commission (FTC)
   c. Securities and Exchange Commission (SEC)
   d. Stock Exchange Monitoring Board (SEMB)

_____ 17. The primary focus of an operational audit is
   a. Compliance with established regulations
   b. Efficiency in meeting an organization's operating objectives
   c. Fairness of the operating results in conformity with accounting standards
   d. none of these

_____ 18. The conclusion reached in an engagement to perform agreed upon procedures is
   a. an opinion on the fairness of the accounts affected by the procedures
   b. a summary of the findings of the procedures
   c. a disclaimer of opinion due to the limited nature of the procedures
   d. negative assurance due to the limited nature of the procedures

_____ 19. The primary focus of audits conducted early in the 20th Century was
   a. detection of illegal acts
   b. assessment of financial viability for creditors
   c. balance sheet errors arising from fraud
   d. establishing the existence of reported assets

_____ 20. Conducting a study of which computer system best fits a client's needs is an example of which type of engagement
   a. agreed upon procedures
   b. an operational audit
   c. a consulting service
   d. a feasibility audit

SOLUTIONS

TRUE OR FALSE STATEMENTS

1. False
2. False
3. True
4. True
5. False
6. True
7. False
8. True
9. True

10. True
11. False
12. False
13. False
14. True
15. False
16. True
17. True

18. True
19. True
20. False
21. True
22. False
23. True
24. False
25. False

COMPLETION STATEMENTS

1. Auditing Standards, CPA Firms, Professional Ethics, Quality Review
2. independence, reporting
3. examination, review, agreed-upon procedures
4. tax, accounting, management advisory
5. degree of correspondence, established criteria
6. Division for Firms, SEC Practice, Private Companies Practice
7. GASB, GAO
8. passing the CPA Examination, obtaining practical experience
9. auditing, expressing an opinion
10. internal
11. governmental
12. State Boards of Accountancy
13. SEC Act of 1933, SEC Act of 1934
14. written conclusion, written assertion, third party
15. Public Oversight Board, Quality Control Inquiry Committee

MULTIPLE CHOICE QUESTIONS

1. a	5. c	9. b	13. d	17. b
2. d	6. c	10. a	14. e	18. b
3. d	7. a	11. d	15. d	19. c
4. a	8. c	12. c	16. c	20. c

Chapter 2

Financial Statement Audits and Auditors' Responsibilities

A. CHAPTER OUTLINE

I. Fundamentals Underlying Financial Statement Audits

   A. Relationship Between Accounting and Auditing

   B. Verifiability of Financial Statement Data

   C. Need for Financial Statement Audits

   D. Economic Benefits of an Audit

   E. Limitations of a Financial Statement Audit

II. Independent Auditor Relationships

   A. Management

   B. Board of Directors and Audit Committee

   C. Internal Auditors

   D. Stockholders

III. Auditing Standards

   A. Statements on Auditing Standards (SASs)

   B. General Accepted Auditing Standards (GAAS)

      1. General Standards

      2. Standards of Field Work

      3. Standards of Reporting

   C. Applicability of Auditing Standards

   D. Relationship of Auditing Standards to Auditing Procedures

IV. The Auditor's Report

   A. The Standard Report

      1. Introductory Paragraph

      2. Scope Paragraph

      3. Opinion Paragraph

B. CHAPTER HIGHLIGHTS

1. There are significant differences in methodology and objectives between accounting and auditing.

	Accounting	**Auditing**
Methodology	Analyze events and transactions and then measure, record, classify and summarize them in the accounting records.	Obtain and evaluate evidence concerning management's financial statements and assess conformity with GAAP.
Objective	Prepare and distribute financial statements.	Express an opinion on the fairness of the financial statements and deliver report to client.

2. Auditing is based on the assumption that financial data are **verifiable**. Verifiability is primarily concerned with the availability of evidence attesting to the validity of the data being considered.

3. Financial statement audits are needed because of (a) conflict of interest between user and preparers, (b) the consequence (importance) of the statements to the users' decision making process, (c) complexity of the data, and (d) remoteness of the users from the accounting records. Collectively, these contribute to **information risk** for financial statement users.

4. Among the **economic benefits** of financial statement audits are (a) companies' access to capital markets that require audits, (b) lower cost of capital through reduced information risk to creditors, (c) deterrent to fraud and inefficiency, (d) improvements in controls and operating activities through auditors' suggestions.

5. Certain **inherent limitations** of an audit exist, including (a) cost/benefit tradeoffs resulting in selective testing, (b) timeliness of releasing audited statements, (c) GAAP related limitations, such as alternative accounting principles for a given transaction.

6. In a financial statement audit, the independent auditor maintains professional relationships with four groups: **(a) management, (b) the board of directors and audit committee, (c) internal auditors, and (d) stockholders.**

7. **Audit committees** of boards of directors strengthen the independence of auditors. The functions of an audit committee include (a) nominating the firm to conduct the annual audit, (b) discussing the scope of the audit with the auditor, (c) inviting auditor communications on major problems encountered during the audit, and (d) reviewing the financial statements and the auditor's report on completion of the engagement.

8. The activities of the Auditing Standards Division of the AICPA include the establishment of auditing standards for the profession. One arm of the Division is the **Auditing Standards Board (ASB)** which has been designated as the senior technical body of the AICPA to issue pronouncements on auditing standards.
   a. The pronouncements of the ASB are called **Statements on Auditing Standards (SASs)**. Compliance with SASs is mandatory for AICPA members, who must be prepared to justify departures from such statements.
   b. The ASB provides guidance in implementing its pronouncements by approving interpretations and audit guides issued by the staff of the Auditing Standards Division.

9. The most widely recognized auditing standards are called **generally accepted auditing standards (GAAS)**.
   a. GAAS establish the quality of performance and the overall objectives to be achieved in a financial statement audit.
   b. GAAS are classified into three groups: **general, field work, and reporting**.

10. The **general standards** relate to the qualifications of the auditor and to the quality of the auditor's work. There are three general standards:
    a. Adequate technical training and proficiency.
    b. Independence in mental attitude.
    c. Due professional care.

11. The **field work standards** pertain primarily to the conduct of the audit. There are three field work standards:
    a. Adequate planning and proper supervision.
    b. Understanding the internal control structure.
    c. Obtaining sufficient competent evidential matter.

12. The **reporting standards** relate to communicating the results of the audit. There are four reporting standards:
    a. Financial statements presented in conformity with GAAP.
    b. Consistency in the application of GAAP.
    c. Adequacy of informative disclosures.
    d. Expression of opinion.

13. Auditing standards are applicable in each financial statement audit.
    a. The ten GAAS are interrelated and interdependent. The concepts of **materiality** and **risk** affect the application of all standards, especially the field work and reporting standards.
    b. While auditing standards guide the overall audit, **auditing procedures** are the specific methods used and the acts performed by the auditor during the audit. They may vary from client to client in complying with auditing standards.

14. The auditor's standard report consists of three paragraphs and prescribed language. The three paragraphs are referred to as the **introductory, scope,** and **opinion paragraphs**, respectively.

15. The **introductory paragraph** contains three factual statements that (a) identify the statements audited, (b) state that the statements are the responsibility of management, and (c) indicate the auditor's responsibility is to express an opinion based on the audit.

16. The **scope paragraph** describes the nature and scope of the audit and several limitations of an audit through such wording as:
    a. conducted audit in accordance with GAAS.
    b. plan and perform audit to obtain reasonable assurance that the financial statements are free of material misstatements.
    c. examining, on a test basis, evidence supporting the financial statements.
    d. assessing the accounting principles used and significant estimates made.
    e. evaluating the overall financial statement presentation, reasonable basis for our opinion.

17. The **opinion paragraph** satisfies the four reporting standards. It contains an opinion that the financial statements:
    a. present fairly, in all material respects,
    b. financial position, results of operations, and cash flows
    c. in conformity with GAAP.

18. Both the second standard of reporting, which relates to **consistency,** and the third standard of reporting, which pertains to **adequate disclosures,** are assumed to be met unless there is specific wording to the contrary in the auditor's report.

19. A **departure from the standard report** occurs when the auditor either (a) adds explanatory language to the standard report or (b) expresses other than an **unqualified opinion** on the financial statements.

20. **Explanatory language** may be added to the standard report, for example, when more than one auditing firm is involved in the audit or when the client has made a change in accounting principles in accordance with GAAP.
    a. The explanatory language may be included in each of the three paragraphs of the standard report or in an explanatory paragraph following the opinion paragraph.
    b. In this type of departure, the opinion paragraph continues to express an unqualified opinion.

21. Audit findings may not support an unqualified opinion when either the statements contain a material departure from GAAP or when the auditor has been unable to obtain sufficient competent evidence to have a reasonable basis for an opinion. When an unqualified opinion cannot be expressed, the auditor may express one of the following opinions:
    a. A **qualified opinion** states that except for the effects of the matter(s) to which the qualification relates, the financial statements present fairly ... in conformity with GAAP.
    b. An **adverse opinion** states that the financial statements do not present fairly in conformity with GAAP.
    c. A **disclaimer of opinion** states that the auditor does not express an opinion on the financial statements.

A summary of the types of auditor's reports and circumstances is as follows:

Circumstance	Standard Report	Departures from Standard Report			
		Standard Report with Explanatory Language	Other Types of Opinions		
	Unqualified Opinion	*Unqualified Opinion*	*Qualified*	*Adverse*	*Disclaimer*
Audit completed in accordance with GAAS, financial statements conform to GAAP, and:					
• Circumstances requiring explanatory language do not exist	√				
• Circumstances requiring explanatory language do exist		√			
Financial statements contain a departure from GAAP			√ Material	√ Extremely Material	
Auditor unable to obtain sufficient competent evidence (scope limitation)			√ Material		√ Extremely Material

22. When other than an unqualified opinion is expressed,
    a. the reason(s) for the opinion should be explained in one or more explanatory paragraphs immediately **before** the opinion paragraph, and
    b. there must be reference to the reason(s) in the opinion paragraph followed by appropriate wording for the type of opinion expressed.

23. An audit made in accordance with GAAS is subject to the following **inherent limitations**:
    a. An auditor works within fairly restrictive economic limits which results in selective testing or sampling.
    b. Time constraints on the audit may affect the evidence that can be obtained concerning events and transactions after the balance sheet date.
    c. The established accounting framework permits alternative GAAP and estimates are an inherent part of the accounting process.

24. To highlight the division of responsibilities between management and the independent auditor, many companies include a **report on management's responsibility** in their annual reports to stockholders. This report contains wording about the integrity and objectivity of the financial statements, internal controls, and the independent auditor's access to the board of directors and audit committee.

25. Users of audited financial statements expect auditors to:
    a. perform the audit with technical competence, integrity, independence, and objectivity;
    b. search for and detect material misstatements, whether intentional or unintentional; and
    c. prevent the issuance of misleading financial statements.

    The term **fraudulent financial reporting** has been used to describe the process by which misleading financial statements are issued by publicly held companies.

26. To narrow the **expectation gap**, the ASB issued nine new SASs in the late 1980's. Seven of the SASs either superseded or expanded existing standards.

27. The term **errors** refers to unintentional misstatements or omissions in financial statements, while the term **irregularities** refers to intentional misstatements or omissions.
    a. An audit made in accordance with GAAS should be designed to provide reasonable assurance that errors and irregularities material to the financial statements will be detected.
    b. When the financial statements are materially affected by an irregularity, they are not prepared in conformity with GAAP. If the financial statements are not revised, the auditor should express either a qualified or adverse opinion and disclose all substantive reasons for the opinion in the audit report.
    c. The auditor is required to communicate to the audit committee any material irregularities detected during the audit. However, except in an unusual circumstance such as in response to a subpoena, the auditor has no responsibility to disclose material irregularities to parties outside the client.

28. An **illegal act** refers to such acts as the payment of bribes, the making of illegal political contributions, and the violation of other specific laws and governmental regulations.
    a. Two characteristics of illegal acts influence the auditor's responsibility for detection.
        • The determination of whether an act is illegal is dependent on legal judgment that normally is beyond the auditor's professional competence.
        • Illegal acts vary considerably in their relation to financial statements. Some laws and regulations, such as income tax laws, have a direct and material effect on the financial statements. However, other laws, such as those pertaining to occupational safety and health and to environmental protection, have only an indirect effect on the financial statements.
    b. The auditor's responsibility for misstatements resulting from **illegal acts having a direct and material effect** on the financial statements is the **same as for errors and irregularities**. Thus, he or she should design the audit to detect such illegal acts.
    c. The auditor's responsibility for misstatements from **other illegal acts** is restricted to information that **comes to his or her attention**. Thus, an audit made in accordance with GAAS provides no assurance that all illegal acts will be detected.
    d. The **effects on the auditor's report** and the auditor's responsibility to communicate illegal acts are the **same as for errors and irregularities**.

29. When there is **doubt about the entity's ability to continue as a going concern**, the auditor should (a) obtain information about management's plans to mitigate the conditions or events, and (b) assess the likelihood that such plans can be effectively implemented.

30. When the auditor concludes that there is substantial doubt, the auditor should state this conclusion in the audit report:
    a. If management's disclosures in the financial statements concerning the entity's ability to continue as a going concern are considered adequate by the auditor, an unqualified opinion should be expressed and an explanatory paragraph should be added following the opinion paragraph describing the uncertainty with reference to management's disclosures.
    b. If management's disclosures in the financial statements are considered inadequate by the auditor, there is a departure from GAAP and the auditor should express either a qualified opinion or an adverse opinion and explain the reasons therefore in an explanatory paragraph preceding the opinion paragraph.

C. TRUE OR FALSE STATEMENTS

Indicate in the space provided whether each of the following statements is true or false.

_____ 1. Information risk is the risk that the financial statements may be incorrect, incomplete, or biased.

_____ 2. Conditions that contribute to the need for financial statement audits include conflict of interest and complexity.

_____ 3. Auditing is based on the assumption that financial data are relevant and reliable.

_____ 4. The Auditing Standards Board makes its pronouncements through Statements on Auditing Standards (SASs) which are interpretations of GAAS.

_____ 5. Generally accept auditing standards (GAAS) establish the quality of performance and the overall objectives to be achieved in a financial statement audit.

_____ 6. During a financial statement audit, the auditor can expect to have direct professional contact with management, internal auditors, and stockholders.

_____ 7. A report on management's responsibility highlights the division of responsibilities between management and internal auditors.

_____ 8. The auditor's standard report contains three paragraphs and prescribed language.

_____ 9. The introductory paragraph of the standard audit report identifies the responsibilities of management and the auditor.

_____ 10. The scope paragraph describes the character of the audit and states that the audit provides a reasonable basis for the opinion.

_____ 11. The opinion paragraph contains implicit reference to financial position, results of operations, and cash flows.

_____ 12. An auditor may issue a four paragraph audit report and still express an unqualified opinion.

_____ 13. Whenever a qualified opinion is expressed, the auditor's report must contain an explanatory paragraph and reference must be made in the opinion paragraph to the explanatory paragraph.

_____ 14. A scope limitation will result in expressing either a qualified opinion or an adverse opinion on the financial statements.

_____ 15. Nonconformity with GAAP will result in expressing either a qualified opinion or a disclaimer of opinion on the financial statements.

_____ 16. The term fraudulent financial reporting describes the process by which misleading financial statements are issued by publicly held companies.

_____ 17. The auditor has a responsibility to design the audit to detect all errors or irregularities material to the financial statements.

_____ 18. The auditor's responsibility under GAAS to detect illegal client acts is the same as for material errors and irregularities.

_____ 19. The auditor has no responsibility to evaluate whether there is substantial doubt about the entity's ability to continue as a going concern.

_____ 20. One of the benefits of financial statement audits is the lower cost of capital for companies through a reduction in information risk to creditors.

_____ 21. A limitation of audits is the inherent flexibility in standards allowed under GAAP.

_____ 22. The term expectations gap refers to the difference between what auditors do in an audit and what management wants them to do.

_____ 23. The Auditing Standards Board is part of the Financial Accounting Standards Board.

_____ 24. Consistency in the application of GAAP is assumed in the audit report unless specifically mentioning the inconsistent application of GAAP.

_____ 25. An unqualified opinion implies that the auditor is not qualified to render an opinion because of limitations imposed by the client.

D. COMPLETION STATEMENTS

Fill in the blanks with the word or words that correctly complete the following statements.

1. The pronouncements of the Auditing _____ are called
    _____.

2. Generally accepted auditing standards (GAAS) are grouped into three categories:
    _____, _____, and _____.

3. The auditor's standard report consists of an _____ paragraph, a
    _____ paragraph, and an _____ paragraph.

4. The opinion paragraph of the auditor's standard report contains an explicit assertion that the
    financial statements are presented fairly, in _____, in conformity
    with _____.

5. In addition to an unqualified opinion, the auditor may express a _____ opinion,
    an _____ opinion, or a _____ of opinion.

6. A departure from the standard audit report occurs when the auditor adds _____
    _____ to the report while expressing a (an) _____ opinion.

7. A qualified opinion may result from either a _____ or nonconformity with
    _____.

8. When there is a scope limitation, the auditor may express either a _____ opinion
    or a _____ opinion.

9. The criteria used by management in discharging its responsibility for financial statements are
    _____; the auditor's criteria in auditing financial statements are
    _____.

10. The Treadway Commission recommended that independent public accountants change and
    the auditor's_____ be changed to better communicate the auditor's role
    and that auditing _____ be changed to better reflect the auditor's responsibility
    to detect _____ , _____ , and _____.

11. An audit made in accordance with GAAS should be designed to provide
    _____that errors and irregularities material to the financial statements will
    be _____.

12. An audit made in accordance with GAAS provides _____ that all illegal client
    acts that have a _____ and _____ effect on the financial statements will be
    _____.

13. When the auditor concludes that there is substantial doubt about the entity's ability to continue as a _____ and the client's disclosures are adequate, the auditor should mention this concern in an _____ paragraph _____the opinion paragraph.

14. When the auditor concludes that there is substantial doubt about the entity's ability to continue as a _____ and the client's disclosures are inadequate, the auditor should issue a _____ opinion and mention this concern in an _____ paragraph _____ the opinion paragraph.

15. A Management Responsibility is intended to highlight the _____ of _____ between management and the independent auditor, and includes comments pertaining to _____ and _____, and the independent auditor's access to the _____ and the _____.

E. MULTIPLE CHOICE

Choose the best answer for each of the following questions and enter the identifying letter in the space provided.

_____ 1. An annual shareholders' report includes audited financial statements and contains a management report asserting that the financial statements are the responsibility of management. Is it permissible for the auditor's report to refer to the management report?
   a. No, because the reference may lead to the belief that the auditor is providing assurances about management's representations.
   b. No, because the auditor has no responsibility to read the other information in a document containing audited financial statements.
   c. Yes, provided the reference is included in a separate explanatory paragraph of the auditor's report.
   d. Yes, provided the auditor reads the management report and discovers no material misrepresentation of fact.

_____ 2. How are auditing procedures related to auditing standards?
   a. Auditing standards are applicable to every audit, while auditing procedures may change between different audits.
   b. Auditing procedure are applicable to every audit, while auditing standards may change between different audits.
   c. Auditing standards are simply the methods used to implement auditing procedures.
   d. None of these, the two are unrelated.

_____ 3. Which of these is not a method recommended as a way to narrow the "expectations gap?"
   a. Using clear engagement letters.
   b. Changing the wording of the standard audit report.
   c. Changing auditing standards to clarify auditor responsibilities for detecting errors, irregularities and illegal acts.
   d. All of these methods are recommended.

_____ 4. Which of the following statements about *Statements on Auditing Standards* is correct?
   a. They are issued by the Auditing Standards Board.
   b. They are optional guidelines for practicing auditors who are members of the AICPA.
   c. They do not include GAAS.
   d. They are interpretations which are intended to clarify the meaning of generally accepted auditing standards.

_____ 5. An independent audit is important to readers of financial statements because it:
   a. determines the future stewardship of the management of the company whose financial statements are audited.
   b. measures and communicates financial and business data included in financial statements.
   c. involves the objective examination of and reporting on management-prepared statements.
   d. reports on the accuracy of all information in the financial statements.

_____ 6. Which of the following best describes why an independent auditor is asked to express an opinion on the fair presentation of financial statements?
   a. It is difficult to prepare financial statements that fairly present a company's financial position, results of operations, and cash flows without the expertise of an independent auditor.
   b. It is management's responsibility to seek available independent aid in the appraisal of the financial information shown in its financial statements.
   c. The opinion of an independent party is needed because a company may not be objective with respect to its own financial statements.
   d. It is a customary courtesy that all stockholders of a company receive an independent report of management's stewardship in managing the affairs of the business.

_____ 7. Which of the following is responsible for the fairness of the representations made in financial statements?
   a. Client's management.
   b. Independent auditor.
   c. Audit committee.
   d. AICPA.

_____ 8. The scope paragraph of the auditor's standard report includes all but one of the following statements.
   a. Our responsibility is to express an opinion on these financial statements based on our audit.
   b. We conducted our audit in accordance with generally accepted auditing standards.
   c. An audit includes examining, on a test basis, evidence supporting the amounts and disclosures in the financial statements.
   d. We believe that our audit provides a reasonable basis for our opinion.

_____ 9. In determining the type of opinion to express, an auditor assesses the nature of the reporting qualifications and the materiality of their effects. Materiality will be the primary factor considered in the choice between:
   a. an unqualified opinion and an adverse opinion.
   b. a qualified opinion and an adverse opinion.
   c. a disclaimer of opinion and an adverse opinion.
   d. an unqualified opinion and a disclaimer of opinion.

_____10. When there are limitations on the scope of the audit that preclude the issuance of a standard report, the auditor will issue:
   a. an unqualified opinion with explanatory language.
   b. an adverse opinion or a disclaimer of opinion.
   c. a qualified opinion or a disclaimer of opinion.
   d. a qualified opinion or an adverse opinion.

_____11. When expressing a qualified opinion, the auditor should include a separate explanatory paragraph describing the effects of the qualification. In addition, in the opinion paragraph the auditor should:
   a. make no reference to the explanatory paragraph.
   b. state that the financial statements do not fairly present.
   c. express a disclaimer of opinion.
   d. make reference to the explanatory paragraph.

_____12. When an adverse opinion is expressed, the opinion paragraph should include a direct reference to:
   a. a footnote to the financial statements which discusses the basis for the opinion.
   b. the scope paragraph which discusses the basis for the opinion rendered.
   c. an explanatory paragraph which discusses the basis for the opinion rendered.
   d. the scope limitation.

_____13. As generally conceived, the "audit committee" of a publicly held company should be made up of:
   a. representatives of the major equity interests (bonds, preferred stock, common stock).
   b. the audit partner, the chief financial officer, the legal counsel, and at least one outsider.
   c. representatives from the client's management, investors, suppliers, and customers.
   d. members of the board of directors who are not officers or employees.

_____14. When, in the auditor's judgment, the financial statements are not presented fairly in conformity with generally accepted accounting principles, the auditor will issue a(n):
   a. qualified opinion or adverse opinion.
   b. unqualified opinion with explanatory language.
   c. disclaimer of opinion or qualified opinion.
   d. adverse opinion or disclaimer of opinion.

_____15. The AICPA classifies its generally accepted auditing standards as:
   a. general, field work, and reporting.
   b. general, examination, and evaluation.
   c. general, field work, and evaluation.
   d. personal, field work, and reporting.

_____16. Which of the following factors is most important concerning an auditor's responsibility to detect errors and irregularities?
   a. The susceptibility of the accounting records to intentional manipulations, alterations, and the misapplication of accounting principles.
   b. The probability that unreasonable accounting estimates result from unintentional bias or intentional attempts to misstate the financial statements.
   c. The possibility that management fraud, defalcations, and the misappropriation of assets may indicate the existence of illegal acts.
   d. The risk that mistakes, falsifications, and omissions may cause the financial statements to contain material misstatements.

_____17. If specific information comes to an auditor's attention that implies the existence of possible illegal acts that could have a material, but indirect, effect on the financial statements, the auditor should next:
   a. apply audit procedures specifically directed to ascertaining whether an illegal act has occurred.
   b. seek the advice of an informed expert qualified to practice law as to possible contingent liabilities.
   c. report the matter to an appropriate level of management at least one level above those involved.
   d. discuss the evidence with the client's audit committee, or others with equivalent authority and responsibility.

_____18. The most likely explanation why an audit cannot reasonably be expected to bring all illegal acts by the client to the auditor's attention is that:
   a. illegal acts are perpetrated by management override of internal controls.
   b. illegal acts by clients often relate to operating aspects rather than accounting aspects.
   c. the client's internal controls may be so strong that the auditor performs only minimal substantive testing.
   d. illegal acts may be perpetrated by the only person in the client's organization with access to both assets and the accounting records.

_____19. Which of the following, if material, would be an irregularity?
   a. Mistakes in the application of accounting principles.
   b. Clerical mistakes in the accounting data underlying the financial statements.
   c. Misappropriation of an asset or groups of assets.
   d. Misinterpretations of facts that existed when the financial statements were prepared.

_____20. Which of the following was not addressed by the "expectation gap" auditing standards issued in the late 1980's?
   a. Responsibilities for detection of illegal acts
   b. Consideration of a client's ability to continue as a going concern
   c. Mandatory observation of physical inventories
   d. Responsibilities for detection of client irregularities

SOLUTIONS

TRUE OR FALSE STATEMENTS

1. True	10. True	18. False
2. True	11. False	19. False
3. False	12. True	20. True
4. True	13. True	21. True
5. True	14. False	22. False
6. False	15. False	23. False
7. False	16. True	24. True
8. True	17. True	25. False
9. True		

COMPLETION STATEMENTS

1. Standards Board, Statements on Auditing Standards (SASs)
2. general, field work, and reporting
3. introductory, scope, opinion
4. all material respects, GAAP
5. qualified, adverse, disclaimer
6. explanatory paragraph, unqualified (standard report)
7. scope limitation, GAAP
8. qualified, disclaimer
9. GAAP, GAAS
10. standard report, standards, errors, irregularities, illegal acts
11. reasonable assurance, detected
12. reasonable assurance, direct, material, detected
13. going concern, explanatory, following
14. qualified or adverse, explanatory, preceding
15. division, responsibility, internal controls, internal auditing, board of directors, audit committee

MULTIPLE CHOICE QUESTIONS

1. a	5. c	9. b	13. d	17. a
2. a	6. c	10. c	14. a	18. b
3. a	7. a	11. d	15. a	19. c
4. a	8. a	12. c	16. d	20. c

Chapter 3

Professional Ethics

A. CHAPTER OUTLINE

   I. Ethics and Morality

      A. General Ethics

      B. Professional Ethics

  II. AICPA Code of Professional Conduct

      A. AICPA Professional Ethics Division

      B. Composition of the AICPA Code

      C. Code Definitions

      D. Principles

         1. Responsibilities

         2. The Public Interest

         3. Integrity

         4. Objectivity and Independence

         5. Due Care

         6. Scope and Nature of Services

 III. Rules of Conduct

      A. Rule 101 - Independence

         1. Interpretation 101-1

         2. Other Independence Matters

      B. Rule 102 - Integrity and Objectivity

      C. Rule 201 - General Standards

      D. Rule 202 - Compliance with Standards

      E. Rule 203 - Accounting Principles

      F. Rule 301 - Confidential Client Information

B. CHAPTER HIGHLIGHTS

1. The profession's framework to ensure high quality in the practice of public accounting consists of four components:
   a. **Standard-setting**. The private sector establishes standards for accounting, auditing, ethics, and quality control to govern the conduct of CPAs and CPA firms.
   b. **Firm regulation**. Each CPA firm adopts policies and procedures to assure that practicing accountants adhere to professional standards.
   c. **Self-regulation.** The AICPA has implemented a comprehensive program of self-regulation including mandatory continuing professional education, peer review, audit failure inquiries, and public oversight.
   d. **Government regulation.** Only qualified professionals are licensed to practice, and auditor conduct is monitored and regulated by state boards of accountancy, the SEC, and the courts. The components involve both the private and public sectors.

2. **Professional ethics** are imposed by a profession on its members who voluntarily accept standards of professional behavior more rigorous than those required by law. Ethics evolve over time as the practice of public accounting changes.

3. CPAs are required to comply with at least **three codes of ethics**. They are the codes promulgated by the:
   a. AICPA,
   b. State Society of CPAs of which the CPA is a member, and
   c. State board of accountancy that has granted the CPA a license to practice.

4. The bylaws of the AICPA provide that there should be a **Professional Ethics Division**. The division functions through an executive committee which serves as the Professional Ethics Committee of the AICPA. The committee is responsible for:
   a. Planning the programs for the division's subcommittees and supervising their implementation.
   b. Issuing formal policy statements and pronouncements.
   c. Establishing prima facie violations of the Code or bylaws for possible disciplinary action.
   d. Proposing changes in the Code.

5. There are two sections in the **AICPA's Code of Professional Conduct**:
   a. **Principles** that express the basic tenets of ethical conduct and provide the framework for the Rules (not enforceable).
   b. **Rules** which establish the minimum standards of acceptable conduct in the performance of professional services by members (enforceable).
   The **Professional Ethics Division** also issues interpretations of the rules of conduct which provide guidelines about the scope and applicability of the rules, and ethics rulings which indicate the applicability of the rules to specific cases and circumstances.

6. There are six principles in the Code:
   a. **Responsibilities**: In carrying out their responsibilities as professionals, members should exercise sensitive professional and moral judgements in all their activities.
   b. **The Public Interest**: Members should accept the obligation to act in a way that will serve the public interest, honor the public trust, and demonstrate commitment to professionalism.
   c. **Integrity**: To maintain and broaden confidence, members should perform all professional responsibilities with the highest sense of integrity.
   d. **Objectivity and Independence**: A member should maintain objectivity and be free of conflicts of interest in discharging professional responsibilities. A member in public practice should be independent in fact and appearance when providing auditing and other attestation services.
   e. **Due Care**: A member should observe the profession's technical and ethical standards, strive continually to improve competence and the quality of services, and discharge professional responsibility to the best of the member's ability.
   f. **Scope and Nature of Services**: A member in public practice should observe the Principles of the Code of Professional Conduct in determining the scope and nature of services to be provided.

7. The **rules** are applicable to all members whenever they perform professional services, except that Rules 101, 301, 502, 503 below pertain only to members in public practice.

8. **Rule 101 - Independence** provides that a member in public practice shall be independent in the performance of professional services as required by standards promulgated by bodies designated by Council. The bodies designated are the Auditing Standards Board and the Accounting and Review Services Committee.
   a. Interpretation 101-1 proscribes certain **financial interests** and **business relationships**. The proscription regarding financial interests applies only during the period of the auditors professional engagement and at the time of expressing an opinion. In contrast, the proscription regarding business relationships also extends to the entire period covered by the financial statements.
   b. For purposes of Interpretation 101-1, a member or a member's firm includes:
      • all proprietors, partners, or shareholders in the firm,
      • all professionals in the firm participating in the engagement,
      • all managerial employees of a firm located in an office participating in a significant portion of the engagement, and
      • any entity whose operating, financial, or accounting policies can be controlled by one or more of the persons described above.

9. A member's independence may also be impaired by the following:
   a. In performing **management advisory services** (MAS), a CPA cannot make management decisions. Also, a CPA firm that is a member of the SEC Practice Section of the Division for Firms must refrain from performing certain types of MAS services for SEC clients, such as executive searches.
   b. **Litigation** that results in an adversary position between a client and a CPA or where the CPA is a co-conspirator with the client in withholding information from stockholders would impair the CPA's independence. However, litigation brought by stockholders against CPAs would not necessarily impair independence.

c. **Unpaid fees** will impair independence if, at the time the CPA's report on the client's current year is issued, the fees pertain to professional services provided more than one year prior to the date of the report.

10. Rule 102 - **Integrity and Objectivity** provides that in the performance of any professional service, a member shall maintain objectivity and integrity, shall be free of conflicts of interest, and shall not knowingly misrepresent facts or subordinate his or her judgement to others.

11. Rule 201 - **General Standards** states that a member shall comply with the following standards and with any interpretation thereof by bodies designated by Council:
    a. **Professional Competence**. Undertake only those professional services that the member or member's firm can reasonably expect to be completed with professional competence.
    b. **Due Professional Care**. Exercise due professional care in the performance of professional services.
    c. **Planning and Supervision**. Adequately plan and supervise the performance of professional services.
    d. **Sufficient Relevant Data**. Obtain sufficient relevant data to afford a reasonable basis for conclusions or recommendations in relation to any professional services performed.

12. Rule 202 - **Compliance with Standards** requires that a member who performs auditing, review, compilation, management advisory, tax, or other professional services shall comply with standards promulgated by bodies designated by Council. The **bodies authorized to issue standards** under this rule are the (a) **Auditing Standards Board**, (b) **Accounting and Review Services Committee**, and (c) the **MAS Executive Committee**.

13. Rule 203 - **Accounting Principles** specifies that a member shall not express an opinion that financial statements are presented in conformity with generally accepted accounting principles if such statements or data contain a material departure from an accounting principle promulgated by bodies designated by Council.
    a. The rule provides for an exception when due to unusual circumstances a departure is required to prevent the statements from being misleading.
    b. Council has **authorized two groups to promulgate accounting principles**: the **GASB** and the **FASB**.

14. Rule 301 - **Confidential Client Information** directs that a member in public practice shall not disclose any confidential client information without the specific consent of the client. Exceptions are allowed in connection with:
    a. Making disclosures required by Rules 202 and 203,
    b. Complying with a validly issued and enforceable subpoena or summons,
    c. Reviewing a member's professional practice under AICPA or state society authorization, and,
    d. Initiating a complaint with or responding to any inquiry made by a recognized investigative or disciplinary body.

15. Rule 302 - **Contingent Fees** states that a member in public practice shall not:
     1. Perform for a contingent fee any professional services for, or receive such a fee from, a client for whom the member or member's firm performs:
         a. an audit or review of a financial statement; or
         b. a compilation of a financial statement when the member expects, or reasonably might expect, that a third party will use the financial statement and the member's compilation report does not disclose a lack of independence; or
         c. an examination of prospective financial information; or
     2. Prepare an original or amended tax return or claim for a tax refund for a contingent fee for any client.

     A member's fee may vary with the complexity of the service rendered. Fees are not regarded as being contingent if fixed by courts or other public authorities.

16. Rule 501 - **Acts Discreditable** enables disciplinary action to be taken against a member for unethical acts not specifically covered by other rules. Such acts would include (a) improper retention of client's records, (b) discrimination in employment, (c) failure to follow government auditing standards in governmental audits, (d) negligence in the preparation of financial statements, and (e) acts resulting in the automatic disciplinary provisions.

17. Rule 502 - **Advertising and Other Forms of Solicitation** specifies that a member in public practice shall not seek to obtain clients by advertising or other forms of solicitation in a manner that is false, misleading, or deceptive. Solicitation by the use of coercion, overreaching, or harassing conduct is prohibited.

18. Rule 503 - **Commissions and Referral Fees** states:
     1. **Prohibited commissions**.
         A member in public practice shall not form a commission, recommended or refer to a client any product or service, or for a commission recommend or refer any product or service to be supplied by a client, or receive a commission, when the member or the member's firm also performs for that client:
         a. an audit or review of a financial statement; or
         b. a compilation of a financial statement when the member expects, or reasonably might expect, that a third party will use the financial statement and the member's compilation report does not disclose a lack of independence; or
         c. an examination of prospective financial information.

         This prohibition applies during the period in which the member is engaged to perform any of the services listed above and the period covered by any historical financial statements involved in such listed services.
     2. **Disclosure of permitted commissions**.
         A member in public practice who is not prohibited by this rule from performing services for or receiving a commission and who is paid or expects to be paid a commission shall disclose that fact to any person or entity to whom the member recommends or refers a product or service to which the commission relates.
     3. **Referral fees**.
         Any member who accepts a referral fee for recommending or referring any service of a CPA to any person or entity or who pays a referral fee to obtain a client shall disclose such acceptance or payment to the client.

19. Rule 505 - **Form of Practice and Name** permits a member to practice in the form of a proprietorship, or professional corporation. A member may use a fictitious firm name or indicate a specialization as long as the name is not misleading.

20. **Enforcement of the Rules of Conduct** rests with two groups: the AICPA and state societies of CPAs. The maximum sanction that may be imposed by each group is loss of membership. The AICPA enforcement includes:
    a. Joint Ethics Enforcement Procedures (JEEP),
    b. Joint Trial Board Procedures, and
    c. Automatic disciplinary provisions.

C. TRUE OR FALSE STATEMENTS

Indicate in the space provided whether each of the following statements is true or false.

_____ 1. The regulatory framework consists of standard setting and two types of regulation.

_____ 2. Professional ethics extend beyond moral principles but not above the letter of the law.

_____ 3. The AICPA Code of Professional Conduct consists of two sections: principles and rules.

_____ 4. An AICPA member can be charged with a violation of the principles or rules of the Code.

_____ 5. Under Rule 101 - Independence, a member may not have any direct or indirect financial interest in a client.

_____ 6. Under Rule 101 - Independence, the prohibition against certain business relationships with a client extends from the beginning of the period covered by the financial statements to the time of expressing an opinion.

_____ 7. For purposes of Interpretation 101-1, "a member or a member's firm" includes all individuals participating in the engagement except those who perform only routine clerical functions.

_____ 8. Rule 201 - General Standards is only applicable when a CPA is involved in audit engagements.

_____ 9. Rule 202 - Compliance with Standards requires members to comply with duly promulgated technical standards in all areas of professional service.

_____10. Under Rule 203 - Accounting Principles, the FASB and GASB have been designated as the promulgating bodies for accounting principles.

_____11.   Under Rule 301 - Confidential Client Information, a member may reveal confidential information to a court of law or other recognized investigative or disciplinary body without the client's permission.

_____12.   Under Rule 302 - Contingent Fees, a fee is not considered to be contingent if fixed by courts, or in tax matters, if based on judicial proceedings.

_____13.   It is permissible under Rule 501 - Acts Discreditable to retain essential client records if fees are not paid.

_____14.   Rule 502 - Advertising and Other Forms of Solicitation permits advertising that is informative, objective, and in good taste.

_____15.   Rule 505 - Form of Practice and Name prohibits a member from practicing in the form of a professional corporation.

_____16.   The AICPA's enforcement machinery resides in its Quality Review Division.

_____17.   The bylaws of the AICPA contain automatic disciplinary provisions for certain types of unethical behavior.

_____18.   For a CPA firm to advertise itself as "members of the AICPA" all partners or shareholders must be individual members of the AICPA and the firm must join the Division for Firms of the AICPA.

_____19.   A member CPA may accept a fee for referring a product to a client as long as proper disclosure of the fee is made to the client.

_____20.   A member CPA may own an interest in a mutual fund that invests in the stock of an audit client as long as the indirect interest is immaterial to the CPA.

_____21.   Professional ethics are generally less stringent than standards required by law.

_____22.   A member CPA may not divulge confidential information concerning a client, even if subpoenaed to do so in court.

_____23.   For purposes of determining independence, a CPA's spouse, who is legally separated from the CPA, cannot impair the CPA's independence.

_____24.   A member CPA may not employ self-laudatory or comparative-claim advertising.

_____25.   A member CPA may not jointly own an investment with a client if the investment is closely held and material to the CPA.

D. COMPLETION STATEMENTS

Fill in the blanks with the word or words that correctly complete the following statements.

1. In addition to standard setting, the profession's regulatory framework consists of the following components of regulation: _____, _____, and _____ .

2. The principles of the AICPA Code express the _____ and provide the _____ for the rules of ethical conduct

3. Guidelines about the scope and applicability of the rules of the AICPA Code are issued in the form of _____ while the applicability of the rules to specific cases and circumstances are indicated in _____ .

4. Rule 101 – Independence contains prohibitions against two basic types of involvement with a client: _____ and _____ .

5. The four general standards in Rule 201 are _____, _____ , _____ and _____ .

6. Under Rule 202 - Compliance with Standards, the groups authorized to promulgate standards for auditing, review, and compilation services are the _____ _____ and the _____ .

7. Under Rule 203 - Accounting Principles, departures from GAAP are permitted when due to _____ the client's financial statements would otherwise be _____ .

8. Exceptions permitted under Rule 301 - Confidential Client Information enable the member to fulfill both _____ and _____ responsibilities.

9. Under Rule 501 - Discreditable Acts, disciplinary action may be taken against a member for _____ not specifically covered by other _____ .

10. A CPA should strive to be independent in _____ and in _____ .

11. A CPA may perform accounting services for a non-public audit client as long as the CPA does not assume the role of an _____ or a _____ position.

12. CPA may not jointly invest with a client if the investment is _____ and _____ to the CPA.

13. Litigation that results in an _____ position between the CPA and the client or that links the client and the CPA as _____ impairs the CPA's independence.

14. Acts discreditable to the profession are designated as _____ ,
_____ , _____ , and _____ .

15. A CPA may advertise as long as it is not _____ , _____ , or
_____ .

E. MULTIPLE CHOICE

Choose the best answer for each of the following questions and enter the identifying letter in the space provided.

_____   1. The profession's ethical standards would most likely be considered to have been violated when a CPA
   a. Continued an audit engagement after the commencement of litigation against the CPA alleging excessive fees filed in a stockholders' derivative action.
   b. Represented to a potential client that the CPA's fees were substantially lower than the fees charged by other CPAs for comparable services.
   c. Issued a report on a financial forecast that omitted a caution regarding achievability.
   d. Accepted an MAS consultation engagement concerning data processing services for which the CPA lacked independence.

_____   2. According to the profession's ethical standards, an auditor would be considered independent in which of the following instances?
   a. The auditor's checking account, which is fully insured by a federal agency, is held at a client financial institution.
   b. The auditor is also an attorney who advises the client as its general counsel.
   c. An employee of the auditor donates service as treasurer of a charitable organization that is a client.
   d. The client owes the auditor fees for two consecutive annual audits.

_____   3. The ethical standards of the profession would most likely be considered to be violated if a CPA
   a. Owns a building and leases a portion of the space to an audit client.
   b. Has an insured account with a brokerage firm that is an audit client and the account is used for occasional cash transactions.
   c. Is asked by an audit client to act as a "finder" in the acquisition of another company on a per diem basis.
   d. Searches for and initially screens candidates for the vacant controllership of an audit client.

_____   4. The concept of materiality would be least important to an auditor when considering the
   a. Adequacy of disclosure of a client's illegal act.
   b. Discovery of weaknesses in a client's internal control structure.
   c. Effects of a direct financial interest in the client on the CPA's independence.
   d. Decision whether to use positive or negative confirmations of receivables.

_____ 5. Which of the following statements best explains why the CPA profession has found it essential to promulgate ethical standards and to establish means for ensuring their observance?
   a. Vigorous enforcement of an established code of ethics is the best way to prevent unscrupulous acts.
   b. Ethical standards that emphasize excellence in performance over material rewards establish a reputation for competence and character.
   c. A distinguishing mark of a profession is its acceptance of responsibility to the public.
   d. A requirement for a profession is to establish ethical standards that stress primarily a responsibility to clients and colleagues.

_____ 6. Which one of the following is an enforceable set of pronouncements of an authoritative body designated to establish accounting principles, according to the AICPA Code of Professional Conduct?
   a. AICPA Statements on Standards for Accounting and Review Services.
   b. AICPA Statements of Position.
   c. FASB Interpretations.
   d. FASB Statements of Financial Accounting Concepts.

_____ 7. The AICPA Code of Professional Conduct states that a CPA shall not disclose any confidential information obtained in the course of a professional engagement except with the consent of the client. This rule should be understood to preclude a CPA from responding to an inquiry made by
   a. The trial board of the AICPA.
   b. A CPA-shareholder of the client corporation.
   c. An investigative body of a state CPA society.
   d. An AICPA voluntary quality review body.

_____ 8. A CPA's retention of client records as a means of enforcing payment of an overdue audit fee is an action that is
   a. Not addressed by the AICPA Code of Professional Conduct.
   b. Acceptable if sanctioned by the state laws.
   c. Prohibited under the AICPA Code of Professional Conduct.
   d. A violation of generally accepted auditing standards.

_____ 9. According to the AICPA Rules of Conduct, contingent fees are permitted by CPAs engaged in tax practice because
   a. This practice establishes fees which are commensurate with the value of the services.
   b. Attorneys in tax practice customarily set contingent fees.
   c. Determinations by taxing authorities are a matter of judicial proceedings which do not involve third parties.
   d. The consequences are based upon findings of judicial proceedings or the findings of tax authorities.

_____ 10. Brown, a non-CPA, has a law practice. Brown has recommended one of his clients to Morrison, CPA. Morrison has agreed to pay Brown 10 percent of the fee for services rendered by Morrison to Brown's client and has informed this client about the referral fee. Who, if anyone, is in violation of the Code of Professional Conduct?
   a. Both Brown and Morrison.
   b. Neither Brown nor Morrison.
   c. Only Brown.
   d. Only Morrison.

_____ 11. Below are the names of four CPA firms and pertinent facts relating to each firm. Unless otherwise indicated, the individuals named are CPAs and partners, and there are no other partners. Which firm name and related facts indicates a violation of the AICPA Code of Professional Conduct?
   a. Arthur, Barry, and Clark, CPAs (Clark died about five years ago; Arthur and Barry are continuing the firm).
   b. Dave and Edwards, CPAs (The name of Fredericks, CPA, a third active partner, is omitted from the firm name).
   c. Jones & Co., CPAs, (The firm is a professional corporation and has ten other stockholders who are all CPAs).
   d. George and Howard, CPAs (Howard died three years ago; George is continuing the firm as a sole proprietorship).

_____ 12. Under procedures administered by the Professional Ethics Division of the AICPA, if a member is found in violation of the Code of Professional Conduct, the Joint Trial Board may impose any of the following penalties except
   a. Censure.
   b. Suspension from membership for up to two years.
   c. Expulsion from membership.
   d. Revocation of the member's license to practice.

_____ 13. A CPA's license to practice will ordinarily be suspended or revoked automatically for
   a. Committing an act discreditable to the profession.
   b. Conviction of willful failure to file personal income tax returns.
   c. Refusing to respond to an inquiry by the AICPA practice review committee.
   d. Accepting compensation while honoring a subpoena to appear as an expert witness.

_____ 14. Which of the following would impair the CPA's independence under strict interpretation of the Code of Professional Conduct?
   a. ownership of a material amount of stock in a publicly-traded company which is also 20% owned by an audit client's President
   b. a manager in the Chicago office of a CPA firm owns stock in a company currently audited by the Chicago office
   c. a partner in the Chicago office owns a material interest in a mutual fund which owns a minor amount of stock in a company audited by the New York office
   d. a Chicago client's purchasing agent is the brother of a senior working in the Chicago office, but not on this client
   e. none of these

_____ 15. The CPA may pay a commission to obtain a client for which of the following engagements, provided the client is informed?
   a. Audits
   b. Normal Tax filings
   c. Compilations, where third parties will rely on the statements
   d. Consulting
   e. all of the above

_____ 16. Which of these would be an "Act Discreditable" to the profession by you under the Code of Professional Conduct?
   a. Withholding audit work papers which contain data, to which the client has no other access, from a successor auditor where you have not been paid for the prior year's audit
   b. Being sued for ordinary negligence by your audit client and losing
   c. Making a clerical error on your tax client's tax return and not informing the IRS when you discover the error (your client chooses not to inform the IRS)
   d. Calling the President a "limelight-seeking coward"
   e. none of these

_____ 17. Under the latest Code of Professional Conduct, a contingent fee may be charged on which of the following engagements?
   a. Reviews
   b. Normal tax filings
   c. Audits
   d. Compilations, where third parties will rely on the statements
   e. None of these

_____ 18. Under the latest Code of Professional Conduct, a member of the AICPA may accept a commission for referring business to IBM for recommending its computers to a client in which type of engagement (assuming the client is informed of the commission)?
   a. Audit
   b. Normal tax filings
   c. Reviews
   d. Compilations where third parties will rely on the statements
   e. None of these

_____ 19. Which of the following is not an acceptable form of organization for a CPA practice?
   a. Proprietorship
   b. LLP or LLC
   c. Professional Corporation
   d. General Corporation
   e. Partnership

_____ 20. Which of the following is not an act that results in automatic suspension or termination of membership in the AICPA?
   a. Filing a fraudulent tax return that the member is required to file.
   b. Willful aiding in the preparation of a fraudulent tax return for a client.
   c. Engaging in discriminatory hiring practices.
   d. Conviction of a crime punishable by more than a one year prison term.

SOLUTIONS

TRUE OR FALSE STATEMENTS

1. False
2. False
3. True
4. False
5. False
6. True
7. True
8. False
9. True
10. True
11. True
12. True
13. False
14. True
15. False
16 False
17. True
18. False
19. True
20. True
21. False
22. False
23. False
24. False
25. True

COMPLETION STATEMENTS

1. firm, self, government
2. basic tenets, framework
3. interpretations of the rules of conduct, ethics rulings
4. financial interest, business relationships
5. professional competence, due professional care, planning and supervision, sufficient relevant data
6. Auditing Standards Board, Accounting and Review Services Committee
7. unusual circumstances, misleading
8. professional, legal
9. unethical acts, rules
10. fact, appearance
11. employee, management
12. closely held, material
13. adversarial, co-conspirators
14. improper retention of client records, employment discrimination, negligence, acts resulting in automatic disciplinary provisions
15. false, misleading, deceptive

MULTIPLE CHOICE QUESTIONS

1. c	5. c	9. d	13. b	17. e
2. a	6. c	10. b	14. b	18. b
3. a	7. b	11. d	15. e	19. d
4. c	8. c	12. d	16. b	20. c

Chapter 4

Auditor's Legal Liability

A. CHAPTER OUTLINE

I. The Legal Environment

    A. The Litigation Crisis

    B. The Need for Legal Reform

II. Liability Under Common Law

    A. Liability to Clients

        1. Contract Law

        2. Tort Law

        3. Cases Illustrating Liability to Clients

    B. Liability to Third Parties

        1. Liability to Primary Beneficiaries

        2. Liability to other Beneficiaries

        3. Cases Illustrating Liability to other Beneficiaries

        4. Recent Developments

    C. Common Law Defenses

III. Liability Under Securities Law

    A. Securities Act of 1933

        1. Bringing Suit Under the 1933 Act

        2. Cases Brought Under the 1933 Act

    B. The Securities Exchange Act of 1934

        1. Section 18 Liability

        2. Section 10 Liability

        3. Section 32 Liability

        4. Bringing Suit Under the 1934 Act

        5. Differences Between the 1933 and 1934 Acts

B. CHAPTER HIGHLIGHTS

1. Growing awareness of the **Litigation Crisis** and the **"Deep Pockets"** syndrome resulted in the 1992 formation of the **Coalition to Eliminate Abusive Securities Suits (CEASS)**, a group of manufacturers, retailers, trade associations, insurance underwriters, accounting firms, and joined by the AICPA to lobby for litigation reform. Among the reforms proposed are: **Proportionate Liability instead of Joint and Several Liability** for accountants, **Transfer of Fees** to losers of lawsuits, **Limitations on Punitive Damages**, and **Form of Organization** changes to allow for limits on liability for partners of firms.

2. Under common law, an auditor is liable to (a) clients and (b) third parties. The term **privity of contract** describes the contractual relationship between the auditor and client.

3. Under common law, an auditor may be liable to a client for **breach of contract** by:
   a. Issuing a standard audit report when he or she has not made an audit in accordance with GAAS.
   b. Failing to deliver the audit report by the agreed upon date.
   c. Violating the client's confidential relationship.

4. The auditor may also be liable to the client under tort law. A tort action may be based on:
   a. **Ordinary Negligence**. Failure to exercise that degree of care a person of ordinary prudence (a reasonable person) would exercise under the same circumstances.
   b. **Gross Negligence**. Failure to use even slight care in the circumstances.
   c. **Fraud**. Intentional deception, such as the misrepresentation, concealment, or nondisclosure of a material fact, that results in injury to another.

5. A **third party** is an individual who is not in privity with the parties to a contract.
   a. A third party is a primary beneficiary when identified by name to the auditor as a primary recipient of the auditor's report.
   b. A third party is an other beneficiary when not named as a recipient of the auditor's report.

6. The auditor has always been held liable to all third parties for gross negligence and fraud. The **auditor's liability** for **ordinary negligence**:
   a. Was limited to **primary beneficiaries** for many years by the decision in the **Ultramares** case.
   b. Has been extended in the past 25 years to two classes of **other beneficiaries**: specifically **foreseen parties** and **foreseeable** parties.

7. A specifically **foreseen class** of beneficiaries includes:
   a. A person or one of a limited group of persons for whose benefit and guidance the information is provided.
   b. Recipients the information is intended to influence in a transaction or substantially similar transaction.

8. Under the specifically foreseen class concept:
   a. A CPA may be liable for pecuniary loss to a limited group of persons for **false information** if he or she fails to exercise reasonable care or competence in obtaining or communicating the information.
   b. An intermediate level of **due care** is imposed on the auditor.
   c. The case that extended the auditor's liability for ordinary negligence to this class was **Rusch Factors Inc. v. Levin.**

9. A **foreseeable parties** class of beneficiaries includes:
   a. Individuals or entities whom the auditor either knew or should have known would rely on the report in making business and investment decisions.
   b. All creditors, stockholders, and present and future investors.

10. Under the foreseeable parties class concept:
    a. The auditors duty of due care is extended to anyone who suffers pecuniary loss from relying on the auditor's representation.
    b. The case that ruled auditors could be tried for ordinary negligence for this class was **Rosenblum v. Adler.**

11. The auditor's primary defenses under common law are **due care** or **contributory negligence**. Contributory negligence occurs when conduct on the part of the plaintiff contributes to his or her own harm. Contributory negligence is a defense for the auditor only when the negligence contributes directly to the accountant's failure to perform.

12. An auditor's liability exposure under statutory law derives primarily from the **Securities Act of 1933** and the **Securities Exchange Act of 1934**, both administered by the **Securities and Exchange Commission (SEC)**. The liability of an auditor under statutory law is more extensive than under common law because certain sections of the statutes:
    a. Grant unnamed third parties rights against auditors for ordinary negligence, and
    b. Provide that criminal indictments may be brought against auditors.

13. Suits against auditors under the 1933 Act are usually based on **Section 11** of the Act, which provides that any person acquiring a security described in a registration statement may sue when such statement contains an **untrue statement of a material fact** or **omits to state a material fact** required to make the statements not misleading.
    a. The term **material** is defined by the SEC in the context of "matters about which an average prudent investor ought reasonably to be informed."
    b. A financial statement filed with the SEC is presumed to be misleading whenever a material matter is presented in accordance with an accounting principle that does not have substantial authoritative support, or where the SEC has rules against its use.

14. Under the 1933 Act, the **plaintiff:**
    a. May be any person acquiring securities described in the registration statement, whether or not he or she is a client of the auditor.
    b. Must base the claim on an alleged material false or misleading financial statement contained in the registration statement.

c. Does not have to prove reliance on the false or misleading statement or that the loss suffered was the proximate result of the statement if purchase was made before the issuance of an income statement covering a period of at least 12 months following the effective date of the registration statement.

d. Does not have to prove that the auditors were negligent or fraudulent in certifying the financial statements involved.

15. Under the 1933 Act the **defendant**:
    a. Has the burden of establishing freedom from negligence by proving that he (or she) had made a reasonable investigation and accordingly had reasonable ground to believe, and did believe, that the statements certified were true at the date of the statements and as of the time the registration statement became effective, or
    b. Must establish, by way of defense, that the plaintiff's loss resulted in whole or in part from causes other than the false or misleading statements.

16. In the **BarChris case**, the court concluded that the accounting firm had not established a due diligence defense because the auditor's S-1 review of subsequent events did not meet professional standards.

17. Suits against auditors under the **1934 Act** are usually brought under (a) **Section 18**, which proscribes making false or misleading statements in a filing under the Act, and (b) **Section 10b and Rule 10b-5**, which prohibit the employment of any manipulative or deceptive device or artifice in the purchase or sale of any security.

18. Under both sections of the 1934 Act, the **plaintiff** must prove the existence of a material false or misleading statement, and must prove reliance on such statement and damage resulting from such reliance. However, the responsibility of the plaintiff differs under the two sections in terms of proof of **auditor fraud**. Under Section 18, the plaintiff does not have to prove that the auditor acted fraudulently, but in a Section 10, Rule 10b-5 action, such proof is required.

19. The defendant (auditor) in a **Section 18 suit** must prove that he or she (a) acted in good faith and (b) had no knowledge of the false or misleading statement. This means that the minimum basis for liability is gross negligence.

20. In the **Hochfelder case**, the U.S. Supreme Court held that an auditor is no longer liable to third parties under Section 10b and Rule 10b-5 of the 1934 Act for ordinary negligence.

21. Section 32(a) establishes **criminal liability** on an auditor for "willfully" and "knowingly" making false or misleading statements in reports filed under the 1934 Act. The leading criminal case is United States v. Simon (Continental Vending) in which auditors were convicted for misrepresenting material facts that made the financial statements false and misleading.

22. The **Racketeer Influenced and Corrupt Organization Act (RICO)** is a fraud statute which surpasses the federal securities laws in terms of both breadth and financial consequences to an auditor who performs a deficient audit, and also can subject the violator to criminal penalties or civil remedies.

a. An important element in RICO is a pattern of racketeering activity which includes the distribution of false audit reports for two years.
b. A plaintiff may be awarded triple damages and attorney's fees.
c. To be liable under RICO, there must be 'scienter' or knowledge of the fraud by the auditor.
d. In a 1995 case, **Reves v. Ernst & Young**, the U.S. Supreme Court ruled that RICO suits "require(s) some participation in the operation or management of the enterprise itself." This provides some relief for auditors under RICO unless a court concludes that the auditor's relationship with the client goes way beyond the traditional role of auditing.

23. The AICPA believes professional standards and expert testimony on these standards should be conclusive in legal decisions, as is indicated by the following:
a. The standard of communication required is measured by specific generally accepted accounting principles (GAAP) and GAAS, and in the absence of specific rules or customs by the views of experts (professional CPAs).
b. The jury (or court in a case of trial without jury) is never authorized to question the wisdom of the professional standard.

24. The **SEC's position** on professional standards and expert testimony is:
a. The auditor has an obligation that goes beyond specific GAAP and GAAS to effectively communicate material information.
b. If GAAP and GAAS are found lacking, the SEC will not hesitate to invoke its authority to establish meaningful standards of performance regardless of expert testimony as to professional standards.

25. Recent court cases suggest that a CPA may **minimize the risk of litigation** by (a) using clear engagement letters, (b) thoroughly investigating prospective clients, (c) emphasizing quality of service rather than growth, (d) complying fully with professional pronouncements, (e) recognizing the limitations of professional pronouncements, (f) establishing and maintaining high standards of quality control, and (g) exercising caution in engagements involving clients in financial difficulty.

C. TRUE OR FALSE STATEMENTS

Indicate in the space provided whether each of the following statements is true or false.

_____ 1. Under common law, auditors may be held liable to clients for breach of contract but not for torts.

_____ 2. Ordinary negligence is the failure to use even slight care in the circumstances.

_____ 3. In an audit engagement, the auditor is in privity of contract with the client as an independent contractor.

_____ 4. The critical issue in the 1136 Tenants' case was the failure of the CPA to inform the client of employee wrongdoings, regardless of the type of service rendered.

_____ 5. Under common law, the auditor is liable for fraud to all third parties who have been damaged and who relied on the audited statements.

_____ 6. In the Ultramares case, the judge ruled that CPAs should not be held liable for ordinary negligence to a primary beneficiary.

_____ 7. The specifically foreseen class concept does not extend the CPA's duty to all users of the information provided by the CPA.

_____ 8. The foreseeable parties class of beneficiaries imposes an intermediate level of due care on the accountant.

_____ 9. The case that extended the accountant's liability for ordinary negligence to foreseen parties was Rosenblum v. Adler.

_____10. In most states, contributory negligence is a significant defense for an auditor only when the negligence indirectly contributes to the auditor's failure to perform.

_____11. The liability of an auditor under statutory law is more extensive than under common law.

_____12. Under the 1933 Act, the plaintiff may be any acquirer of the securities described in the registration statement.

_____13. Under the 1933 Act, the plaintiff does not have to prove that the auditor failed to perform the audit in accordance with GAAS.

_____14. The defendant can only avoid liability under Section 18 of the 1934 Act by proving he or she acted in good faith.

_____15. Both the buyer and seller of securities may bring suit under the 1934 Act.

_____16. Section 10b and Rule 10b-5 of the 1934 Act are often referred to as the antifraud provisions.

_____17. The Hochfelder case held that the auditor is no longer liable under Rule 10b-5 of the 1934 Act to third parties for ordinary negligence.

_____18. The Fund of Funds case found that the requisite of scienter was met through the accountant's recklessness.

_____19. In the Continental Vending case, the court ruled that in reporting whether the financial statements are fairly presented, the auditor must only establish compliance with GAAP.

_____20. The provisions of RICO have been extended to losses suffered from fraudulent financial securities offerings and failures of legitimate businesses.

_____21. To be held liable under RICO, the CPA must have some participation in the operation or management of the company perpetrating the fraud.

_____22. The use of engagement letters is recommended as a way to help avoid litigation.

_____23. In the BarChris case, the major issue was the inadequacy of the review of events subsequent to the balance sheet date (S-1 Review).

_____24. Under Section 10b-5 of the SEC Act of 1934, some degree of "scienter" must be present for the CPA to be held liable to third parties bringing suit.

_____25. The SEC defines "material" to be anything more than 5% of net income.

D. COMPLETION STATEMENTS

Fill in the blanks with the word or words that correctly complete the following statements.

1. Based on common law, an accountant may be held liable to a client under either _____ _____ law or _____ law.

2. The two classes of third parties under common law are _____ and _____ .

3. In the Ultramares case, the judge ruled that accountants should not be liable to any third party for _____ except to a _____ .

4. The foreseen class concept extends the accountant's liability to a _____of persons for whose benefit the CPA intends to _____ .

5. The foreseeable parties concept extends the accountant's duty of _____to _____ who suffers a pecuniary loss from relying on the accountant's representation.

6. The accountant's primary defenses under common law are _____ and _____ .

7. Statutory law is more extensive than common law because the auditor may be held liable to _____ and _____ may be brought against auditors.

8. To establish freedom from negligence in a 1933 Act suit, the auditor may use a _____ defense, or establish that the plaintiff's loss resulted from causes other than the _____ statements.

9. In the Hochfelder decision, the U.S. Supreme Court ruled that in the absence of any _____ the auditor is not liable to third parties for _____ .

10. In the Continental Vending case, the critical test was whether the balance sheet _____ the company's financial position without reference to _____ .

11. An accountant may be liable under RICO for _____ or actual knowledge of the fraud, but not for _____ .

12. Two ways to minimize the risk of litigation are _____ and _____ .

13. To be held liable under RICO, the CPA must be shown to have a _____ of _____ activities.

14. The SEC defines material as being matters about which the _____ _____ _____ ought reasonably to be informed.

15. In the BarChris case, the CPA performed an insufficient _____ Review of a public client, and too easily accepted the client's _____ as evidence.

E. MULTIPLE CHOICE

Choose the best answer for each of the following questions and enter the identifying letter in the space provided.

_____ 1. Which of the following third parties would be considered a member of a foreseen class?
   a. A Savings and Loan specifically named at the time of engaging in the audit.
   b. A major supplier of inventory on credit.
   c. A bank not specifically named, when the purpose of the audit is to aid in obtaining a loan.
   d. A stockholder of the client.

_____ 2. When a client sues a CPA for failure to detect a misappropriation of funds by a client employee, which of these would not be a valid defense for the CPA?
   a. Contributory Negligence
   b. Due Care
   c. Lack of Privity
   d. Due Diligence

_____ 3. A CPA firm issues an unqualified opinion on financial statements not prepared in accordance with GAAP. The CPA firm will have acted with scienter in all the following circumstances except where the firm
   a. Intentionally disregards the truth.
   b. Has actual knowledge of fraud.
   c. Negligently performs auditing procedures.
   d. Intends to gain monetarily by concealing fraud.

_____ 4. In a common law action against an accountant, lack of privity is a viable defense if

the plaintiff
   a. Can prove the presence of gross negligence which amounts to a reckless disregard for the truth.
   b. Bases the action upon fraud.
   c. Is the client's creditor who sues the accountant for negligence.
   d. Is the accountant's client.

_____ 5. Mix and Associates, CPAs, issued an unqualified opinion on the financial statements of Glass Corp. for the year ended December 31, 19X9. It was determined later that Glass' treasurer had embezzled $300,000 from Glass during 19X9. Glass sued Mix because of Mix's failure to discover the embezzlement. Mix was unaware of the embezzlement. Which of the following is Mix's best defense?
   a. The audit was performed in accordance with GAAS.
   b. The treasurer was Glass' agent and, therefore, Glass was responsible for preventing the embezzlement.
   c. The financial statements were presented in conformity with GAAP.
   d. Mix had no actual knowledge of the embezzlement.

_____ 6. As a result of a series of legal decisions, the auditor's common law liability for ordinary negligence extends to
   a. The client only.
   b. The client and primary beneficiaries.
   c. The client, and foreseen limited classes of persons.
   d. The client, primary beneficiaries, and foreseen and foreseeable parties.

_____ 7. A CPA's liability for breach of contract does not extend to
   a. The client for failing to deliver the audit report by the agreed-upon date.
   b. The client for violation of the confidential relationship.
   c. Subrogees for losses resulting from defalcations not discovered as the result of the CPA's negligence.
   d. Unforeseen third parties for losses resulting from the CPA's negligence.

_____ 8. A third-party purchaser of securities has brought suit based upon the Securities Act of 1933 against a CPA firm. The CPA firm will prevail in the suit brought by the third party even though the CPA firm issued an unqualified opinion on materially incorrect financial statements if
   a. The CPA firm was unaware of the defect.
   b. The third-party plaintiff had no direct dealings with the CPA firm.
   c. The CPA firm can show that the third-party plaintiff did not rely upon the audited financial statements.
   d. The CPA firm can establish that it was not guilty of actual fraud.

_____ 9. Under the Securities Act of 1933, an accountant may be held liable for any materially false or misleading financial statements, including an omission of a material fact therefrom, provided the purchaser
   a. Proves reliance on the registration statements or prospectus.
   b. Proves negligence or fraud on the part of the accountant.
   c. Brings suit within four years from the date the security is offered to the public.
   d. Bases the claim on an alleged material false or misleading financial statement contained in the registration statement.

_____10. A CPA is subject to criminal liability if the CPA
   a. Refuses to turn over the working papers to the client.
   b. Performs an audit in a negligent manner.
   c. Willfully omits a material fact required to be stated in a registration statement.
   d. Willfully breaches the contract with the client.

_____11. In bringing suit under the Securities Exchange Act of 1934, the plaintiff need not
   a. Be a buyer of securities registered under the Act.
   b. Prove the existence of a false or misleading statement.
   c. Prove reliance on a false or misleading statement.
   d. Prove that damage was suffered from relying on a false or misleading statement.

_____12. Based on the Hochfelder decision, an auditor is not liable under the 1934 Act for
   a. Employing any device, scheme, or artifice to defraud.
   b. Making any untrue statement of a material fact or omitting a material fact.
   c. Engaging in any act, practice, or course of business which would operate as a fraud or deceit in connection with the purchase or sale of any security.
   d. Ordinary negligence.

_____13. Which of the following statements best describes the court's position on the importance of professional standards and the conclusiveness of expert testimony concerning the standards?
   a. A jury or court is never authorized to question the wisdom of a standard.
   b. If GAAP or GAAS are found lacking, the courts will not hesitate to invoke their authority to establish meaningful standards of performance, regardless of expert testimony as to professional standards.
   c. Where the profession has established specific standards for reasonably dealing with a perceived problem, the professional duty of an auditor will be limited to conformance with the standard; but where communication of findings is involved, expert testimony as to compliance with GAAP will be persuasive but not conclusive.
   d. The standard of communication required is measured by specific GAAP and GAAS, and in the absence of specific rules or customs, by the views of experts (professional CPAs).

_____14. Gleam is contemplating a common law action against Moore & Co., CPAS, based upon fraud. Gleam loaned money to Lilly & Company relying upon Lilly's financial statements which were audited by Moore. Gleam's action will fail if
   a. Gleam shows only that Moore failed to meticulously follow GAAP.
   b. Moore can establish that they fully complied with the statute of frauds.
   c. The alleged fraud was in part committed by oral misrepresentations and Moore pleads the parole evidence rule.
   d. Gleam is not a third party beneficiary in light of the absence of privity.

_____15. In an action for negligence against a CPA, 'the custom of the profession' standard is used at least to some extent in determining whether the CPA is negligent. Which

of the following statements describes how this standard is applied?
a. If the CPA proves he or she literally followed GAAP and GAAS, it will be conclusively presumed that the CPA was not negligent.
b. The custom of the profession argument may only be raised by the defendant.
c. Despite adherence to professional custom, negligence may still be present.
d. Failure to satisfy the custom of the profession is equivalent to gross negligence.

_____16. A CPA firm is being sued by a third party purchaser of securities sold in interstate commerce to the public. The third party is relying upon the Securities Act of 1933. The CPA firm had issued an unqualified opinion on incorrect financial statements. Which of the following represents the best defense available to the CPA firm?
a. The securities sold had not been registered with the SEC.
b. The CPA firm had returned the entire engagement fee to the corporation.
c. The third party was not in privity of contract with the CPA firm.
d. The action is not commenced within one year after discovery.

_____17. Generally, the decision to notify parties outside the client's organization regarding an illegal act is the responsibility of (the)
a. Independent auditor.
b. Management.
c. Outside legal counsel.
d. Internal auditors.

_____18. When the auditor concludes that the financial statements are materially affected by an irregularity, the auditor should
a. Revise the financial statements.
b. Express a qualified or adverse opinion if the financial statements are not revised.
c. Communicate the matter to the audit committee only if the financial statements are not revised.
d. Disclose the irregularity to parties outside the client.

_____19. Which of these is not a litigation reform sought by organizations such as CEASS?
a. Limits on Punitive Damage awards
b. Forms of organization that limit liability for CPA firm owners
c. Transfer of fees to lawsuit losers
d. Joint and Several Liability

_____20. Which of the following cases provided relief from RICO laws?
a. Hochfelder
b. Reves vs. Ernst & Young
c. Ultramares vs. Touche
d. BarChris

SOLUTIONS

TRUE OR FALSE STATEMENTS

1. False	10. False	18. True
2. False	11. True	19. False
3. True	12. True	20. True
4. True	13. True	21. True
5. True	14. False	22. True
6. False	15. True	23. True
7. True	16. True	24. True
8. False	17. True	25. False
9. True		

COMPLETION STATEMENTS

1. contract, tort
2. primary beneficiaries, other beneficiaries
3. ordinary negligence, primary beneficiary
4. limited group, supply the information
5. due care, anyone (who is damaged and relies on the statements)
6. due care, contributory negligence
7. unnamed third-party beneficiaries, criminal indictments
8. due diligence, false or misleading
9. intent to deceive or defraud (scienter), ordinary negligence
10. presented fairly, GAAP
11. scienter, ordinary negligence
12. engagement letters, investigating prospective clients, emphasizing quality not growth, complying with professional pronouncements and recognizing their limitations, caution in dealing with financially-troubled clients, maintaining quality controls (any 2).
13. pattern, racketeering
14. average, prudent, investor
15. S-1, verbal representations

MULTIPLE CHOICE QUESTIONS

1. c	5. a	9. d	13. c	17. b
2. c	6. d	10. c	14. a	18. b
3. c	7. d	11. a	15. c	19. d
4. c	8. d	12. d	16. d	20. b

Chapter 5

Audit Objectives, Evidence, and Working Papers

A. CHAPTER OUTLINE

I. Audit Objectives

A. Management's Financial Statement Assertions

1. Existence or Occurrence

2. Completeness

3. Rights and Obligations

4. Valuation or Allocation

5. Presentation and Disclosure

B. Specific Audit Objectives

II. Audit Evidence

A. Statement and Purpose of the Third Standard of Field Work

1. Sufficiency of Evidential Matter

2. Competency of Evidential Matter

3. Reasonable Basis

B. Types of Corroborating Information

1. Analytical Evidence

2. Documentary Evidence

3. Confirmations

4. Written Representations

5. Mathematical Evidence

6. Oral Evidence

7. Physical Evidence

8. Electronic Evidence

III. Audit Procedures

    A. Types of Audit Procedures

        1. Analytical Procedures

        2. Inspecting

        3. Confirming

        4. Inquiring

        5. Counting

        6. Tracing

        7. Vouching

        8. Observing

        9. Reperforming

        10. Computer-Assisted Audit Techniques

    B. Relationships Among Audit Procedures, Types of Evidence, and Assertions

    C. Classification of Auditing Procedures

        1. Procedures to Obtain an Understanding

        2. Tests of Controls

        3. Substantive Tests

    D. Evaluation of Evidence Obtained

IV. Working Papers

    A. Types of Working Papers

        1. Working Trial Balance

        2. Schedules and Analyses

        3. Audit Memoranda and Corroborating Information

        4. Adjusting and Reclassifying Entries

    B. Preparing Working Papers

    C. Reviewing Working Papers

    D. Working Paper Files

    E. Ownership and Custody of Working Papers

V. Summary

B. CHAPTER HIGHLIGHTS

1. The **overall objective** of a financial statement audit is the expression of an opinion on whether the client's financial statements are presented fairly, in all material respects, in conformity with GAAP.

2. Financial statements include both explicit and implicit **management assertions.** There are **five** categories of financial statement assertions:
    a. Assertions about **existence or occurrence** deal with whether assets or liabilities of the entity exist at a given date and whether recorded transactions have occurred during a given period.
    b. Assertions about **completeness** deal with whether all transactions and accounts that should be presented in the financial statements are so included.
    c. Assertions about **rights and obligations** deal with whether assets are the rights of the entity and liabilities are the obligations of the entity at a given date.
    d. Assertions about **valuation or allocation** deal with whether asset, liability, revenue, and expense components have been included in the financial statements at appropriate amounts.
    e. Assertions about **presentation and disclosure** deal with whether particular components of the financial statements are properly classified, described, and disclosed.

3. In obtaining evidence to support an opinion on the financial statements, the auditor develops **specific audit objectives for each account** in the financial statements. The categories of management's financial statement assertions are a useful starting point for developing the objectives.

4. In performing the audit, the auditor
    a. Obtains **evidence** concerning each specific objective,
    b. Reaches a **conclusion** as to whether any of management's assertions are misrepresentations, and
    c. **Combines the conclusions** about the individual assertions to reach an **opinion** on the fairness of the financial statements as a whole.

5. In auditing, **evidential matter** consists of **underlying accounting data** (e.g., the underlying accounting or financial records) and **corroborating information** (e.g., documents, confirmations, etc.) available to the auditor.

6. The third standard of field work states that **sufficient competent evidential matter** is to be obtained through inspection, observation, inquiries, and confirmations to afford a reasonable basis for an opinion regarding the financial statements under audit.
    a. The **sufficiency** of corroborating information depends on the auditor's judgment as to (1) **materiality and risk,** (2) **economic factors,** and (3) **size and characteristics of the population**.
    b. The **competency** of underlying accounting data depends on the **effectiveness of the client's internal controls**.
    c. The competency of corroborating information is affected by the (1) **relevance,** (2) **source,** (3) **timeliness,** and (4) **objectivity of the evidence.**

7. **Three presumptions** can be made on the effects of the source of information on the competency of evidential matter.
   a. When evidential matter can be obtained from **independent sources outside an enterprise**, it provides greater assurance of reliability for the purposes of an independent audit than that secured solely within the enterprise.
   b. When accounting data and financial statements are **developed under satisfactory conditions of internal control**, there is more assurance as to their reliability than when they are developed under unsatisfactory conditions of internal control.
   c. **Direct personal knowledge** of the independent auditor obtained through physical examination, observation, computation, and inspection is more persuasive than information obtained indirectly.

8. The auditor is only required to have a reasonable basis for an opinion. Factors that influence the auditor's judgment about a reasonable basis include:
   a. Professional considerations
   b. Integrity of management
   c. Public versus private ownership
   d. Financial condition

9. The principal types of corroborating information are: (a) physical evidence, (b) confirmations, (c) documentary evidence, (d) written representations, (e) mathematical evidence, (f) oral evidence, and (g) analytical evidence.

10. **Physical evidence** is obtained from physical examination of tangible resources. This type of evidence enables the auditor to obtain direct personal knowledge of:
    a. The existence of assets (existence or occurrence assertion).
    b. The quality or condition of assets (valuation or allocation assertion).

11. **Confirmations** are direct written responses by knowledgeable third parties to specific requests for financial information. This type of evidence may support any of the assertions but it is primarily related to the existence or occurrence assertion.

12. **Documentary evidence** includes checks, invoices, contracts, and minutes of meetings.
    a. Evidence created outside the client organization and obtained directly by the auditor has a higher degree of reliability than other types of documentary evidence.
    b. This type of evidence may pertain to all categories of financial statement assertions.

13. A **written representation** is a signed statement by a responsible and knowledgeable individual about a particular account, circumstance, or event.
    a. This type of evidence includes **management representation letters** (rep letters) and written communications from outside specialists.
    b. Written representations may relate to all financial statement assertions.

14. **Mathematical evidence** results from recomputations by the auditor. This type of evidence relates to the valuation or allocation assertion.

15. **Oral evidence** is obtained from verbal answers to auditor inquiries by management and key personnel. Such evidence may pertain to all financial statement assertions.

16. **Analytical evidence** involves the use of ratios and comparisons of data. This type of evidence relates to three assertions: existence or occurrence, completeness, and valuation or allocation.

17. The auditing procedures that may be used in obtaining corroborating information are:
    a. Analyzing ratios and other comparative data.
    b. Inspecting physical assets and documents.
    c. Confirming information directly from independent sources outside the entity.
    d. Inquiring of management and key employees either orally or in writing.
    e. Counting cash and prenumbered documents.
    f. Tracing documents through the accounting process.
    g. Vouching recorded data to supporting documentation.
    h. Observing or watching the performance of some activity.
    i. Reperforming calculations and reconciliations.
    j. Computer-assisted audit techniques.

18. The procedure of **tracing** is useful in detecting the understatement of an account balance (completeness assertion). The procedure of **vouching** is useful in detecting the overstatement of an account balance (existence or occurrence assertion).

19. The **relationships** between types of audit evidence and auditing procedures are:

Type of Audit Evidence	Auditing Procedure
Documentary	Tracing, vouching, inspecting
Physical	Inspecting, counting, observing
Written representations	Inquiring
Oral	Inquiring
Confirmations	Confirming
Mathematical	Reperforming
Analytical	Analyzing

20. **Auditing procedures** are classified by purpose into the following categories: (a) procedures to obtain an understanding of the internal control structure, (b) tests of controls, and (c) substantive tests.

21. **Procedures to obtain an understanding of the internal control structure** include:
    a. Inquiry of management.
    b. Inspection of accounting manuals and flowcharts.
    c. Observing the entity's activities and operations.
    These procedures focus on the **design of internal control policies and procedures**. They are required in every financial statement audit.

22. **Tests of controls** are made to provide evidence about the **effectiveness** of **the design and operation** of internal control policies and procedures.
    a. The procedures identified in Highlight 21 and reperformance of controls by the auditor may be used in performing tests of controls.
    b. These tests are not required in an audit. However, they are performed in most audits.

23. **Substantive tests** consist of (a) **tests of details of transactions and balances** and (b) **analytical procedures.**
    a. These tests provide evidence as to the fairness of management's financial statement assertions.
    b. These tests are required in every financial statement audit.

24. **Working papers** may be defined as the records kept by the independent auditor of the procedures followed, the tests performed, the information obtained, and the **conclusions reached** pertinent to the audit. They provide:
    a. The principal support for the auditor's report.
    b. A means for coordinating and supervising the audit.
    c. Evidence that the audit was made in accordance with GAAS.

25. Working papers have direct application to **GAAS.** They should provide evidence of compliance with each of the ten standards. For example,
    a. The conclusions reached demonstrate the auditor's objectivity and independence.
    b. The completeness of the working papers provides evidence of due care.
    c. Working papers document the audit evidence obtained during the **audit.**

26. Working papers are **classified** into the following groupings: (a) audit plans and audit programs, (b) working trial balance, (c) schedules and analyses, (d) audit memoranda and corroborating information, and (e) adjusting and reclassifying entries.

27. There are several **levels of review** of working papers within a CPA firm. The first level review is made by the preparer's supervisor to evaluate the evidence obtained, the judgment exercised, and the conclusions reached. Other reviews are made when field work has been completed.

28. One major category of working papers is the **permanent file**. This file contains data that are expected to be useful to the auditor on many future engagements with the client.

29. A second major category of working papers is the current file. This file contains corroborating information pertaining to the execution of the current year's audit.

30. Working papers belong to the auditor and he or she is responsible for their safekeeping.

C. TRUE OR FALSE STATEMENTS

Indicate in the space provided whether each of the following statements is true or false.

_____   1. Assertions about valuation or allocation relate to whether individual components have been included in the financial statements at appropriate amounts.

_____ 2. There are four broad categories of financial statement assertions.

_____ 3. Specific audit objectives are tailored to fit each client.

_____ 4. In making an audit in accordance with GAAS, the auditor only needs to obtain corroborating information.

_____ 5. Most of the auditor's work in forming an opinion involves obtaining and evaluating evidential matter concerning management's financial statement assertions.

_____ 6. The third standard of field work requires the auditor to have a conclusive basis for his or her opinion.

_____ 7. Factors that affect the sufficiency of corroborating information include the size and characteristics of the population and relevance.

_____ 8. There is an inverse relationship between the materiality level for an account balance and the quantity of corroborating information required by the auditor.

_____ 9. Timeliness and objectivity are two factors that affect the competency of corroborating information.

_____ 10. Direct personal knowledge of the auditor is more persuasive than information obtained indirectly.

_____ 11. Professional considerations permit substantial diversity in the quality and amount of evidence that is required.

_____ 12. Physical evidence provides the auditor with direct personal knowledge of the existence of an asset.

_____ 13. Confirmations are especially useful in verifying the existence or occurrence of an account balance.

_____ 14. Documentary evidence is infrequently used in auditing.

_____ 15. Written representations are a form of documentary evidence.

_____ 16. The auditor is required by GAAS to obtain a written representation (rep letter) from management.

_____ 17. The auditor obtains corroborating information through the application of auditing procedures.

_____ 18. Tracing is an important procedure in obtaining evidence about the existence or occurrence assertion.

_____ 19. Vouching is an important procedure in obtaining evidence about the completeness assertion.

_____ 20. Two classifications of auditing procedures are tests of controls and substantive tests.

_____ 21. To have a reasonable basis for an opinion on the financial statements, the auditor needs conclusive evidence about each financial statement assertion that is material.

_____ 22. GAAS do not require the auditor to express an opinion in reporting the findings.

_____ 23. Working papers provide the principal support for the auditor's report.

_____ 24. A lead schedule summarizes working paper data pertaining to a material account.

_____ 25. Custody of working papers rests with the auditor who is responsible for their safekeeping.

D. COMPLETION STATEMENTS

Fill in the blanks with the word or words that correctly complete the following statements.

1. The financial statement _____ that pertains to the overstatement of an account balance is the _____ assertion.

2. Assertions about completeness deal with whether all _____ that should be presented in the _____ are so included.

3. In performing the audit, the auditor obtains _____ concerning each _____ objective.

4. The auditor obtains physical evidence from the following audit procedures: _____ _____, _____, and _____ .

5. The two categories of evidential matter are _____ and _____ .

6. The third standard of field work requires the auditor to obtain sufficient competent _____ _____ to have a reasonable basis for an _____ on the financial statements.

7. The reliability of the accounting records is _____ related to the effectiveness of the client's _____ .

8. Evidential matter obtained from _____ outside an enterprise is more reliable than that secured from _____ the enterprise.

9. Mathematical evidence provides the auditor with _____ knowledge about the _____ of an account balance.

10. Auditing procedures are the _____ or the _____ utilized by the auditor during the audit.

11. Inspecting involves careful scrutiny of _____ and _____of tangible resources.

12. Auditing procedures are classified into the following categories: _____ _____ , _____ , and _____ .

13. In issuing a report without a reasonable basis for an opinion concerning a material financial statement assertion, the auditor may express a _____ opinion or _____ of opinion on the financial statements.

14. Working papers provide the principal support for the _____ and evidence that the audit was made in accordance with _____ .

15. Working papers are generally filed under two categories: (a) _____ and (b) _____ .

E. MULTIPLE CHOICE

Choose the best answer for each of the following questions and enter the identifying letter in the space provided.

_____ 1. The third standard of field work states that sufficient competent evidential matter is to be obtained through inspection, observation, inquiries, and confirmations to afford a reasonable basis for an opinion regarding the financial statements under audit. The substantive evidential matter required by this standard may be obtained, in part, through:
a. Flowcharting the internal control structure.
b. Proper planning of the audit engagement.
c. Analytical procedures.
d. Auditor working papers.

_____ 2. Which of the following statements concerning the auditor's use of the work of a specialist is correct?
a. If the auditor believes that the determinations made by the specialist are unreasonable, only a qualified opinion may be issued.
b. If the specialist is related to the client, the auditor is still permitted to use the specialist's findings as corroborative evidence.
c. The specialist need not have an understanding of the auditor's corroborative use of the specialist's findings.
d. The specialist may be identified in the auditor's report when the auditor issues an unqualified opinion.

_____ 3. Which of the following statements concerning evidential matter is correct?
   a. Competent evidence supporting management's assertions should be convincing rather than merely persuasive.
   b. An effective internal control structure contributes little to the reliability of the evidence created within the entity.
   c. The cost of obtaining evidence is not an important consideration to an auditor in deciding what evidence should be obtained.
   d. A client's accounting data cannot be considered sufficient audit evidence to support the financial statements.

_____ 4. Most of the independent auditor's work in formulating an opinion on financial statements consists of:
   a. Studying and evaluating the internal control structure.
   b. Obtaining and examining evidential matter.
   c. Examining cash transactions.
   d. Comparing recorded accountability with assets.

_____ 5. Evidential matter supporting the financial statements consists of the underlying accounting data and all corroborating information available to the auditor. Which of the following is an example of corroborating information?
   a. Minutes of meetings.
   b. General and subsidiary ledgers.
   c. Accounting manuals.
   d. Worksheets supporting cost allocations.

_____ 6. Evidential matter is generally considered sufficient when:
   a. It is competent.
   b. There is enough of it to afford a reasonable basis for an opinion on financial statements.
   c. It has the qualities of being relevant, objective, and free from unknown bias.
   d. It has been obtained by random selection.

_____ 7. The strongest criticism of the reliability of audit evidence which the auditor physically observes is that:
   a. The client may conceal items from the auditor.
   b. The auditor may not be qualified to evaluate the items he or she is observing.
   c. Such evidence is too costly in relation to its reliability.
   d. The observation must occur at a specific time, which is often difficult to arrange.

_____ 8. Although the validity of evidential matter is dependent on the circumstances under which it is obtained, there are three general presumptions which have some usefulness. The situations given below indicate the relative reliability a CPA has placed on two types of evidence obtained in different situations. Which of these is an exception to one of the general presumptions?
   a. The CPA places more reliance on the balance in the scrap sales account at plant A where the CPA has made limited tests of transactions because of good internal control than at plant B where the CPA has made extensive tests of transactions because of poor internal control.
   b. The CPA places more reliance on the CPA's computation of interest payable on outstanding bonds than on the amount confirmed by the trustee.
   c. The CPA places more reliance on the report of an expert on an inventory of precious gems than on the CPA's physical observation of the gems.
   d. The CPA places more reliance on a schedule of insurance coverage obtained from the company's insurance agent rather than one prepared by the internal audit staff.

_____ 9. Audit evidence can come in different forms with different degrees of persuasiveness. Which of the following is the least persuasive type of evidence?
   a. Vendor's invoices.
   b. Bank statement obtained from client.
   c. Computations made by the auditor.
   d. Prenumbered client invoices.

_____10. Which of the following types of documentary evidence should the auditor consider to be the most reliable?
   a. A sales invoice issued by the client and supported by a delivery receipt from an outside trucker.
   b. Confirmation of an account-payable balance mailed by and returned directly to the auditor.
   c. A check issued by the company and bearing the payee's endorsement which is included with the bank statement mailed directly to the auditor.
   d. A working paper prepared by the client's controller and reviewed by the client's treasurer.

_____11. A representation letter issued by a client:
   a. Is essential for the preparation of the audit program.
   b. Is a substitute for testing.
   c. Does not reduce the auditor's responsibility.
   d. Reduces the auditor's responsibility only to the extent that it is relied upon.

_____12. Which of the following best describes the primary purpose of audit procedures?
   a. To detect errors or irregularities.
   b. To comply with generally accepted accounting principles.
   c. To gather corroborative information.
   d. To verify the accuracy of account balances.

_____13. The following statements were made in a discussion of audit evidence between two CPAs. Which statement is not valid concerning evidential matter?
a. "I am seldom convinced beyond all doubt with respect to all aspects of the statements being audited."
b. "I would not undertake that procedure because at best the results would only be persuasive and I'm looking for convincing evidence."
c. "I evaluate the degree of risk involved in deciding the kind of evidence I will gather."
d. "I evaluate the usefulness of the evidence I can obtain against the cost of obtaining it."

_____14. The sufficiency and competency of evidential matter ultimately is based on the:
a. Availability of corroborating data.
b. Generally accepted auditing standards.
c. Pertinence of the evidence.
d. Judgement of the auditor.

_____15. To be competent, evidence must be both:
a. Timely and substantial.
b. Reliable and documented.
c. Valid and relevant.
d. Useful and consistent.

_____16. An auditor ordinarily uses a working trial balance resembling the financial statements without footnotes, but containing columns for:
a. Reclassifications and adjustments.
b. Reconciliations and tickmarks.
c. Accruals and deferrals.
d. Expense and revenue summaries.

_____17. The current file of an auditor's working papers most likely would include a copy of the:
a. Bank reconciliation.
b. Pension plan contract.
c. Articles of incorporation.
d. Flowchart of the internal control procedures.

_____18. Although the quantity, type, and content of working papers will vary with the circumstances, the working papers generally would include the:
a. Copies of those client records examined by the auditor during the course of the engagement.
b. Evaluation of the efficiency and competence of the audit staff assistants by the partner responsible for the audit.
c. Auditor's comments concerning the efficiency and competence of client management personnel.
d. Auditing procedures followed, and the testing performed in obtaining evidential matter.

_____19. An auditor's working papers will generally be least likely to include documentation showing how the:
   a. Client's schedules were prepared.
   b. Engagement has been planned.
   c. Client's internal control structure had been studied and evaluated.
   d. Unusual matters were resolved.

_____20. Working papers are used to record the results of the auditor's evidence-gathering procedures. When preparing working papers the auditor should remember that
   a. Working papers should be kept on the client's premises so that the client can have access to them for reference purposes.
   b. Working papers should be the primary support for the financial statements being examined.
   c. Working papers should be considered as a substitutes for the client's accounting records.
   d. Working papers should be designed to meet the circumstances and the auditor's needs on each engagement.

SOLUTIONS

TRUE OR FALSE STATEMENTS

1. True	10. True	18. False
2. False	11. False	19. False
3. True	12. True	20. True
4. False	13. True	21. False
5. True	14. False	22. True
6. False	15. True	23. True
7. False	16. True	24. False
8. True	17. True	25. True
9. True		

COMPLETION STATEMENTS

1. assertion, existence or occurrence
2. transactions and accounts, financial statements
3. evidence, specific audit
4. inspecting, counting, observing
5. underlying accounting data, corroborating information
6. evidential matter, opinion
7. directly, internal controls
8. independent sources, solely within
9. direct personal, accuracy
10. acts performed, methods and techniques
11. documents and records, physical examination
12. procedures to obtain an understanding of the internal control structure, tests of controls, substantive tests
13. qualified, disclaimer
14. auditor's report, GAAS
15. permanent, current

MULTIPLE CHOICE QUESTIONS

1. c	5. a	9. d	13. b	17. a
2. b	6. b	10. b	14. d	18. d
3. c	7. b	11. c	15. c	19. a
4. b	8. c	12. c	16. a	20. d

Chapter 6

Accepting the Engagement and Planning the Audit

A. CHAPTER OUTLINE

I. **Overview of a Financial Statement Audit**

    A. Accepting the Audit Engagement

    B. Planning the Audit

    C. Performing Audit Tests

    D. Reporting the Findings

II. **Accepting the Engagement**

    A. Evaluating Integrity of Management

        1. Communicate with Predecessor Auditor

        2. Make Inquiries of Other Third Parties

        3. Review Previous Experience with Existing Clients

    B. Identifying Special Circumstances and Unusual Risks

        1. Identify Intended Users of Audited Statements

        2. Assess Prospective Client's Legal and Financial Stability

        3. Evaluate Entity's Auditability

    C. Assessing Competence to Perform the Audit

        1. Identify the Audit Team

        2. Consider Need for Consultation and the Use of Specialists

    D. Evaluating Independence

    E. Determining Ability to Use Due Care

        1. Assess Timing of Appointment

        2. Consider the Scheduling of Field Work

    F. Preparing the Engagement Letter

III. **Planning the Audit**

    A. Steps in Planning the Audit

B. CHAPTER HIGHLIGHTS

1. The **four phases** of a financial statement audit are:
    a. Accepting the audit engagement.
    b. Planning the audit.
    c. Performing audit tests.
    d. Reporting the findings.

2. The **steps in accepting an audit engagement** include:
    a. Evaluating the integrity of management.
    b. Identifying special circumstances and unusual risks.
    c. Assessing competence to perform audit.
    d. Evaluating independence.
    e. Determining ability to use due care.
    f. Preparing engagement letter.

3. When management lacks integrity, there is a greater likelihood that material efforts and irregularities may occur in the accounting process from which the financial statements are developed. In **evaluating management's integrity**, the auditor should:
    a. Communicate with the predecessor auditor.
    b. Make inquiries of other third parties.
    c. Review previous experience with existing clients.

4. In **communicating with the predecessor auditor**, the successor auditor should inquire about:
    a. The integrity of management.
    b. Disagreements between the predecessor and management about accounting principles and auditing procedures.
    c. The predecessor's understanding of the reasons for a change in auditors.

5. **Identifying special circumstances and unusual risks** includes:
    a. Identifying the intended users of the audited statements.
    b. Assessing the prospective client's legal and financial stability.
    c. Evaluating the entity's auditability.

6. **Assessing competence** to perform an audit engagement involves:
    a. Determining that the firm can comply with the first general standard of GAAS.
    b. Identifying the key members of the audit team which typically includes a partner, one or more managers, one or more seniors, and staff assistants.
    c. Considering the need for consultation during the engagement with experts within the auditor's firm (such as EDP or industry experts), or the use of specialists outside the firm (such as appraisers, engineers, actuaries, and attorneys).

7. **Evaluating independence** involves determining that:
    a. The firm can comply with the second general standard of GAAS.
    b. The firm can comply with Rule 101 - Independence of the Code of Professional Conduct.
    c. Acceptance of the client will not result in any conflicts of interest with other clients.

8. Factors pertaining to the ability to use **due care** involve:
    a. Complying with the **third general standard of GAAS** and **Rule 201** of the Code of Professional Conduct, both of which require the critical review at every level of supervision of both the work done and the judgments exercised by those assisting in the audit.
    b. **Early appointment**, which facilitates audit planning.
    c. Scheduling the field work, which includes developing **time budgets** and considering the use of **client personnel**.

9. **Field work** is generally classified into two categories:
    a. **Interim work** that is typically performed within the three- to four-month period immediately prior to the balance sheet date.
    b. **Year-end work** that is typically performed within a period extending from shortly before the balance sheet date to as long as three months following the balance sheet date.

10. An **engagement letter** is a legal contract that is used to:
    a. Confirm the terms of the engagement with the client.
    b. Provide a clear statement of the nature of the audit and the professional responsibilities assumed by the auditor.
    c. Indicate the basis for determining the audit fee.
    d. Identify any limitations on the scope of the audit.
    e. Obtain written acceptance of the terms by the client via his or her signature on a duplicate copy.

11. The **steps in planning an audit** are:
    a. Obtaining an understanding of client's business and industry.
    b. Performing analytical procedures.
    c. Making preliminary judgments about materiality levels.
    d. Considering audit risk.
    e. Developing preliminary audit strategies for significant assertions.
    f. Obtaining an understanding of client's internal control structure.

12. **Obtaining an understanding of client's business and industry** includes events, transactions, and practices that may have a significant effect on the financial statements, such as types of products and services, company locations, company and industry operating characteristics, vulnerability to changing economic conditions, related party transactions, government regulations and reporting requirements, and the entity's internal control structure.

13. **Procedures** to acquire the **understanding of the client's business and industry** include:
    a. Reviewing prior years' working papers.
    b. Reviewing industry and business data.
    c. Touring client operations.
    d. Making inquiries of the audit committee.
    e. Making inquiries of management.
    f. Determining existence of related parties.
    g. Considering the impact of applicable accounting and auditing pronouncements.

14. In **reviewing prior years' working papers**, the auditor seeks information on problem areas that occurred in prior audits and may be expected to have continued, and other matters of continuing audit significance such as analyses of balance sheet accounts and contingencies.

15. Reviewing **industry and business data** includes:
    a. Reviewing the articles of incorporation and bylaws.
    b. Reading the minutes of directors' and stockholders' meetings.
    c. Analyzing recent annual and interim financial statements, tax returns, and reports to regulatory agencies.
    d. Becoming familiar with applicable government regulations.
    e. Reading important continuing contracts such as loan agreements, leases, and labor contracts.
    f. Reading current trade and industry publications.

16. **Touring client operations** enables the auditor to become familiar with:
    a. The layout of the plant, manufacturing processes, and storage facilities.
    b. Trouble spots such as unlocked storerooms, obsolete materials, and excessive scrap.
    c. The types and locations of accounting records and EDP facilities.
    d. Personnel who occupy key positions within the client's organization.

17. **Inquiries of the audit committee and management** may provide the auditor with (a) special insights into the client's business and industry, including current developments such as the effects of new regulations, and (b) information about significant changes in management and such matters as the entity's organizational structure, internal controls, and EDP systems.

18. Specific auditing procedures used to determine the existence of **related parties** include:
    a. Evaluating the company's procedures for identifying and properly accounting for related party transactions.
    b. Reviewing filings with the SEC and other regulatory agencies that include related party disclosures.
    c. Reviewing prior years' working papers for names of known related parties.
    d. Reviewing material investment transactions to determine whether their nature and extent created new related parties.

19. In addition to being generally knowledgeable of GAAP and GAAS, the auditor should consider the **applicability of accounting and auditing pronouncements** such as AICPA Accounting and Audit Guides and Statements of Position, pronouncements of regulatory agencies such as the SEC, and newly effective SFASs and SASs.

20. **Analytical procedures** consist of evaluations of financial information made by a study of plausible relationships among both financial and nonfinancial data.

21. Analytical procedures serve the following **purposes** in an audit:
    a. In the planning phase, to assist the auditor in planning the nature, timing, and extent of substantive tests (required).
    b. In the testing phase, as an alternative, or complement, to substantive tests of details to obtain evidence about particular assertions (optional).
    c. At the conclusion of the audit, in a final review of the overall reasonableness of the audited financial statements (required).

22. Analytical procedures can assist the auditor in **planning** by (a) enhancing the auditor's understanding of the client's business and (b) identifying unusual relationships and unexpected fluctuations in data that may indicate areas of greater risk of misstatement.

23. To effectively use analytical procedures in the planning phase, the auditor should systematically complete the following **steps**:
    a. Identify the calculations/comparisons to be made.
    b. Develop expectations (estimated probable outcomes).
    c. Perform the calculations/comparisons.
    d. Analyze data and identify significant differences.
    e. Investigate significant unexpected differences.
    f. Determine effects on audit planning.

24. The types of **calculations and comparisons** commonly used in analytical procedures include
    a. Absolute data comparisons.
    b. Common-size financial statements (vertical analysis).
    c. Ratio analysis.
    d. Trend analysis (horizontal analysis).

25. A **basic premise** underlying the use of analytical procedures in auditing is that relationships among data may be expected to continue in the absence of known conditions to the contrary.

26. Sources of data used in **developing expectations** include:
    a. Client financial information for comparable prior period(s) giving consideration to known changes.
    b. Anticipated results based on formal budgets or forecasts.
    c. Relationships among elements of financial information within the period.
    d. Industry data.
    e. Relationships of financial information with relevant nonfinancial information.

27. Because **performing calculations/comparisons** in the planning phase usually occurs several months before current year-end account balances are available, this step may involve the use of actual year-to-date company data.

28. In **identifying significant differences**, some firms use statistical models, but most firms continue to use simple rules of thumb such as differences in excess of a predetermined dollar amount, a percentage, or a combination of both.

29. **Investigating significant unexpected differences** usually involves (a) reconsidering the methods and factors used in developing the expectations and (b) making inquiries of management and corroborating their responses with other evidential matter.

30. The **effects on audit planning** of unexplained significant differences will be to cause the auditor to view the account or accounts involved in the calculations or comparisons as having an increased risk of misstatement. Accordingly, the auditor will plan more detailed tests of these areas.

C.   TRUE OR FALSE STATEMENTS

Indicate in the space provided whether each of the following statements is true or false.

_____ 1.   Audit planning is usually done three to six months prior to the end of the client's fiscal year.

_____ 2.   The initial phase of an audit engagement is planning the audit.

_____ 3.   The third phase of the audit, performing audit tests, is also referred to as performing the field work.

_____ 4.   Both the general and reporting standards of GAAS apply to the final phase of an audit which is reporting the findings.

_____ 5.   In accepting an audit engagement, the auditor takes on responsibilities only to the client and other members of the profession.

_____ 6.   An important step in accepting an audit engagement is evaluating the integrity of management.

_____ 7.   Before accepting an audit engagement, a successor auditor is required to take the initiative to communicate with the predecessor auditor.

_____ 8.   It is unethical for auditors to attempt to identify and reject prospective clients that pose a high risk of litigation.

_____ 9.   The key members of the audit team are typically identified after acceptance of the engagement but before starting the interim field work.

_____ 10.   In determining whether to accept the engagement, it is appropriate to consider using consultants within the firm to assist the audit team in performing the audit, but it is not appropriate to plan to use outside specialists to obtain competent evidential matter.

_____ 11.   When it is concluded that independence requirements cannot be met, the prospective audit client should be informed that the firm will be required to issue a qualified opinion on the financial statements.

_____ 12.   It may be possible to accept an audit engagement even when appointment of the auditor occurs after the end of the client's fiscal year.

_____ 13.   An engagement letter is a letter from the client to the auditor legally appointing the audit firm.

_____ 14.   The auditor should plan the audit with an attitude of professional skepticism about such matters as the integrity of management, errors and irregularities, and illegal acts.

_____15.   In planning the audit, provision should be made for more supervision when several members of the audit team are inexperienced than when they are all experienced.

_____16.   Knowledge of the existence of related party transactions is not needed in planning the audit.

_____17.   A predecessor auditor is not expected to allow a successor auditor to review, with the client's consent, the predecessor's working papers for matters of continuing audit significance.

_____18.   In a recurring engagement, the tour of client operations is often limited to areas of major changes that have occurred since the completion of last year's audit.

_____19.   Inquiries of the audit committee of the board of directors may provide the auditor with special insights into the client's business and industry.

_____20.   Analytical procedures are required at three points in all audits: in the planning phase to assist in planning, in the testing phase as a substantive test of particular assertions, and at the conclusion of the audit as part of a final overall review.

_____21.   The use of analytical procedures in identifying areas of greater risk of misstatement is often described as the attention directing objective of analytical procedures.

_____22.   Trend analysis which involves comparing certain data elements for more than two accounting periods is also known as vertical analysis.

_____23.   Generally, analytical procedures performed in the planning phase use highly aggregated, company-wide data based on year-to-date or projected annual data.

_____24.   Sources of data used in developing expectations include both historical and future-oriented internal (client) and external (industry) data, and both financial and nonfinancial data.

_____25.   The process of determining whether a difference between actual and expected data is significant involves the exercise of judgment and the concept of materiality.

D. COMPLETION STATEMENTS

Fill in the blanks with the word or words that correctly complete the following statements.

1. The four phases of an audit engagement are _____ the audit engagement, _____the audit, performing _____ and _____ the findings.

2. In accepting an audit engagement, the auditor accepts responsibilities to the _____, the _____, and other members of the _____.

3. A successor auditor should make inquiries of a predecessor auditor about such matters as the _____ of management, disagreements with management about _____ , and the predecessor's understanding of the reasons for the _____ .

4. Information about management's integrity may also be obtained from knowledgeable third parties such as _____ , _____ , and others in the financial and business community who have had _____ with the prospective client.

5. Matters pertaining to identifying special circumstances and unusual risks include identifying the _____ of the audited financial statements, making a preliminary assessment of the prospective client's _____ stability, and evaluating the entity's _____ .

6. Assessing competence to perform the audit involves identifying the key members of the _____ and considering the need to seek assistance from _____ and _____ during the course of the audit.

7. Independence requirements include the second _____ , Rule _____ of the *Code of Professional Conduct*, and, in the case of audits of public companies, the _____ requirements.

8. It is customary to classify the timing of field work into _____ and _____ .

9. It is good professional practice to confirm the terms of each engagement in an _____ that constitutes a _____ between the auditor and the client.

10. Audit planning involves the development of an overall _____ or game plan for the expected conduct and _____ of the audit.

11. Supervision involves directing the _____ on the audit team who participate in accomplishing the _____ of the audit.

12. The concern about related party transactions results from the realization that one of the participants may be in a position to _____ the other participant to the extent that _____ of terms and conditions is not possible.

13. Analytical procedures are defined as evaluations of financial information made by a study of _____ among both _____ data.

14. A basic premise underlying the use of analytical procedures in auditing is that _____ may be expected to continue in the absence of _____ .

15. Because the process of developing expectations generally requires considerable audit _____ and business _____ , this step is usually performed by the _____ on the audit team.

E. MULTIPLE CHOICE

Choose the best answer for each of the following questions and enter the identifying letter in the space provided.

_____   1. In the "performing audit tests" phase of an audit engagement, the following GAAS apply:
       a. General standards only.
       b. Field work standards only.
       c. General and field work standards.
       d. General, field work, and reporting standards.

_____   2. Each of the following steps should be performed prior to accepting an audit engagement except:
       a. Evaluating the integrity of management.
       b. Identifying special circumstances and unusual risks.
       c. Making preliminary judgments about materiality levels.
       d. Evaluating independence.

_____   3. Prior to the acceptance of an audit engagement with a client who has terminated the services of the predecessor auditor, the CPA should:
       a. Contact the predecessor auditor without advising the prospective client and request a complete report of the circumstance leading to the termination with the understanding that all information disclosed will be kept confidential.
       b. Accept the engagement without contacting the predecessor auditor since the CPA can include audit procedures to verify the reason given by the client for the termination.
       c. Not communicate with the predecessor auditor because this would in effect be asking the auditor to violate the confidential relationship between auditor and client.
       d. Advise the client of the intention to contact the predecessor auditor and request permission for the contact.

_____   4. In an audit situation, communication between successor and predecessor auditors should be:
       a. Authorized in an engagement letter.
       b. Acknowledged in a representation letter.
       c. Either written or oral.
       d. Written and included in the working papers.

_____ 5. Competence as a certified public accountant includes all of the following except:
   a. Having the technical qualifications to perform an engagement.
   b. Possessing the ability to supervise and evaluate the quality of staff work.
   c. Warranting the infallibility of the work performed.
   d. Consulting others if additional technical information is needed.

_____ 6. In evaluating independence prior to accepting an audit engagement, all of the following are relevant except:
   a. The general standards of GAAS.
   b. The field work standards of GAAS.
   c. The _Code of Professional Conduct._
   d. The quality control elements.

_____ 7. Due professional care requires:
   a. A critical review of the work done at every level of supervision.
   b. The examination of all corroborating evidence available.
   c. The exercise of error-free judgment.
   d. A study of internal controls that includes tests of controls.

_____ 8. The scope and nature of the auditor's contractual obligation to a client ordinarily is set forth in the:
   a. Management letter.
   b. Scope paragraph of the auditor's report.
   c. Engagement letter.
   d. Introductory paragraph of the auditor's report.

_____ 9. With respect to the auditor's planning of a year-end audit, which of the following statements is always true?
   a. An engagement should not be accepted after the fiscal year end.
   b. An inventory count must be observed at the balance sheet date.
   c. The client's audit committee should not be told of the specific audit procedures which will be performed.
   d. It is an acceptable practice to carry out substantial parts of the audit at interim dates.

_____ 10. The auditor will least likely engage in a discussion with the audit committee concerning:
   a. Significant changes in the client's management or organizational structure.
   b. Additions or modifications to the auditor's audit plan requested by the audit committee.
   c. Details of the procedures which the auditor plans to apply.
   d. Details of potential problems which the auditor believes might cause a qualified opinion.

_____ 11. Which of the following events most likely indicates the existence of related parties?
   a. Borrowing a large sum of money at a variable rate of interest.
   b. Selling real estate at a price that differs significantly from its book value.
   c. Making a loan without scheduled terms for repayment of the funds.
   d. Discussing merger terms with a company that is a major competitor.

_____ 12. The attention directing objective of analytical procedures refers to their use:
   a. In enhancing the auditor's understanding of the client's business.
   b. In identifying unusual relationships and unexpected fluctuations in data that may indicate areas of greater risk of misstatement.
   c. As an alternative, or complement, to a substantive test of details for a particular assertion.
   d. In a final review of the overall reasonableness of the audited financial statements.

_____ 13. Which of the following is not a typical analytical procedure?
   a. Study of relationships of the financial information with relevant nonfinancial information.
   b. Comparison of the financial information with similar information regarding the industry in which the entity operates.
   c. Comparison of financial information with budgeted amounts.
   d. Comparison of recorded amounts of major disbursements with appropriate invoices.

_____ 14. Following are several steps involved in using analytical procedures in the planning phase of an audit:
   I.   Investigate significant unexpected differences.
   II.   Perform calculations/comparisons.
   III.   Determine effects on audit planning.
   IV.   Develop expectations.
   V.   Identify calculations/comparisons to be made.
   VI.   Analyze data and identify significant differences.

   The order in which these steps should be performed is
   a. III, IV, I, V, II, VI.
   b. V, IV, II, VI, I, III.
   c. V, II, IV, VI, I, III.
   d. IV, V, II, IV, III, I.

_____ 15. Which of the following is not an example of vertical analysis?
   a. Calculating the percentage of inventories to total assets.
   b. Calculating the percentage of cost of sales to sales.
   c. Comparing the client's gross margin percentage to the industry average.
   d. Comparing actual sales to budgeted sales.

_____ 16. An advantage of trend analysis is that it:
   a. Does not require the calculation of percentages.
   b. Does not require the development of expectations.
   c. May identify important changes that may not be obvious from comparisons limited to just the current and prior period.

d. Does not require specifying the magnitude of difference or fluctuation that should trigger a decision to investigate.

_____ 17. For companies with diverse operations:
   a. Analytical procedures are inappropriate.
   b. Some disaggregation of data by product line or division may be necessary for analytical procedures to be effective.
   c. Only highly aggregated, company-wide data should be used in analytical procedures.
   d. It is necessary to perform analytical procedures on monthly or quarterly data rather than year-to-date data.

_____ 18. Which of the following factors would least influence an auditor's consideration of the reliability of data for purposes of analytical procedures?
   a. Whether the data were processed in an EDP system or in a manual accounting system.
   b. Whether sources within the entity were independent of those who are responsible for the data being audited.
   c. Whether the data were subjected to audit testing in the current or prior year.
   d. Whether the data were obtained from independent sources outside the entity or from sources within the entity.

_____ 19. A basic premise underlying the application of analytical procedures is that:
   a. The study of financial ratios is an acceptable alternative to the investigation of unusual fluctuations.
   b. Statistical tests of financial information may lead to the discovery of material errors in the financial statements.
   c. Plausible relationships among data may reasonably be expected to exist and continue in the absence of known conditions to the contrary.
   d. These procedures cannot replace tests of details of balances and transactions.

_____ 20. Which of the following statements about the inventory turnover ratio is least likely to be valid?
   a. Some auditors prefer to use ending, rather than average, inventory values in calculating the ratio because the use of an average would make an error in the ending inventory more difficult to detect.
   b. A low value for the ratio may indicate excessively high inventories and slow-moving items.
   c. A value for the ratio that is much higher than the industry average might indicate insufficient merchandise to meet customer demand resulting in lost sales.
   d. An unexpected increase in the ratio compared to the prior year may be due to the overstatement of the ending inventory in the current year.

SOLUTIONS

TRUE OR FALSE STATEMENTS

1. True	10. False	18. True
2. False	11. False	19. True
3. True	12. True	20. False
4. True	13. False	21. True
5. False	14. True	22. False
6. True	15. True	23. True
7. True	16. False	24. True
8. False	17. False	25. True
9. False		

COMPLETION STATEMENTS

1. accepting, planning, audit tests, reporting
2. public, client, public accounting profession
3. integrity, accounting principles or auditing procedures, change of auditors
4. attorneys, bankers, business relationships
5. intended users, legal and financial, auditability
6. audit team, consultants, specialists
7. general standard of GAAS, 101, SEC's
8. interim work, year-end work
9. engagement letter, legal contract
10. strategy, scope
11. assistants, objectives
12. significantly influence, arm's length bargaining
13. plausible relationships, financial and nonfinancial
14. relationships among data, known conditions to the contrary
15. judgment, expertise, senior or manager

MULTIPLE CHOICE QUESTIONS

1. c	5. c	9. d	13. d	17. b
2. c	6. b	10. c	14. b	18. a
3. d	7. a	11. c	15. d	19. c
4. c	8. c	12. b	16. c	20. d

Chapter 7

Materiality, Risk, and Preliminary Audit Strategies

A. CHAPTER OUTLINE

I. Materiality

   A. The Concept of Materiality

   B. Preliminary Judgments About Materiality

   C. Materiality at the Financial Statement Level

      1. Quantitative Guidelines

      2. Qualitative Considerations

   D. Materiality at the Account-Balance Level

   E. Allocating Financial Statement Materiality to Accounts

   F. Relationship Between Materiality and Audit Evidence

II. Audit Risk

   A. Audit Risk Components

      1. Inherent Risk

      2. Control Risk

      3. Detection Risk

   B. Relationship Among Risk Components

      1. Audit Risk Model

      2. Risk Components Matrix

   C. Audit Risk at the Financial Statement and Account-Balance Levels

   D. Relationship between Audit Risk and Audit Evidence

   E. Interrelationships among Materiality, Audit Risk, and Audit Evidence

   F. Audit Risk Alerts

III. Preliminary Audit Strategies

   A. Components of Preliminary Audit Strategies

B. CHAPTER HIGHLIGHTS

1. **Materiality** has been defined by the FASB as the magnitude of an omission or misstatement of accounting information that, in the light of surrounding circumstances, makes it probable that the judgment of a reasonable person relying on the information would have been changed or influenced by the omission or misstatement.

2. Materiality underlies the **application or GAAS**, particularly the standards of field work and reporting.

3. Materiality has a pervasive effect on the audit. **Preliminary judgments** about materiality levels used in **planning** the audit may differ from **materiality levels** used at the conclusion of the audit in **evaluating audit findings** because the surrounding circumstances may change and additional information about the client will have been obtained during the course of the audit.

4. In planning the audit, the auditor should assess materiality at:
    a. The **financial statement level** because the auditor's opinion on fairness extends to the statements taken as a whole.
    b. The **account balance level** because the auditor verifies account balances in reaching an overall conclusion on the statements.

5. The auditor initially determines the **aggregate (overall) level of materiality for each statement** (balance sheet and income statement). For planning purposes, the auditor then uses the **smallest aggregate level** of misstatements considered to be material to any one of the statements.

6. Materiality judgments involve both **quantitative and qualitative** considerations.
    a. In the absence of official guidelines in accounting and auditing standards, firms use **quantitative rules of thumb** based on fixed or variable percentages of financial variables such as net income, total assets, and total revenues.
    b. **Qualitative considerations** may result in an auditor concluding that an irregularity of a given magnitude is material while an error of the same magnitude is not material.

7. At the **account balance level**:
    a. Materiality is also known as **tolerable misstatement**.
    b. A distinction must be made between the concept of **materiality**, which pertains to the amount of misstatement that could affect a user's decision, and the term **material account balance**, which refers to the size of a recorded balance (a seemingly immaterial (small) account balance could contain an understatement that exceeds materiality).

8. In **allocating financial statement materiality to account balances**, the auditor may choose to allocate relatively larger amounts to accounts that (a) have a higher likelihood of misstatements and/or (b) are more costly to audit.

9. Other things equal, the following **relationships to audit evidence** pertain:
    a. The lower the materiality level for an account, the greater the amount of evidence needed (inverse relationship).
    b. The larger (or more significant or material) an account balance is, the greater the amount of evidence needed (direct relationship).

10. **Audit risk** is the risk that the auditor may unknowingly fail to appropriately modify his or her opinion on financial statements that are materially misstated.

11. The objective is to **restrict audit risk at the account balance level** so that at the conclusion of the audit, the audit risk in expressing an opinion on the financial statements as a whole will be at an appropriately low level.

12. Audit risk has **three components:** inherent risk, control risk, and detection risk.

13. **Inherent risk** is the susceptibility of an assertion to a material misstatement, assuming that there are no related internal control structure policies or procedures.

14. The assessment of inherent risk requires consideration of:
    a. **Matters that may have a pervasive effect** on assertions for all or many accounts (such as going concern status, management turnover, and impact of technological developments).
    b. **Matters that may pertain only to assertions for specific accounts** (such as contentious accounting issues, susceptibility to misappropriation, and complexity of calculations).

15. The **actual level of inherent risk** may be greater for some assertions than for others and exists independently of the audit.

16. The **assessed level of inherent risk** is based on the auditor's evaluation of inherent risk factors. The auditor may forego the evaluation and choose to simply assess inherent risk at the maximum when he or she concludes that the evaluation effort would exceed the benefits from using a lower assessment.

17. **Control risk** is the risk that a material misstatement that could occur in an assertion will not be prevented or detected on a timely basis by the entity's internal control structure policies or procedures.

18. **Control risk can never be zero** because internal controls cannot provide complete assurance that all material misstatements will be prevented or detected.

19. The **actual level of control risk** for an assertion cannot be changed by the auditor. However, the auditor's assessed level can vary based on evidence from (a) procedures to obtain an understanding of relevant controls and (b) tests of the controls. The lower the assessed level the auditor wishes to support, the more extensive will be his or her use of these two classes of procedures to obtain the required evidence.

20. Normally, auditors determine a **planned assessed level of control risk** for each significant assertion in the planning phase of the audit **based on assumptions** about the effectiveness of

relevant portions of the internal control structure. An **actual assessed level of control risk** is subsequently determined for each assertion **based on evidence** obtained from the auditor's study and evaluation of the internal control structure during interim work.

21. **Detection risk** is the risk that the auditor will not detect a material misstatement that exists in an assertion.

22. Unlike inherent and control risk, the **actual level of detection risk** can be changed by the auditor by varying the nature, timing, and extent of substantive tests performed on an assertion. Lower levels of detection risk result from using more rather than less effective procedures, performing the procedures at or near the balance sheet date rather than at an interim date, and performing the procedures on larger rather than smaller samples.

23. For each significant assertion, a **planned acceptable level of detection risk** is determined in the planning phase of the audit. This planned level may be subsequently **revised** based on evidence obtained about the effectiveness of relevant internal controls.

24. The components of audit risk can be expressed in **quantitative terms**, such as percentages, and the **relationship** between the components can be expressed **through an audit risk model**. Alternatively, the components can be expressed in **nonquantitative terms**, such as very low, low, moderate, high, and maximum, and the **relationship** between the components can be expressed **through a risk components matrix** which is based on the relationships contained in the audit risk model.

25. The audit risk model expresses the relationship between the risk components as follows:

$$AR = IR \times CR \times DR$$

where the symbols represent audit, inherent, control, and detection risk, respectively. The auditor generally specifies the desired level of overall audit risk to be achieved and his or her levels of inherent and control risk for an assertion, and then solves for detection risk using the following variation of the model:

$$DR = AR / (IR \times CR)$$

Thus, based on the model, the auditor can control audit risk at the desired level by varying detection risk inversely with the assessed levels of inherent and control risk.

26. The following **relationships between audit risk and audit evidence** pertain:
    a. The lower the level of overall audit risk to be achieved, the greater the amount of evidence needed (inverse relationship).
    b. For a given level of audit risk, the lower the acceptable level of detection risk, the greater the amount of evidence needed (inverse relationship). Conversely, the lower the assessed levels of inherent or control risk, the less evidence needed. However, it is not appropriate under GAAS to conclude that inherent and control risks are so low that it is not necessary to perform any substantive tests for all assertions pertaining to an account.

27. A **preliminary audit strategy**:
   a. Represents the auditor's preliminary judgments about an audit approach for obtaining evidence about an assertion. (It is not a detailed specification of auditing procedures.)
   b. Is based on certain assumptions about the conduct of the audit which affect the specification of four components of the audit strategy.

28. The four components of an audit strategy and differences in their specification for two common preliminary audit strategies may be summarized as follows:

Preliminary Audit Strategies

Component	Primarily Substantive Approach	Lower Assessed Level of Control Risk Approach
The planned assessed level of control risk	Maximum or slightly below the maximum	Moderate or low
The extent of understanding of the internal control structure to be obtained	Minimum	Extensive
Tests of controls to be performed in assessing control risk	Few, if any	Extensive
The planned level of substantive tests to be performed to reduce audit risk to an appropriately low level	Extensive tests based on low planned acceptable level of detection risk	Restricted tests based on moderate or high planned acceptable level of detection risk

29. Frequently, a common audit strategy is applied to groups of assertions affected by a **transaction class** within a transaction cycle. The rationale is that many internal controls focus on the processing of a single type of transaction within one of the cycles.

30. The following framework of transaction cycles and major classes of transactions is used in the text and is representative of practice:

Cycle	Major Classes of Transactions
Revenue	Sales, cash receipts, and sales adjustments
Expenditure	Purchases and cash disbursements
Personnel services	Payroll
Production	Manufacturing
Investing	Temporary and long-term investments
Financing	Long-term debt and capital stock

C. TRUE OR FALSE STATEMENTS

Indicate in the space provided whether each of the following statements is true or false.

_____ 1. The definition of materiality used by auditors requires consideration of both (a) the circumstances pertaining to the entity and (b) the information needs of those who will rely on the audited financial statements.

_____ 2. An amount that is material to the audited financial statements of one entity may not be material to the financial statements of another entity of a different size or nature.

_____ 3. Planning materiality and the materiality level used at the conclusion of the audit in evaluating the audit findings should always be the same.

_____ 4. Errors or irregularities that, in the aggregate, may prevent financial statements from being presented fairly in conformity with GAAP include misstatements resulting from misapplications of GAAP, departures from fact, or omissions of necessary information.

_____ 5. Auditors' preliminary judgments about materiality made several months before the balance sheet date may be based on annualized interim financial statement data or one or more prior years' financial results adjusted for current changes.

_____ 6. Materiality judgments involve both quantitative and qualitative considerations.

_____ 7. Materiality at the financial statement level is also known as tolerable misstatement.

_____ 8. In allocating financial statement materiality to accounts, the auditor should consider the likelihood of misstatements in an account but not the probable cost of verifying the account.

_____ 9. The higher the materiality level for an account, the greater the amount of evidence needed.

_____10. Audit risk is the risk that the auditor will not detect a material misstatement that exists in an assertion.

_____11. Inherent risk is the susceptibility of an assertion to a material misstatement, assuming that there are no related internal control structure policies or procedures.

_____12. Effective internal controls over an assertion reduce inherent risk, whereas ineffective internal controls increase inherent risk.

_____13. Detection risk is a function of the effectiveness of auditing procedures and of their application by the auditor.

_____14. The audit risk model can be used in the planning phase of the audit to determine planned detection risk for an assertion based on the auditor's planned assessed level of control risk, and reapplied later in the audit to determine a revised detection risk based on the actual assessed level of control risk.

_____15. The use of either the audit risk model or a risk components matrix should result in acceptable levels of detection risk for an assertion that are inversely related to the auditors assessments of inherent and control risk.

_____16. Expressions of the levels of inherent, control, and detection risk ordinarily pertain to the financial statements taken as a whole.

_____17. When inherent and control risks are assessed as low, it may be appropriate to eliminate substantive tests for some, but not all, assertions pertaining to a significant account balance.

_____18. There is an inverse relationship between audit risk and the amount of evidence needed to support the auditor's opinion on the financial statements.

_____19. Periodically, the Financial Accounting Standards Board issues audit risk alerts.

_____20. The four components of an audit strategy are inherent risk, control risk, detection risk, and audit risk.

_____21. A preliminary audit strategy is a detailed specification of auditing procedures to be performed in completing the audit.

_____22. Under the primarily substantive approach, the auditor should specify a planned assessed level of control risk of maximum or slightly below the maximum.

_____23. Under the lower assessed level of control risk approach, the auditor should plan restricted substantive tests based on a moderate or high planned acceptable level of detection risk.

_____24. The auditor is most likely to use the primarily substantive approach for accounts that are affected by a high volume of transactions such as sales, accounts receivable, inventory, and payroll expenses.

_____25. Sales, cash receipts, purchases, and cash disbursements are examples of transaction cycles.

D. COMPLETION STATEMENTS

Fill in the blanks with the word or words that correctly complete the following statements.

1. Materiality is defined as the magnitude of an _____ of accounting information that, in the light of surrounding circumstances, makes it probable that the judgment of a _____ relying on the information would have been _____ by the omission or misstatement.

2. In planning the audit, the auditor should assess materiality at both the _____ level and the _____ level.

3. For planning purposes, the auditor should use the _____ aggregate level of misstatements considered material to any one of the _____ .

4. The auditor should plan the audit to detect misstatements that may be _____ , but that, when _____ with misstatements in other account balances, may be material to the financial statements _____ .

5. In allocating financial statement materiality to accounts, the auditor should consider the _____ in the account and the _____ of verifying the account.

6. Materiality is one of the factors that affects the auditor's _____ about the sufficiency of _____ .

7. Audit risk is the risk that the auditor may unknowingly _____ his or her opinion on financial statements that are _____ .

8. The three components of audit risk are _____ , _____ , and _____ .

9. Control risk is the risk that a material misstatement that could occur in an assertion will not be _____ or _____ on a timely basis by the entity's internal control structure.

10. Detection risk is a function of the effectiveness of _____ and of their _____ .

11. For a specified level of audit risk, there is an _____ of inherent and control risks for an assertion and the level of _____ that the auditor can accept for that assertion.

12. When the components of audit risk are expressed quantitatively, they can be mathematically related through the _____ while nonquantitative expressions for the risk components can be related through the use of a _____ .

13. A preliminary audit strategy represents the auditor's preliminary judgments about an _____ ; it is not a _____ of auditing procedures to be performed in completing the audit.

14. Two alternative preliminary strategies commonly used in auditing are the _____ and the _____ .

15. Frequently, a common strategy is applied to groups of assertions affected by a _____ within a _____ .

E. MULTIPLE CHOICE

Choose the best answer for each of the following questions and enter the identifying letter in the space provided.

_____   1. Which of the following parts of the definition of materiality is incorrect?
a. The magnitude of an omission or misstatement of accounting information...
b. ...that, in the light of surrounding circumstances, makes it probable...
c. ...that the judgment of a reasonable auditor examining the financial statements...
d. ...would have been changed or influenced by the omission or misstatement.

_____   2. Which of the following statements about materiality is correct?
a. It is essential that the same materiality level be used in planning the audit and in evaluating the findings at the conclusion of the audit.
b. It may be appropriate to use lower materiality levels for working capital accounts for a company on the brink of bankruptcy than for a company that is financially sound.
c. What is material to the financial statements of a particular entity should not change from one period to another.
d. The definition of materiality requires the auditor to consider circumstances pertaining to the entity, but not the information needs of users of the financial statements.

_____   3. Which of the following statements regarding qualitative considerations pertaining to materiality is incorrect?
a. Qualitative considerations relate to the causes of misstatements.
b. In most cases, the auditor is expected to design procedures to detect misstatements that are either qualitatively or quantitatively material.
c. Qualitative considerations might lead an auditor to conclude that a misstatement resulting from an irregularity of a given magnitude is material while a misstatement resulting from an error of the same magnitude is not material.
d. Discovery of an illegal act that results in a small misstatement might be considered qualitatively material if the auditor concludes there is a significant risk of additional similar misstatements.

_____   4. The term tolerable misstatement relates most closely to:
a. The level of materiality set by management.
b. The amount determined by applying a variable percentage to either total assets or total revenues.
c. The concept of financial statement materiality.
d. The concept of account balance materiality.

_____   5. Regarding the allocation of financial statement materiality to accounts, it is correct to say that:
a. The process is heavily dependent on the subjective judgment of the auditor.
b. The auditor should allocate smaller amounts for materiality to accounts with a greater likelihood of misstatements.

    c. The auditor should allocate smaller amounts for materiality to accounts that are more costly to verify.

    d. It is never appropriate to revise the allocation of the preliminary estimate of materiality as the field work progresses.

6. Upon giving proper consideration to the relationship between materiality and audit evidence, the auditor would conclude that:

    a. The lower the materiality level, the greater the amount of evidence needed.

    b. The higher the materiality level, the greater the amount of evidence needed.

    c. No evidence is needed for any account which has a balance that is less than tolerable misstatement.

    d. The amount of evidence needed in not affected by materiality.

7. Audit risk is:

    a. The risk that the auditor will incur legal liability for performing a substandard audit.

    b. The risk that the auditor's procedures will fail to detect a material misstatement that exists in an assertion.

    c. The risk that the auditor may unknowingly fail to appropriately modify his or her opinion on financial statements that are materially misstated.

    d. The risk that the financial statements contain misstatements in excess of financial statement materiality.

8. The components of audit risk are:

    a. Financial statement risk, account balance risk, and opinion risk.

    b. Inherent risk, business risk, and control risk.

    c. Inherent risk, control risk, and detection risk.

    d. Business risk, control risk, and financial statement risk.

9. Of the following inherent risk factors, the one that is most likely to pertain to a specific account rather than to all or many accounts is:

    a. Going concern problems such as lack of sufficient working capital.

    b. Management turnover, reputation, and accounting skills.

    c. The impact of technological developments on the company's operations and competitiveness.

    d. Susceptibility to misappropriation.

10. The auditor might choose to forego attempting to assess inherent risk for an assertion at an appropriate level and simply assess it at the maximum when he or she:

    a. Elects to perform more extensive tests of controls instead.

    b. Agrees with a management imposed scope limitation on assessing this risk.

    c. Concludes that the effort required to evaluate inherent risk would exceed the potential reduction in the extent of auditing procedures derived from using a lower assessment.

    d. Decides that inherent risk is inseparable from detection risk.

_____ 11. Based on inherent risk considerations, which of the following statements is least likely to be valid?
   a. The existence or occurrence assertion for cash is more susceptible to misstatement than the same assertion for plant assets.
   b. The presentation and disclosure assertion for equipment acquired under capital leases is more susceptible to misstatements than the same assertion for equipment purchased for cash.
   c. The completeness assertion for accounts receivable is more susceptible to misstatement than the same assertion for accounts payable.
   d. The valuation or allocation assertion for inventories is more susceptible to misstatement than the same assertion for gross plant assets.

_____ 12. Which of the following statements about control risk is incorrect?
   a. Control risk can never be zero because internal controls cannot provide complete assurance that all material misstatements will be prevented or detected.
   b. The assessed level of control risk for an assertion can vary based on the extent of (1) the auditor's procedures to obtain an understanding of the internal control structure and (2) the auditor's tests of controls.
   c. The planned assessed level of control risk for an assertion is based on assumptions about the effectiveness of the design and operation of relevant portions of the client's internal control structure.
   d. Control risk is inversely related to inherent risk and detection risk.

_____ 13. Detection risk is:
   a. Directly related to inherent risk and inversely related to control risk.
   b. Inversely related to both inherent and control risks.
   c. Determined independently of either inherent or control risk.
   d. The risk that the client's internal controls will fail to detect material misstatements.

_____ 14. When the acceptable level of detection risk for an assertion is high, the auditor is more likely to:
   a. Select an auditing procedure that is more effective and more costly rather than less effective and less costly.
   b. Perform a procedure at an interim date rather than at year end.
   c. Apply a procedure to a larger sample rather than a smaller sample.
   d. Forego extensive tests of controls.

_____ 15. The audit risk model is used to:
   a. Assess the risk that the auditor may suffer losses from audit failures.
   b. Identify inherent risk factors that may affect all or many assertions.
   c. Provide a means for calculating control risk based on the auditor's assessments of inherent and detection risk.
   d. Show how the components of audit risk relate to each other.

_____ 16. For a particular assertion, the auditor specified an overall audit risk of 10%, assessed inherent and control risks as 50% and 20%, respectively, and calculated detection risk to be 100%. The implication of this situation is that:
   a. The auditor made an error in calculating detection risk.
   b. Inherent and control risks are sufficiently low that it may not be necessary to perform any substantive tests for this particular assertion.
   c. The auditor will need to perform extensive substantive tests to compensate for the high level of detection risk.
   d. The auditor should reduce the extent of tests of controls so that the assessed level of control risk will be higher and detection risk will be lower.

_____ 17. Audit risk alerts are issued by:
   a. The auditor to inform management and the audit committee when control risk is assessed as high or maximum.
   b. The FASB to inform auditors about the implications of newly effective _Statements of Financial Accounting Standards._
   c. The AICPA staff to provide auditors with an overview of recent economic, professional, and regulatory developments.
   d. The audit committee to advise the board of directors of problems encountered in the audit.

_____ 18. A preliminary audit strategy:
   a. Represents the auditor's preliminary audit judgments about an audit approach to obtaining evidence about an assertion or group of assertions.
   b. Is a detailed specification of auditing procedures to be performed.
   c. Is intended to characterize the auditor's approach to the overall audit, not an individual assertion.
   d. Contains separate components dealing with inherent risk, control risk, detection risk, and audit risk.

_____ 19. Each of the following strategy components is consistent with the primarily substantive approach for an assertion except:
   a. Use a planned assessed level of control risk of moderate or low.
   b. Plan to obtain a minimum understanding of relevant portions of the internal control structure.
   c. Plan few, if any, tests of controls.
   d. Plan extensive substantive tests based on a low planned acceptable level of detection risk.

_____ 20. In developing preliminary audit strategies for accounts receivable assertions, the auditor should consider expectations about the effectiveness of controls pertaining to:
   a. Sales transactions.
   b. Cash receipts transactions.
   c. Sales adjustments transactions.
   d. All of the above.

SOLUTIONS

TRUE OR FALSE STATEMENTS

1. True	10. False	18. True
2. True	11. True	19. False
3. False	12. False	20. False
4. True	13. True	21. False
5. True	14. True	22. True
6. True	15. True	23. True
7. False	16. False	24. False
8. False	17. True	25. False
9. False		

COMPLETION STATEMENTS

1. omission or misstatement, reasonable person, changed or influenced
2. financial statement, account balance
3. smallest, financial statements
4. immaterial individually, aggregated, taken as a whole
5. likelihood of misstatements, probable cost
6. judgment, evidential matter
7. fail to appropriately modify, materially misstated
8. inherent risk, control risk, detection risk
9. prevented, detected
10. auditing procedures, application by the auditor
11. inverse relationship between, detection risk
12. audit risk model, risk components matrix
13. audit approach, detailed specification
14. primarily substantive approach, lower assessed level of control risk approach
15. transaction class, transaction cycle

MULTIPLE CHOICE QUESTIONS

1. c	5. a	9. d	13. b	17. c
2. b	6. a	10. c	14. b	18. a
3. b	7. c	11. c	15. d	19. a
4. d	8. c	12. d	16. b	20. d

Chapter 8

Understanding the Internal Control Structure

A. CHAPTER OUTLINE

I. Introduction to Internal Control

    A. Importance of Internal Control

    B. Definition, Fundamental Concepts, and Components

    C. Entity Objectives and Related Internal Controls Relevant to an Audit

    D. Limitations of an Entity's Internal Control Structure

    E. Roles and Responsibilities

II. Components of an Internal Control Structure

    A. Control Environment

        1. Integrity and Ethical Values

        2. Commitment to Competence

        3. Board of Directors and Audit Committee

        4. Management's Philosophy and Operating Style

        5. Organizational Structure

        6. Assignment of Authority and Responsibility

        7. Human Resource Policies and Practices

    B. Risk Assessment

    C. Information and Communication

    D. Control Activities

        1. Information Processing Controls

        2. Segregation of Duties

        3. Physical Controls

        4. Performance Reviews

    E. Monitoring

    F. Application of Components to Small and Midsize Entities

B. CHAPTER HIGHLIGHTS

1. During the last five decades, internal control has become more important to **management, independent auditors, and external parties**, such as regulators.

2. The **Foreign Corrupt Practices Act (FCPA)** requires companies subject to SEC regulation to maintain a satisfactory system of internal control and to comply with antibribery standards.

3. The **National Commission on Fraudulent Financial Reporting (Treadway Commission)** recognized the importance of internal control in reducing the incidence of fraudulent financial reporting.

4. **SAS 55** expanded the meaning of internal control and the auditor's responsibilities for satisfying the second standard of field work.

5. In 1992, the **Committee of Sponsoring Organizations (COSO)** of the Treadway Commission issued a report entitled Internal Control-Integrated Framework.

6. COSO defines internal control as a **process** effected by an entity's board of directors, management, and other personnel, designed to provide reasonable assurance regarding the achievement of objectives in:
    a. Reliability of financial reporting
    b. Compliance with laws and regulations
    c. Effectiveness and efficiency of operation (including safeguarding of assets)

7. COSO also identifies **five interrelated components** of internal control:
    a. Control environment
    b. Risk assessment
    c. Information and communication
    d. Control activities
    e. Monitoring

8. **Inherent limitations** exist in any internal control structure, including:
    a. Mistakes in judgment by management or others because of inadequate information, time constraints, etc.
    b. Breakdowns in established controls due to carelessness, distractions or fatigue.
    c. Collusion among individuals to both perpetrate and conceal an irregularity.
    d. Management override of controls for illegitimate purposes (inflating earnings, maximizing bonuses or stock values, or hiding noncompliance with debt covenants or laws).
    e. Cost/benefit tradeoffs.

9. COSO recognizes the following **parties** as **having key responsibilities** for internal controls:
    a. Management should set a "tone at the top" for control consciousness.
    b. The board of directors and its audit committee should determine that management meets its responsibilities.
    c. Internal auditors should periodically evaluate the control structure and recommend improvements.
    d. Other personnel should communicate any noncompliance with controls.

e. Independent auditors should understand controls sufficient to plan the audit and should report any discovered deficiencies to the audit committee.

f. External parties establish minimum standards for establishment of controls (e.g., FCPA, FDIC regulations for banks).

10. Factors affecting the **control environment** are:
    a. Integrity and ethical values, including moral guidance and reduction of temptations.
    b. Commitment to competence at every organizational level.
    c. Board of directors and audit committee.
    d. Management's philosophy and operating style, including approaches to risk and attitudes toward accounting options and controls.
    e. Organizational structure clearly defined to assign responsibility and monitor effectiveness.
    f. Human resources policies and practices to ensure integrity, ethical values and competence of employees.

11. Establishing a relevant **information system**, of which an **accounting information system** is a subset, to maintain accountability and clear communication of individual roles and responsibilities under the system is critical to establishing control. Accounting systems focus on identifying and measuring **transactions** in sufficient detail to permit proper financial presentation.

12. **Control activities** consist of:
    a. Information processing controls, including general data center organization, hardware, software, and backup/recovery controls. Also, application controls such as authorization, documents and records, and independent checks are included.
    b. Segregation of incompatible duties to prevent an individual from committing and concealing an error or irregularity.
    c. Physical controls to limit direct and indirect access to assets and records.
    d. Performance reviews, including summarization of detail balances, actual vs. budget comparisons, financial and nonfinancial data comparisons.
    e. Monitoring activities to focus management's attention on problem areas.

13. **Documents** provide evidence of the occurrence of transactions while records provide summaries of issued documents. **Prenumbering** of documents and appropriate follow-up and filing provides assurance that all transactions are recorded and recorded only once (the completeness assertion). **Independent comparison** of records with document details provides additional assurance that all recorded transactions are documented (the existence/occurrence assertion) and that the transactions are properly priced (the valuation/allocation assertion).

14. **Independent checks** involve the verification of (1) work previously performed by other individuals, and (2) the proper valuation of the recorded amounts. Examples include supervisor's counts of bank teller drawers and independent comparisons of recorded prices with authorized price lists. These checks can be performed manually or by computer programs.

15. **Duties should be segregated** in the following ways:
    a. Responsibility for executing a transaction, recording the transaction, and maintaining custody of the assets resulting from the transaction should be assigned to different individuals or departments.
    b. The various steps involved in executing a transaction should be assigned to different individuals or departments.
    c. Responsibility for certain accounting operations should be segregated.
    d. There should be proper segregation of duties within the EDP department and between EDP and user departments.

16. **Physical controls** limit access to assets or important records. Access can be accomplished either directly (i.e., physical access to cash or inventories) or indirectly (i.e., preparing and processing documents that allow access to assets). Measures to limit access include fireproof safes, vaults, locks, offsite storage, cash registers. When EDP systems are in use, the computer, records, programs, data files, and EDP output should be access-controlled. Passwords, keys and identification badges help ensure proper control. Periodic physical counts for comparison to control records provides additional physical control.

17. Periodic assessment of the quality of control procedures is termed **monitoring** and is often the responsibility of internal audit departments.

18. The degree of formality and implementation of the these five control components vary with the organization's size, business, organization and ownership, complexity, and legal/regulatory requirements. **Small entities** are less likely to have formal written policies, outside directors, sufficient employees to implement segregation of duties, or internal auditors. Owner manager involvement in certain critical tasks can aid controls.

19. Whether the auditor chooses the primarily substantive approach or the lower assessed control risk approach, an **understanding** of the internal control systems **sufficient to plan the audit** is required by the second standard of fieldwork. This understanding of the ICS is used to identify types of potential misstatements, consider risk, and design substantive testing procedures. Developing an understanding of the ICS extends only to whether controls and policies are being used, not to their effectiveness, which is assessed later in making control risk estimates.

20. **Procedures** to obtain an understanding include:
    a. Reviewing previous experience with the client.
    b. Preliminary inherent risk and materiality assessments.
    c. Understanding the client's industry.
    d. The complexity and sophistication of the client's operations and accounting systems.

21. The auditor's **understanding** of the internal control structure should be **documented** through completed questionnaires, flowcharts, decision tables, and narrative memoranda.

22. A **transaction walk-through** review consists of tracing one or a few transactions within a major class of transactions through the transaction trail and identifying related control procedures.

23. An **internal control questionnaire** consists of a series of questions about whether controls necessary to prevent or detect errors and irregularities in the financial statements are included in the control structure.

24. A **flowchart** is a schematic diagram using standardized symbols, interconnecting flow lines, and annotations that portray the steps involved in processing information through the accounting system.

25. A **narrative memorandum** consists of written comments concerning the auditor's consideration of the internal control structure.

C. TRUE OR FALSE STATEMENTS

Indicate in the space provided whether each of the following statements is true or false.

_____ 1. Internal control is important to both management and independent auditors.

_____ 2. The Foreign Corrupt Practices Act requires all companies to maintain a satisfactory system of internal control.

_____ 3. The National Commission on Fraudulent Financial Reporting (Treadway Commission) provided sponsorship for COSO to investigate the relationship of internal controls with fraudulent financial reporting.

_____ 4. An entity's control environment reflects the overall tone of employees regarding the importance of control in the company.

_____ 5. COSO's three assurances to be provided by internal controls are reliable financial reporting, compliance with laws/regulations, and promoting effectiveness and efficiency within an organization.

_____ 6. The major components of internal control are control environment, accounting system, and control procedures.

_____ 7. One factor affecting the control environment is proper human resources policies to ensure the hiring of ethical and moral employees.

_____ 8. One inherent limitation of any control system is the possibility of collusion.

_____ 9. The primary objective of segregation of duties is the prevention or prompt detection of errors and irregularities in the performance of assigned responsibilities.

_____ 10. The use of, and accounting for the sequence of, documents relates to the presentation and disclosure assertion.

_____ 11. Access controls relate to both direct physical access to assets and indirect access through the preparation or processing of documents.

_____ 12. Independent checks involve activities such as checking actual financial results to budgeted expectations.

_____ 13. Access controls are relevant in assessing control risk for the existence or occurrence assertion.

_____ 14. For planning purposes, the understanding of the control structure is limited to the design of controls.

_____ 15. The control environment may have pervasive effects on control risk for numerous financial statement assertions.

_____ 16. Monitoring is the periodic assessment of the effectiveness of control procedures and is the primary responsibility of independent auditors.

_____ 17. Consideration of previous experience with the client in prior audits ordinarily is not relevant in obtaining an understanding of the internal control structure in the current audit.

_____ 18. When the auditor chooses the primarily substantive approach to auditing a given assertion, an assessment as to the effectiveness of the applicable controls needs to be performed.

_____ 19. Procedures performed by internal auditors to monitor an entity's internal control structure policies and procedures may provide useful information for the external auditor.

_____ 20. In a small entity, owner/manager involvement in tasks such as signing checks is a good way to compensate for the inability to properly segregate duties.

_____ 21. An internal control questionnaire consists of a series of questions pertaining to the effectiveness of specific controls.

_____ 22. Questionnaires reduce the possibility of overlooking important aspects of an entity's control structure and they are easy to use and to complete.

_____ 23. Flowcharts may be prepared for the accounting system as a whole or for a specific transaction class.

_____ 24. A flowchart is an end in itself, not a means to an end.

_____ 25. Narrative memoranda are useful because they are tailored to the client, but they may lead to overlooking necessary, but missing, controls .

D. COMPLETION STATEMENTS

Fill in the blanks with the word or words that correctly complete the following statements.

1. An entity's internal control structure consists of five elements: the _____ , the _____ , the _____ , the _____ , and _____ .

2. Five inherent limitations of any control system are _____ , _____ , _____ , _____ , and _____ .

3. The commission that investigated fraudulent financial reporting in the 1980's was commonly termed the _____ Commission.

4. The organization that provided sponsorship for the commission in 3. and that issued the most recent report on internal controls was the _____ .

5. When considering management's philosophy as it affects controls, the auditor should consider management's approaches to _____ and attitudes toward _____ and _____ .

6. Accounting systems focus on identifying and measuring _____ to permit proper _____ .

7. Control activities consist of _____ , _____ , _____ , _____ , and _____ .

8. The auditor's primary objective in obtaining an understanding of the client's internal control structure is to be able to _____ the audit, identify _____ , and design _____ tests.

9. Periodic assessment of the quality of control procedures is termed _____ and is often performed by _____ auditors.

10. In performing a transaction walk-through review, one or a few transactions within each major _____ is traced through the _____ and the related control policies and procedures are _____ .

11. Two types of information processing controls are _____ and _____ .

12. Physical controls limit access to assets, which can be accomplished either _____ or _____ through preparation and processing of _____ .

13. Working paper documentation of the auditor's understanding of the internal control structure may be in the form of _____ , _____ , _____ , and/or _____ .

14. Small entities are less likely to have _____ , _____ ,
_____ , or _____ .

15. A flowchart is a schematic diagram using standardized _____ , interconnecting
_____ , and _____ that portray the steps involved in processing
information through the accounting system.

E. MULTIPLE CHOICE

Choose the best answer for each of the following questions and enter the identifying letter in the
space provided.

_____   1. Proper segregation of functional responsibilities in an effective internal control
structure calls for separation of the functions of:
a. Authorization, execution, and payment.
b. Authorization, recording, and custody.
c. Custody, execution, and reporting.
d. Authorization, payment, and recording.

_____   2. Internal controls are not designed to provide reasonable assurance that:
a. Transactions are executed in accordance with management's authorization.
b. Irregularities will be eliminated.
c. Access to assets is permitted only in accordance with management's
authorization.
d. The recorded accountability for assets is compared with the existing assets at
reasonable intervals.

_____   3. The concept that the cost of internal control should not exceed the benefits expected
to be derived is known as:
a. Relative risk
b. Reasonable assurance.
c. Comparative cost.
d. Management justification.
e. Management objective.

_____   4. Establishing and maintaining an internal control structure is the responsibility of the:
a. Internal auditor.
b. External auditor.
c. Management.
d. Audit committee.
e. Financial vice-president.

_____ 5. Which of the following factors are included in an entity's control environment?

	Board of Directors/ Audit Committee	Internal Audit Function	Organizational Structure
a.	Yes	Yes	No
b.	Yes	No	Yes
c.	No	Yes	Yes
d.	Yes	Yes	Yes

_____ 6. A well prepared flowchart should make it easier for the auditor to:
   a. Prepare audit procedure manuals.
   b. Prepare detailed job descriptions.
   c. Trace the origin and disposition of documents.
   d. Assess the degree of accuracy of financial data.

_____ 7. The auditor's understanding of the client's internal control structure is documented in order to substantiate:
   a. Conformity of the accounting records with generally accepted accounting principles.
   b. Compliance with generally accepted auditing standards.
   c. Adherence to requirements of management.
   d. The fairness of the financial statement presentation.

_____ 8. Which of the following statements regarding auditor documentation of the client's internal control structure is correct?
   a. Documentation must include flowcharts.
   b. Documentation must include procedural writeups.
   c. No documentation is necessary although it is desirable.
   d. No one particular form of documentation is necessary, and the extent of documentation may vary.

_____ 9. Which of the following is a provision of the Foreign Corrupt Practices Act?
   a. It is a criminal offense for an auditor to fail to detect and report a bribe paid by an American business entity to a foreign official for the purpose of obtaining business.
   b. The auditor's detection of illegal acts committed by officials of the auditor's publicly held client in conjunction with foreign officials should be reported to the Enforcement Division of the Securities and Exchange Commission.
   c. If the auditor of a publicly held company concludes that the effects on the financial statements of a bribe given to a foreign official are not susceptible of reasonable estimation, the auditor's report should be modified.
   d. Every publicly held company must devise, document, and maintain a system of internal control sufficient to provide reasonable assurances that internal control objectives are met.

_____ 10. The correct labeling, in order, for the following flowchart symbols is

  a. Document, display, on-line storage, and on-line computer process.
  b. Manual operation, processing, off-line storage, and input/output activity.
  c. Display, document, on-line storage, and off-line storage.
  d. Manual operation, document, on-line storage, and on-line computer process.

_____ 11. An auditor's flowchart of a client's internal control structure is a diagrammatic representation which depicts the auditor's:
  a. Understanding of the control structure
  b. Program for tests of controls.
  c. Documentation of the evaluation of the control structure.
  d. Understanding of the types of irregularities which are probable, given the present structure.

_____ 12. Which of the following best describes an inherent limitation that should be recognized by an auditor when considering the potential effectiveness of an internal control structure?
  a. Procedures whose effectiveness depends on segregation of duties can be circumvented by collusion.
  b. The competence and integrity of client personnel provides an environment conducive to internal control and provides assurance that effective control will be achieved.
  c. Procedures designed to assure the execution and recording of transactions in accordance with proper authorizations are effective against irregularities perpetrated by management.
  d. Despite proper separation of duties, collusion among two or more employees may allow them to commit and conceal an irregularity.

_____ 13. Developing an understanding of the control system extends to:
  a. Determining whether controls are being used.
  b. Determining whether controls are being used and whether they are effective.
  c. Oral inquiries of client personnel.
  d. Review of control procedures and testing compliance with the procedures.

_____ 14. The organization that investigated fraudulent financial reporting in the 1980's was:

Name	Sponsored by
a. COSO	Cohen Commission
b. Treadway Commission	COSO
c. Cohen Commission	AICPA
d. Metcalf Committee	U.S. Congress

_____ 15. Which of the following is not one of the components of internal control as identified in *Internal Control-Integrated Framework*?
   a. Control Environment
   b. Control Activities
   c. Management Override
   d. Monitoring

_____ 16. Which of the following is not an example of an application information processing control?
   a. Authorization
   b. Independent checks
   c. Backup/ Recovery procedures
   d. Documents and Records

_____ 17. Which of the following symbolic representations indicates that a file has been consulted?

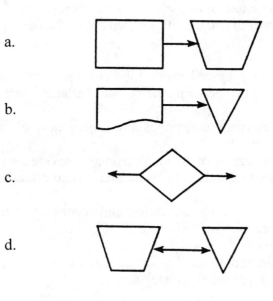

   a.

   b.

   c.

   d.

_____ 18. Which of the following symbolic representations indicates that a sales invoice has been filed?

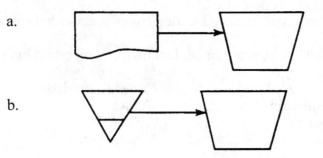

   a.

   b.

c.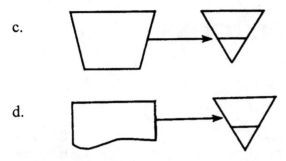

d.

_____ 19. The Jones Company has a competent and objective internal auditing staff. In performing the financial statement audit, the independent auditor should recognize that:
   a. The audit programs, working papers, and reports of internal auditors can often be used as a substitute for the work of the independent auditor's staff.
   b. The procedures performed by the internal audit staff may eliminate the independent auditor's need for an extensive study and evaluation of internal control.
   c. The work performed by internal auditors may be a factor in determining the nature, timing, and extent of the independent auditor's procedures.
   d. The understanding of the internal audit function is an important substantive test to be performed by the independent auditor.

_____ 20. What is the independent auditor's principal purpose in conducting a study and evaluation of the internal control structure?
   a. To comply with generally accepted accounting principles.
   b. To obtain a measure of assurance of management's efficiency.
   c. To maintain a state of independence in mental attitude in all matters relating to the audit.
   d. To plan the audit and to determine the nature, timing, and extent of subsequent audit work.

SOLUTIONS

TRUE OR FALSE STATEMENTS

1. True	10. False	18. False
2. False	11. True	19. True
3. False	12. False	20. True
4. True	13. True	21. False
5. True	14. False	22. True
6. False	15. True	23. True
7. True	16. False	24. False
8. True	17. False	25. True
9. True		

COMPLETION STATEMENTS

1. control environment, risk assessment, information and communication, control activities, monitoring
2. judgment mistakes, breakdowns, collusion, management override, cost/benefit
3. Treadway
4. Committee of Sponsoring Organizations
5. risk, accounting options, controls
6. transactions, financial presentation
7. information processing, segregation of duties, physical controls, performance reviews, monitoring
8. plan, potential misstatements, substantive
9. monitoring, internal
10. class of transactions, transaction trail, identified and observed
11. general, application
12. directly, indirectly, documents
13. questionnaires, flowcharts, decision tables, and narrative memoranda
14. written policies, outside directors, segregation of duties, internal auditors
15. symbols, flow lines, annotations

MULTIPLE CHOICE QUESTIONS

1. b	5. d	9. d	13. a	17. d
2. b	6. c	10. d	14. b	18. d
3. b	7. b	11. a	15. c.	19. c
4. c	8. d	12. a	16. c.	20. d

Chapter 9

Assessing Control Risk/ Tests of Controls

A. CHAPTER OUTLINE

I. **Assessing Control Risk**

   A. Consider Knowledge Acquired from Procedures to Obtain an Understanding

   B. Identify Potential Misstatements

   C. Identify Necessary Controls

   D. Perform Tests of Controls

   E. Evaluate Evidence and Make Assessment

   F. Effects of Preliminary Strategies

      1. Primarily Substantive Approach

      2. Lower Assessed Level of Control Risk Approach

II. **Tests of Controls**

   A. Concurrent Tests of Controls

   B. Additional or Planned Tests of Controls

   C. Designing Tests of Controls

      1. Nature of Tests

      2. Timing of Tests

      3. Extent of Tests

   D. Audit Programs for Tests of Controls

   E. Using Internal Auditors in Tests of Controls

      1. Coordination of Audit with Internal Auditors

      2. Direct Assistance

   F. Dual Purpose Tests

III. **Additional Considerations**

    A. Assessing Control Risk for Account Balance Assertions Affected by a Single Transaction Class

    B. Assessing Control Risk for Account Balance Assertions Affected by Multiple Transaction Classes

    C. Combining Different Control Risk Assessments

    D. Documenting the Assessed Level of Control Risk

    E. Communication of Internal Control Structure Related Matters

IV. **Summary**

B. CHAPTER HIGHLIGHTS

1. The **methodology** for meeting the **second standard of field work** involves three major activities: (1) obtaining sufficient understanding of the internal control structure (ICS) to plan the audit, (2) assessing control risk for assertions in account balances, transaction classes, or disclosure components of financial statements, and (3) designing substantive tests at the assertion level.

2. **Control risk is assessed for individual assertions** to evaluate the effectiveness of the design and operation of client controls in preventing and detecting material misstatements.

3. In making control risk assessments for financial statement assertions, the auditor should:
    a. Considers **knowledge obtained while developing an understanding** of the ICS concerning whether controls are properly designed and placed in operation.
    b. Identify **potential misstatements**.
    c. Identify **necessary controls to prevent or detect** these misstatements.
    d. Perform **tests of controls** to assess the ICS's effectiveness.
    e. Make a **control risk assessment**.

4. In **developing an understanding of the ICS**, the auditor carefully considers the information in **questionnaires, flowcharts, or narratives** to identify potential misstatements and to determine whether controls have been adequately designed and put into place.

5. In identifying **potential misstatements and identifying necessary compensating controls,** the auditor usually relies on firm-developed checklists. Certain control procedures may simultaneously affect assertions for several transaction classes and account balances.

6. A **compensating control** is one that is primarily designed for one purpose but its application may also be relevant in offsetting a weakness associated with an ineffective or missing control.

7.   After identifying potential misstatements and compensating controls, the auditor may make an initial assessment of control risk, before performing any tests of controls. **Even with a thorough understanding** of the design and placement of controls, the auditor should **not assess control risk at less than the maximum** since no information on effectiveness (obtained through tests of controls) is present.

8. Each test of control should provide **evidence about the effectiveness of the design and/or operation** of the tested control. In determining which tests to perform, the auditor considers the type of evidence provided and the cost of performing the test.

9. The **final control risk assessment** is based on both the procedures to obtain an understanding of the ICS and the related tests of controls. In forming a conclusion about effectiveness, the auditor uses guidelines about tolerable frequencies of deviations (i.e., noncompliance with a prescribed control). Other qualitative considerations, such as the cause of the deviation, enter into assessing the importance of each deviation. For instance, one deviation involving an irregularity may be more important than several deviations involving errors.

10. Under the **primarily substantive approach,** the auditor plans little or no reliance on **internal** control (maximum or high control risk). Reasons for adopting this strategy are:
    a. No significant control procedures pertaining to the assertion being audited.
    b. Relevant control policies or procedures are likely to be ineffective.
    c. It would not be efficient to obtain evidence about the effectiveness of controls for this assertion (i.e., the costs of performing tests of controls exceed the reduction in related substantive tests).

11. The **final decision in the primarily substantive approach** is to determine whether the **actual level of assessed control risk supports the planned level of substantive testing.** Evidence from **concurrent tests of controls** obtained while developing an understanding of the ICS may allow a control risk assessment at less than maximum even when extensive tests of controls are not performed.

12. Under **the lower assessed level of control risk approach,** the auditor expects to perform extensive tests of controls and restricted substantive tests. The steps under this strategy are:
    a. Obtain and document the understanding.
    b. Plan and perform tests of controls.
    c. Assess control risk.
    d. Document the control risk assessment.
    e. Determine whether the assessed level of control risk supports the planned level of substantive tests. (If yes, skip to g).
    f. Revise the planned level of substantive tests.
    g. Design substantive tests.

13. **Tests of controls** are auditing procedures performed to determine the effectiveness of the design and/or operation of control structure policies and procedures.
    a. Tests of controls pertaining to the **effectiveness of design** are concerned with whether the policy or procedure is suitably designed to prevent or detect material misstatements in a specific financial statement assertion.
    b. Tests of controls pertaining to the **effectiveness of operation** are concerned with whether control policies and procedures are actually working and focus on three questions:
       • How was the control performed?
       • Was it applied consistently during the year?
       • By whom was it applied?

14. **Concurrent tests of controls:**
    a. Are performed during audit planning in conjunction with obtaining the understanding of the internal control structure. For example, observation of segregation of duties provides evidence about the design, placement, and effectiveness of this control procedure.
    b. May provide evidence to support an assessed level of control risk in the range *slightly below the maximum to moderate.*

15. **Additional or planned tests of controls:**
    a. Are performed during interim field work.
    b. Are only performed when it is cost-efficient to do so.
    c. May provide evidence sufficient to support an assessed level of control risk of *moderate* or *low.*

16. The auditor's choices as to the **nature of tests** of controls are:
    a. *Inquiring* of personnel concerning the performance of their duties.
    b. *Observing* personnel in the performance of their duties.
    c. *Inspecting* documents and reports indicating performance of controls.
    d. *Reperforming* the controls by the auditor.

17. The **timing of tests** of controls refers to (a) when they are performed, and (b) the part of the accounting period to which they relate (when evidence is obtained about effectiveness of controls, it must pertain to the entire year covered by the financial statements).

18. The **extent of tests** of controls is directly affected by (a) the auditor's planned assessed level of control risk and (b) evidence about effectiveness of controls from prior audits.

19. The auditor's decisions about the nature, timing, and extent of tests of controls should be documented in an **audit program and related working papers**. Work papers should contain cross-references to other work papers, who performed the tests, and the date completed.

20. When a client has an **internal audit function**, the external auditor may:
    a. Coordinate his or her audit work with the internal auditors.
    b. Use the internal auditors to provide direct assistance in the audit.

21. When there is **coordination of the work**, the independent auditor should **evaluate the quality and effectiveness** of the internal auditors' work **by testing** it and determining whether the:
    a. Scope of work is appropriate to meet the objectives.
    b. Audit programs are adequate.
    c. Working papers adequately document work performed, including evidence of supervision and review.
    d. Conclusions are appropriate in the circumstances.
    e. Reports are consistent with the work performed.

22. When **internal auditors provide direct assistance** in the audit, the independent auditor should:
    a. Consider the internal auditors' competence and objectivity, and supervise, review, evaluate, and test the work performed.
    b. Inform the internal auditors of their responsibilities, the objectives of the procedures they are to perform, and matters that may affect the nature, timing, and extent of the tests.
    c. Inform the internal auditors that all significant accounting and auditing issues identified during their work should be brought to the external auditor's attention.

23. **Dual purpose testing**:
    a. Involves performing both tests of controls and substantive tests of details on the same transactions.
    b. Should be designed to obtain evidence about both the effectiveness of controls and monetary errors in the accounts.
    c. May be used when it is more cost efficient to perform the tests simultaneously than separately.

24. **Assessing control risk** is the process of evaluating the effectiveness of an entity's internal control structure policies and procedures in preventing or detecting material misstatements in the financial statements.

25. For account balance assertions that are **affected by only a single transaction class** (i.e., the sales account is almost exclusively affected by only the revenue transaction class) risk assessments for assertions are equivalent at the account balance and the transaction class levels. This is the case for most income statement accounts.

26. For account balance assertions that are **affected by multiple transaction classes** (i.e., the cash account is affected by the revenue transaction class through cash collections and by the expenditure transaction class through cash disbursements) risk assessments for assertions are the combination of transaction class assessments. This is most common for balance sheet accounts.

27. When **control risk assessments about an assertion for different transaction classes** (i.e., completeness assertion from both the revenue transaction class and the expenditure transaction class) affecting the **same account** (i.e., cash) **differ**, the auditor may **judgmentally weigh** the significance of each assessment in arriving at a combined account-level assessment.

28. An assessed level of control risk:
    a. Should be determined for **each significant financial statement assertion**.
    b. Represents the auditor's **judgment of the effectiveness** of relevant control policies and procedures.

29. **Control risk** for an assertion may be **assessed at the maximum** when the auditor believes that control policies and procedures:
    a. Are unlikely to pertain to the assertion.
    b. Are unlikely to be effective.
    c. Cannot be efficiently evaluated as to their effectiveness.

30. **Control risk** for an assertion is **assessed below the maximum** when the auditor concludes that:
    a. There are relevant control policies and procedures.
    b. Evidence has been obtained from tests of controls supporting their effectiveness.

31. For assessments **at the maximum**, only the **conclusion needs to be documented**. For assessments **below the maximum**, both the **conclusion and the basis for the conclusion** need to be documented.

32. The auditor is required to **identify and report to the audit committee** conditions that relate to an entity's internal control structure observed during an audit of financial statements. A **reportable condition** is defined as a significant deficiency in the design or operation of the internal control structure, which could adversely affect the organization's ability to record, process, summarize, and report financial data consistent with the assertions of management in the financial statements.

C. TRUE OR FALSE STATEMENTS

Indicate in the space provided whether each of the following statements is true or false.

_____ 1. Even with a thorough understanding of the ICS, the auditor should not assess control risk below the maximum unless tests of controls are performed.

_____ 2. A compensating control is one that relates to the payroll or compensation system.

_____ 3. Performing additional tests of controls is a required step under the primarily substantive approach.

_____ 4. Evidence from additional tests of controls would normally be expected to support a control risk assessment in the range of slightly below the maximum to moderate.

_____ 5. When the auditor chooses the lower assessed control risk approach, an implicit decision has been made that the cost of performing tests of controls is exceeded by the cost reduction in substantive testing due to performing tests of controls.

_____ 6. Under the lower assessed level of control risk approach, the auditor may choose to make only one assessment of control risk for an assertion after both the procedures to obtain an understanding and the planned tests of controls have been performed.

_____ 7. Under the lower assessed level of control risk approach, when the planned level of substantive tests is based on a planned assessed level of control risk that is moderate or low and the actual assessed level of control risk is high, the planned level of substantive tests must be increased.

_____ 8. In designing substantive tests, the auditor may use the primarily substantive approach for some assertions and the lower assessed level of control risk approach for other assertions.

_____ 9. Qualitative considerations, such as whether a noted deviation from controls involves an irregularity, may affect the auditors ultimate judgment about the effectiveness of a given control.

_____10. Tests of controls should only be performed on controls that are considered relevant in preventing or detecting a material misstatement in a financial statement assertion.

_____11. Tests of controls may be performed on transactions occurring anytime between audit planning up through the end of field work.

_____12. Concurrent tests of controls provide both substantive evidence and test of control effectiveness evidence.

_____13. Dual purpose tests provide evidence about both developing an understanding of a control and about whether the control is effective.

_____14. Inquiring and observing are especially useful in obtaining evidence about the control: segregation of duties.

_____15. Inspecting documents and records is applicable when there is a transaction trail of performance in the form of signatures and validation stamps that indicate whether the control was performed.

_____16. If the client's internal audit staff is used to provide direct assistance, the independent auditor need not test the internal auditor's work provided that the competence and objectivity of the internal auditors can be established.

_____17. More extensive tests of controls will be required to document a moderate assessed level of control risk than for a low assessed level of control risk.

_____18. Evidence about effectiveness from tests of controls performed in the previous year's audit may affect the amount of testing in the current audit.

_____19. The auditor is only required to obtain evidence of the effectiveness of controls from the beginning of the year to the date of the tests.

_____20. If an account is affected by multiple transaction classes, the auditor may have to judgmentally weigh differing risk assessments about a given assertion for the account.

_____21. Obtaining evidence from tests of controls is not required when control risk for an assertion is assessed at the maximum.

_____22. A reportable condition is an item that needs to be disclosed in the footnotes to the financial statements.

_____23. When an account is affected largely by a single transaction class, the auditor's account-level risk assessment for a given assertion will correspond with the auditor's transaction-class level risk assessment for this assertion.

_____24. When control risk is assessed at the maximum for an assertion, the basis for this assessment should be documented in the auditor's working papers.

_____25. The auditor is required to identify and report to the audit committee deficiencies that relate to an entity's internal control structure observed during an audit of financial statements.

D. COMPLETION STATEMENTS

Fill in the blanks with the word or words that correctly complete the following statements.

1. The methodology for meeting the second standard of fieldwork involves _____, _____, and _____.

2. Concurrent tests of controls are performed in conjunction with _____ while additional tests of controls are performed during _____.

3. Three procedures used both in obtaining an understanding and in tests of controls are _____, _____, and _____, and a fourth procedure used in tests of controls is _____.

4. Compensating controls are controls designed for _____, but their application may be relevant in offsetting a weakness associated with an _____ or _____ control.

5. Each test of control should provide evidence about the effectiveness of the _____ and the effectiveness of _____ of the tested control.

6. Whenever a client has an internal audit function, the independent auditor may _____ his or her audit work with the internal auditors, and/or use the internal auditors to provide _____ in the audit.

7. When dual purpose testing is done, the auditor should exercise care in designing the tests to ensure that evidence is obtained as to both the _____ and _____ in the accounts.

8. The final control risk assessment is based both on procedures to _____ and on _____ of _____.

9. An assessment of control risk at the maximum means there is a very high probability that a _____ in an assertion will not be _____ on a timely basis by the _____.

10. Most auditing firms have developed _____ that enumerate the types of _____ that could occur in financial statement assertions.

11. In identifying relevant controls, the auditor should recognize that some accounts are affected by multiple _____; therefore, control risk assessments about an _____ affecting this account may differ between _____ and may have to be judgmentally _____.

12. The evaluation of evidence from additional tests of controls involves both _____ and _____ considerations.

13. When control risk is assessed below the maximum, both the auditor's _____ and the _____ need to be documented.

14. As to the timing of tests of controls, they are normally performed at _____; however the auditor is required to obtain evidence about the effectiveness of controls for the _____ covered by the financial statements.

15. GAAS defines a reportable condition as a _____ in the design or operation of the _____ which could adversely affect the organization's ability to record, process, summarize, and report financial data consistent with the _____ in the financial statements.

E. MULTIPLE CHOICE

Choose the best answer for each of the following questions and enter the identifying letter in the space provided.

_____   1.   When the auditor adopts the primarily substantive approach for an assertion, the methodology for meeting the second standard of field work always involves each of the following except:
  a. Obtaining and documenting the understanding of relevant controls.
  b. Considering whether any concurrent tests of controls were performed in obtaining the understanding.
  c. Performing additional tests of controls.
  d. Documenting the control risk assessment.

_____   2.   When the auditor has initially adopted the primarily substantive approach for an assertion, he or she may decide to modify the preliminary audit strategy and seek a further reduction in the assessed level of control risk in each of the following situations except when:
  a. Tests of controls performed while obtaining an understanding support an initial assessment of control risk below the maximum.
  b. It is likely that additional evidential matter can be obtained to support a lower assessed level of control risk.
  c. It is likely to be cost efficient to obtain the additional evidence needed.
  d. The extent of the likely reduction in control risk would have a minimal effect on the planned level of substantive tests.

_____   3.   The following steps may be involved in meeting the second standard of field work when the lower assessed level of control risk approach is adopted for an assertion:

  I.   Plan and perform tests of controls.
  II.   Revise planned level of substantive tests.
  III.   Design substantive tests.
  IV.   Obtain understanding of controls and document understanding.
  V.   Assess control risk and document assessment.
  VI.   Determine whether assessed level of control risk supports the planned level of substantive tests.

  The order in which these steps should occur is
  a. III, IV, I, V, VI, II.
  b. IV, I, V, VI, II, III.
  c. VI, IV, I, II, V, III
  d. IV, V, I, 11, VI, III.

_____ 4. Tests of control structure policies and procedures are least likely to be performed to provide evidence about:
a. The effectiveness of their design.
b. The effectiveness of their operation.
c. The frequency of deviations from the controls.
d. The amount of monetary errors in a related assertion.

_____ 5. Tests of controls pertaining to effectiveness of operation focus on each of the following questions except:
a. How was the control applied?
b. How material was the control?
c. Was the control applied consistently during the year?
d. By whom was the control applied?

_____ 6. Which of the following terms is least preferable as a general description of failures by client personnel to properly and consistently apply controls during the year?
a. Deviations.
b. Errors.
c. Occurrences.
d. Exceptions.

_____ 7. Which of the following statements about concurrent tests of controls is correct?
a. They are performed simultaneously with substantive tests.
b. They are always required under either audit strategy.
c. They may occur as a by-product of obtaining an understanding or they may be planned.
d. They normally provide evidence of the proper and consistent application of a control policy or procedure during the entire year.

_____ 8. Each of the following statements about planned tests of controls is correct except:
a. They are required under the lower assessed level of control risk approach.
b. They are performed to support the auditor's planned level of substantive tests.
c. They should provide sufficient evidence to support a moderate or low assessment of control risk for some assertions.
d. They can be performed only for those controls for which there is a transaction trail of performance in the form of signatures and validation stamps that indicate whether the controls were performed and who performed them.

_____ 9. Choices as to the nature of tests of controls include:
a. Inquiring, observing, confirming, and reperforming.
b. Analyzing, counting, observing, and inspecting.
c. Inspecting, confirming, reperforming, and inquiring.
d. Inquiring, observing, inspecting, and reperforming.

_____ 10. An example of reperforming by the auditor is:
   a. Examining invoices for the initials of client personnel who performed an independent check of agreement of unit selling prices with an authorized price list.
   b. Observing client personnel in processing cash receipts to see that there is appropriate segregation of duties.
   c. Recalculating invoices to determine that invoices with initials indicating performance of an independent check of mathematical accuracy by client personnel are indeed correct.
   d. Inquiring of client personnel about procedures used in approving credit for customers.

_____ 11. The extent of tests of controls:
   a. Is inversely related to the auditor's planned assessed level of control risk.
   b. Should not be affected by the availability of evidence about effectiveness of controls from the prior audit.
   c. Is greater under the primarily substantive approach than under the lower assessed level of control risk approach.
   d. Is greater for concurrent tests of controls than for additional tests of controls.

_____ 12. When tests of controls are performed at an interim date, the need to perform additional tests of controls later in the year depends on all of the following except:
   a. The significance of the assertion to which the controls relate.
   b. The length of time between the interim testing date and the balance sheet date.
   c. Whether any significant changes in controls have occurred since the interim testing date.
   d. The auditor's ability to design dual-purpose tests.

_____ 13. Performing tests of controls and substantive tests of details simultaneously on the same transactions is known as:
   a. Concurrent testing.
   b. Dual-purpose testing.
   c. Analytical testing.
   d. Reperformance testing.

_____ 14. Control risk should be assessed in terms of individual:
   a. Financial statements.
   b. Accounts.
   c. Transactions.
   d. Assertions.

_____ 15. In making an assessment of control risk for an assertion, when the assessment is at the maximum it is not necessary to:
   a. Identify potential misstatements that could occur.
   b. Identify the controls that could likely prevent or detect the misstatements.
   c. Obtain evidence from tests of controls.
   d. Document the assessment.

_____ 16. Each of the following is an example of a potential misstatement in the completeness assertion for sales transactions except:
a. Goods shipped may not be billed.
b. Recorded sales may not be shipped.
c. Billed sales may not be journalized.
d. Billed sales may not be posted to the accounts receivable ledger.

_____ 17. A significant deficiency in the design or operation of a control is termed a:
a. Material weakness.
b. Reportable condition.
c. Control structure deviation.
d. Either a or b, depending on the financial statement effect.

_____ 18. Which of the following statements about evidence from tests of controls is incorrect?
a. Evidence obtained directly by the auditor through reperformance and observation generally provides more assurance than evidential matter obtained indirectly or by inference such as inquiry of client personnel.
b. When different types of evidence support the same conclusion about the effectiveness of a control, the degree of assurance increases.
c. In reaching a conclusion about the effectiveness of controls, the auditor should consider the number or rate of deviations but not the causes of the deviations.
d. Evidence of one deviation due to an irregularity may be more important to the auditor than more frequent deviations caused by errors.

_____ 19. Which of the following statements about control risk assessments is incorrect?
a. Making control risk assessments is a matter of professional judgment.
b. In making a control risk assessment for a specific financial statement assertion, it is imperative that the auditor recognize the interaction of the three elements of the internal control structure.
c. If control risk is assessed too low, more substantive testing may be done than is necessary, which would result in an inefficient audit.
d. Evidence of effective policies and procedures pertaining to the control environment may negate ineffective control procedures and vice versa.

_____ 20. The correct statement regarding requirements for documentation of the control risk assessment is:
a. When control risk is below the maximum, the basis for the assessment must be documented.
b. When control risk is at the maximum, the basis for the assessment must be documented.
c. When control risk is at the maximum, both this conclusion and the basis for the assessment must be documented.
d. Both the conclusion and the basis for the assessment must always be documented regardless of the level of the assessment.

SOLUTIONS

TRUE OR FALSE STATEMENTS

1. True	10. True	18. True
2. False	11. False	19. False
3. False	12. False	20. True
4. False	13. False	21. True
5. True	14. True	22. False
6. True	15. True	23. True
7. True	16. False	24. False
8. True	17. False	25. True
9. True		

COMPLETION STATEMENTS

1. obtaining an understanding, assessing control risk, designing substantive tests
2. obtaining an understanding, interim field work
3. inquiring, observing, inspecting, reperforming
4. one purpose, ineffective, missing
5. design, operation
6. coordinate, direct assistance
7. effectiveness of controls, monetary errors
8. obtain an understanding, tests, controls
9. material misstatement, prevented or detected, internal control structure
10. checklists, potential misstatements
11. transaction classes, assertion, transaction classes, weighed
12. quantitative, qualitative
13. conclusion, basis for the assessment
14. interim, entire year
15. significant deficiency, internal control structure, assertions of management

MULTIPLE CHOICE QUESTIONS

1. c	5. b	9. d	13. b	17. d
2. d	6. b	10. c	14. d	18. c
3. b	7. c	11. a	15. c	19. c
4. d	8. d	12. d	16. b	20. a

Chapter 10

Detection Risk and the Design of Substantive Tests

A. CHAPTER OUTLINE

I. Determining Detection Risk

A. Evaluating the Planned Level of Substantive Tests

B. Revising Planned Detection Risk

C. Specifying Detection Risk for Different Substantive Tests of the Same Assertion

II. Designing Substantive Tests

A. Nature

1. Analytical Procedures

2. Tests of Details of Transactions

3. Tests of Details of Balances

4. Illustration of Nature of Substantive Tests

B. Timing

1. Substantive Tests Prior to the Balance Sheet Date

C. Extent

D. Summary of the Relationships Among Audit Risk Components and the Nature, Timing, and Extent of Substantive Tests

III. Developing Audit Programs for Substantive Tests

A. Relationships Among Assertions, Specific Audit Objectives, and Substantive Tests

B. Illustrative Audit Program for Substantive Tests

C. General Framework for Developing Audit Programs for Substantive Tests

D. Audit Programs in Initial Engagements

E. Audit Programs in Recurring Engagements

IV. Special Considerations In Designing Substantive Tests

A. Income Statement Accounts

B. CHAPTER HIGHLIGHTS

1. In the planning phase of the audit, a **planned acceptable level of detection risk** is determined for each significant financial statement assertion based on the relationships of the risk components expressed in the audit risk model. These relationships indicate that for a given level of audit risk, **(a) planned detection risk** for an assertion is inversely related to the **assessed level of inherent risk** (ordinarily determined in the planning phase) and (b) the **planned assessed level of control risk** that is based on assumptions about the nature and extent of the auditor's yet-to-be-completed study and evaluation of relevant portions of the internal control structure.

2. The planned detection risk for an assertion in turn affects the auditor's **preliminary audit strategy** as follows:

    a. When planned detection risk is low, the auditor is more likely to adopt the primarily substantive approach, a component of which is a planned level of substantive tests that is extensive because more effort will be required to achieve the low planned detection risk.
    b. When planned detection risk is high, the auditor is more likely to adopt the lower assessed level of control risk approach, a component of which is a planned level of substantive tests that is restricted because less effort will be required to achieve the high planned detection risk.

3. Before designing substantive tests for an assertion, the auditor must **evaluate the planned level of substantive tests** specified in the preliminary audit strategy to determine whether it is supported by the **actual assessed level of control risk** determined after the study and evaluation of relevant portions of the internal control structure has been completed during interim work. For example, if the planned assessed level of control risk for an assertion was low but the actual assessed level turned out to be high, detection risk and the planned level of substantive tests should be revised before designing substantive tests.

4. Because controls often pertain to the processing of a class of transactions rather than to an account balance, many auditors first assess control risk for particular **transaction class assertions** (e.g., the existence or occurrence assertion for cash receipts transactions). These assessments are then used to assess control risk for **account balance assertions.**

5. For **accounts affected by a single transaction class,** the control risk assessment for each account balance assertion is the same as the control risk assessment for the same assertion for the transaction class that increases the account. For example, control risk for the existence or occurrence assertion for the sales account balance is the same as control risk for the same assertion for sales transactions. Similarly, control risk for the valuation or allocation assertion for many expense accounts is the same as control risk for the same assertion for purchases transactions.

6. For accounts affected by **more than one transaction class**:
    a. Assessing control risk for each account balance assertion requires consideration of the relevant control risk assessments for each transaction class that significantly affects the account (e.g., determining control risk for cash balance assertions requires consideration

of the control risk assessments for relevant cash receipts transaction assertions and relevant cash disbursements transaction assertions).

b. In general, control risk assessments for account balance assertions are based on combining the control risk assessments for the same assertion for each transaction class that affects the balance with the following exception: the control risk assessments for the existence or occurrence and completeness assertions for a transaction class that decreases an account balance should be considered in determining control risk for the opposite assertion for the account balance affected. For example, the control risk assessment for the existence or occurrence assertion for the cash balance is determined by combining the control risk assessment for the existence or occurrence assertion for cash receipts transactions which increase the cash balance with the control risk assessment for the completeness assertion for cash disbursements transactions which decrease the cash balance.

7. When the control **risk assessments differ for two or more transaction class assertions** that are to be combined in determining control risk for an account balance assertion, the auditor may judgementally weigh the relative significance of the separate assessments in affirming at the combined assessment, or use the most conservative (highest) of the relevant assessments as the combined assessment.

8. The auditor may elect to specify **different detection risk levels for different substantive tests** of the same assertion when the evidence obtained from one or more tests significantly reduces the risk of misstatements remaining to be detected by additional tests. For example, detection risk for a particular substantive test of details may be reduced based on the effectiveness of previous analytical procedures and other tests of details performed to detect misstatements in the same assertion.

9. **Designing substantive tests** to achieve a specified acceptable level of detection risk involves determining their nature, timing, and extent.

10. The **nature of substantive tests** refers to the type and effectiveness of the auditing procedures performed. When the acceptable level of detection risk is low, the auditor selects more effective, rather than less effective, procedures.

11. Three **types of substantive tests**, in order, generally, of increasing effectiveness and cost, are (a) analytical procedures, (b) tests of details of transactions, and (c) tests of details of balances. Procedures applicable to the last two types of tests include tracing, vouching, inspecting, counting, observing, inquiring, confirming, and reperforming.

12. **Analytical procedures** involve comparisons of financial and nonfinancial data with expectations. The effectiveness and efficiency of such procedures depend on the:
    a. Nature of the assertion to which they are applied.
    b. Plausibility and predictability of the relationship.
    c. Availability and reliability of the data used to develop the expectation.
    d. Precision of the expectation.

13. When the **results** of analytical procedures **conform to expectations**, and the acceptable level of detection risk for the assertion is high, it may not be necessary to perform tests of details.

14. **Tests of details of transactions** primarily involve tracing the details of transactions from source documents to accounting records and vouching the details of transactions from accounting records to documents in company files. These tests focus on finding monetary errors in the individual debits and credits in an account.

15. **Tests of details of balances** often involve the use of external documentation and/or the direct personal knowledge of the auditor to obtain evidence directly about an account balance rather than the individual debits and credits comprising the balance.

16. The **timing of substantive tests** refers to when they are performed. When the acceptable level of detection risk is high, the tests may be performed up to several months before year end; when detection risk is low, the tests should be performed at or near the balance sheet date.

17. **Early substantive testing** of an account balance:
    a. Is not done unless tests of controls have provided convincing evidence that internal controls are effective.
    b. Do not eliminate the need for additional substantive tests at the balance sheet date.

18. The **extent of substantive tests** means both the number of different types of substantive tests performed, and the number of items to which a particular test is applied. Generally, the lower the acceptable level of detection risk, the more extensive substantive tests should be.

19. An **audit program** is a list of auditing procedures to be performed which includes columns for the initials of the individual who performed each procedure, the date the procedure was performed, and a cross-reference to other working papers containing the evidence obtained from the procedure.

20. **Audit programs should be sufficiently detailed** to provide:
    a. An outline of the work to be done.
    b. A basis for coordinating, supervising, and controlling the audit.
    c. A record of the work performed.

21. The **detailed specification of substantive tests** in audit programs:
    a. In initial engagements, is generally not completed until after the study and evaluation of the internal control structure has been completed and the appropriate level of detection risk has been determined for each significant assertion.
    b. In recurring engagements, is often done before the auditor completes the current study and evaluation of the internal control structure based on the presumption that the risk levels and audit programs used in the previous period will be appropriate for the current period, with modifications to be made subsequently if necessary.

22. **Substantive tests of income statement accounts** typically rely more heavily on analytical procedures and less on tests of details of transactions and balances.

23. **Analytical procedures for income statement accounts**:
    a. May be direct, such as when a revenue or expense account is compared with other relevant data to determine the reasonableness of its balance (e.g., sales commissions to sales).
    b. May be indirect, such as when evidence concerning income statement balances is derived from analytical procedures applied to related balance sheet accounts (e.g., relating the accounts receivable turnover ratio to bad debts expense).
    c. Often involve comparisons of financial information with nonfinancial information (e.g., hotel room revenue with number of rooms and occupancy rates).
    d. May eliminate the need for tests of details of some accounts when detection risk is high.

24. **Tests of details of income statement accounts** may be necessary when:
    a. Inherent risk is high.
    b. Control risk is high.
    c. Analytical procedures reveal unusual relationships or unexpected fluctuations.
    d. An account requires analysis, such as one that requires special disclosure in the income statement, contains information needed in preparing tax returns or reports for regulatory agencies, or has a general account title that suggests the likelihood of misclassifications and errors.

25. Examples of **income statement accounts requiring separate analysis** include legal expense and professional fees, maintenance and repairs, travel and entertainment, officers' salaries and expenses, rents and royalties, contributions, advertising, and taxes, licenses, and fees.

26. The auditor's objective in auditing **accounting estimates** is to provide reasonable assurance that:
    a. All accounting estimates that could be material to the statements have been developed.
    b. They are reasonable in the circumstances.
    c. They are presented in conformity with applicable accounting principles and properly disclosed.

27. Procedures for **determining the reasonableness of a management estimate** include:
    a. Performing procedures to review and test management's process in making the estimate.
    b. Preparing an independent expectation of the estimate.
    c. Reviewing subsequent transactions and events occurring prior to completing the audit that pertain to the estimate.

28. The auditor's objective in auditing **related party transactions** is to obtain evidential matter as to the purpose, nature, and extent of these transactions and their effect on the financial statements.

29. **Evidence about related party transactions** should extend beyond responses to inquiries of management and include the results of substantive tests that involve:
    a. Obtaining an understanding of the business purpose of the transaction.
    b. Examining invoices, contracts, and other pertinent documents.
    c. Determining whether board of directors approval was obtained.
    d. Testing the reasonableness of amounts to be disclosed.
    e. Examining intercompany accounts as of concurrent dates.
    f. Evaluating the transferability and value of collateral.

30. The **testing phase** of the audit consists primarily of tests of controls and substantive tests. These tests can be differentiated as to type, purpose, nature of test measurement, applicable auditing procedures, timing, audit risk component to which related, primary field work standard to which related, and whether or not required by GAAS.

C. TRUE OR FALSE STATEMENTS

Indicate in the space provided whether each of the following statements is true or false.

_____   1. Planned detection risk is the basis for the planned level of substantive tests that is specified as one of the components of a preliminary audit strategy for an assertion.

_____   2. Before designing substantive tests, the auditor must determine whether the planned assessed level of control risk for an assertion supports the planned level of substantive tests.

_____   3. When combining control risk assessments for multiple transaction class assertions to determine control risk for an account balance assertion, the auditor should use the lowest of the transaction class assessments as the account balance assessment.

_____   4. The control risk assessments for the existence or occurrence and completeness assertions for a transaction class that increases an account balance relate to the opposite assertion for the account balance affected.

_____   5. When the actual assessed level of control risk for an assertion differs from the planned assessed level, the planned levels of detection risk and substantive tests should be revised.

_____   6. In some cases, it may be appropriate to specify different levels of detection risk for different substantive tests of the same assertion.

_____   7. Designing substantive tests involves determining the nature, timing, and extent of the tests necessary to meet the acceptable level of detection risk for each assertion.

_____   8. The nature of substantive tests refers to whether they are designed to determine the effectiveness of controls or the amount of monetary misstatements in an account.

_____   9. When the acceptable level of detection risk is high, the auditor is likely to make more extensive use of tests of details of balances and less extensive use of analytical procedures.

_____   10. Analytical procedures are generally more costly to perform than tests of details.

_____   11. Tests of details of balances focus on obtaining evidence directly about the individual debits and credits comprising the balance.

_____ 12. Tests of details of transactions often involve the use of external documentation and/or the direct personal knowledge of the auditor.

_____ 13. When detection risk is high, some substantive tests may be performed several months before the end of the year.

_____ 14. Early substantive testing of account balances is not done unless tests of controls have provided convincing evidence that internal controls are operating effectively.

_____ 15. Generally, when the acceptable level of detection risk is high, more extensive substantive tests should be performed.

_____ 16. Audit programs are lists of audit objectives to be achieved.

_____ 17. In initial engagements, audit programs are generally completed during the planning phase of the audit.

_____ 18. Traditionally, tests of details of balances focus on financial statement assertions that pertain to balance sheet accounts rather than income statement accounts.

_____ 19. Analytical procedures are a powerful audit tool in obtaining audit evidence about income statement balances.

_____ 20. When controls over sales adjustments transactions are effective, the auditor might elect to restrict substantive tests of the sales returns and allowances account balance to analytical procedures.

_____ 21. An auditor is expected to determine that accounting estimates made by management are accurate.

_____ 22. In some cases, it may be useful for the auditor to obtain the opinion of a specialist regarding the reasonableness of the assumptions used by management in developing an accounting estimate.

_____ 23. Management's responses to inquiries by the auditor represent sufficient evidence concerning related party transactions.

_____ 24. In auditing a related party transaction, the auditor should determine what the exchange price and terms would have been had the transaction been with an unrelated party.

_____ 25. The third phase of the audit consists primarily of performing tests of controls and substantive tests.

D. COMPLETION STATEMENTS

Fill in the blanks with the word or words that correctly complete the following statements.

1. Before designing substantive tests, the auditor must determine whether the _____ for an assertion supports the _____.

2. To determine the combined control risk assessment for the completeness assertion for the cash balance, the auditor should consider his or her control risk assessments for the completeness assertion for _____ transactions and the_____ assertion for cash disbursements transactions.

3. When the control risk assessments differ for two or more transaction class assertions that affect the determination of control risk for an account balance assertion, the auditor may _____ the significance of each assessment or simply elect to use the _____ of the relevant assessments.

4. Designing substantive tests involves determining the _____, _____, and _____ of the tests necessary to meet the acceptable level of _____ for each assertion.

5. Three types of substantive tests are analytical procedures, tests of details of _____, and tests of details of _____.

6. It may not be necessary to perform tests of details for an assertion when the results of _____ conform to expectations and the acceptable level of detection risk is _____.

7. Tests of details of transactions primarily involve _____ the details of transactions from source documents to accounting records and _____ the details of transactions from accounting records to source documents.

8. Tests of details of balances often involve the use of _____ documentation and the _____ of the auditor.

9. The decision to perform substantive tests prior to the balance sheet date should be based on whether the auditor can control the _____ that material misstatements existing in the account at the balance sheet date will not be detected, and _____ of substantive tests necessary at the balance sheet date to meet planned audit objectives.

10. The _____ of substantive tests refers to both the number of substantive tests performed and the number of _____ to which a particular substantive test is applied.

11. Audit programs are lists of procedures performed and should include columns for the _____ who performed each procedure, the _____ the procedures were performed, and _____ to other working papers

containing the evidence obtained from the procedures.

12. As compared with substantive tests of balance sheet accounts, tests of income statement accounts rely more heavily on _____ and less on _____ of transactions and balances.

13. An accounting estimate is an _____ of a financial statement element, item, or account in the absence of _____.

14. Related party transactions, which should be identified in the _____ phase of the audit, are a concern to the auditor because they may not be executed on an _____.

15. The nature of the test measurement for substantive tests is _____ and the tests relate to the _____ component of audit risk.

E. MULTIPLE CHOICE

Choose the best answer for each of the following questions and enter the identifying letter in the space provided.

_____ 1. An auditor assesses control risk because it:
   a. Indicates where inherent risk may be the greatest.
   b. Affects the level of detection risk the auditor may accept.
   c. Determines whether audit risk is sufficiently low.
   d. Includes the aspects of audit risk that are controllable.

_____ 2. To determine a control risk assessment for the completeness assertion for the cash balance, the auditor should consider his or her control risk assessments for the following transaction class assertions:
   a. Completeness assertion for cash receipts and completeness assertion for cash disbursements.
   b. Existence or occurrence assertion for cash receipts and completeness for cash disbursements.
   c. Completeness assertion for cash receipts and existence or occurrence for cash disbursements.
   d. Completeness assertions for sales, cash receipts, and sales adjustments.

_____ 3. The auditor uses the knowledge provided by the understanding of the internal control structure and the actual assessed level of control risk for account balance assertions to:
   a. Determine the nature, timing, and extent of tests of controls.
   b. Evaluate the planned level of substantive tests before designing the specific substantive tests to be performed.
   c. Identify the areas of greatest inherent risk.
   d. Determine an appropriate level for overall audit risk.

_____ 4. The acceptable level of detection risk is inversely related to the:
   a. Assurance provided by substantive tests.
   b. Risk of misapplying auditing procedures.
   c. Preliminary judgment about materiality levels.
   d. Risk of failing to discover material misstatements.

_____ 5. In the context of an audit of financial statements, substantive tests are audit procedures that:
   a. May be eliminated for a material account balance under certain conditions.
   b. Are designed to discover significant weaknesses in internal control.
   c. May be either tests of details of transactions and balances or analytical procedures.
   d. Will vary inversely with the assessed level of control risk.

_____ 6. An auditor may compensate for a weakness in the internal control structure by increasing the:
   a. Level of detection risk.
   b. Extent of tests of controls.
   c. Preliminary judgment about audit risk.
   d. Extent of tests of details of transactions and balances.

_____ 7. Before applying substantive tests to the details of asset and liability accounts at an interim date, the auditor should:
   a. Assess the difficulty in controlling incremental audit risk.
   b. Investigate significant fluctuations that have occurred in the asset and liability accounts since the previous balance sheet date.
   c. Select only those accounts which can effectively be sampled during the year-end audit work.
   d. Consider the tests of controls that must be applied at the balance sheet date to extend the audit conclusions reached at the interim date.

_____ 8. As the acceptable level of detection risk decreases, an auditor may change the:
   a. Timing of substantive tests by performing them at an interim date rather than at year end.
   b. Nature of substantive tests from less effective to more effective procedures.
   c. Timing of tests of controls by performing them at several dates rather than at one time.
   d. Assessed level of inherent risk to a higher amount.

_____ 9. The procedures specifically outlined in an audit program are primarily designed to:
   a. Protect the auditor in the event of litigation.
   b. Gather evidence.
   c. Enable the auditor to assess detection risk.
   d. Provide the auditor with an understanding of the internal control structure.

_____ 10. An audit program should be sufficiently detailed to provide all of the following except:
   a. An outline of the work to be done.
   b. A basis for coordinating, supervising, and controlling the audit.
   c. A basis for the client's clear understanding of the responsibilities being assumed by the auditor.
   d. A record of the work performed.

_____ 11. As compared to audit programs in recurring engagements, audit programs in initial engagements:
   a. Should be prepared earlier in the process of completing the audit.
   b. Need not address whether the accounting principles used in the preceding period are consistent with those used in the previous period.
   c. Will include more extensive use of analytical procedures and less extensive use of tests of details.
   d. Must be designed with special consideration for determining the propriety of the account balances at the beginning of the period.

_____ 12. As compared with substantive tests of balance sheet accounts, tests of income statement accounts usually rely more heavily on analytical procedures and less on tests of details of transactions and balances because:
   a. Income statement accounts are typically less material than balance sheet accounts.
   b. Each income statement account is linked to one or more balance sheet accounts, permitting the results of tests of details of the balance sheet accounts to be used in evaluating the fairness of the income statement accounts as well, thus reducing the need for additional direct tests of details.
   c. For income statement accounts, analytical procedures are always more effective than tests of details.
   d. It is too costly to apply extensive tests of details to income statement accounts.

_____ 13. Circumstances which may contribute to the need to perform direct tests of details of income statement accounts include all of the following except:
   a. Inherent risk is high.
   b. Control risk is low.
   c. Analytical procedures reveal unusual relationships or unexpected fluctuations.
   d. The account contains information needed in preparing tax returns or reports of regulatory agencies.

_____ 14. The income statement account that is least likely to require separate analysis is:
   a. Maintenance and repairs.
   b. Utilities expense.
   c. Legal expense and professional fees.
   d. Contributions.

_____ 15. Which of the following statements is incorrect concerning accounting estimates?
  a. Management is responsible for establishing the process and controls for preparing accounting estimates.
  b. The auditor should obtain sufficient competent evidential matter to provide reasonable assurance that all accounting estimates that could be material to the financial statements have been developed.
  c. An entity's internal control structure cannot be relied upon to reduce the likelihood of material misstatements of accounting estimates.
  d. The auditor should evaluate the reasonableness and consistency of the assumptions used by management in developing the estimates.

_____ 16. Regarding related party transactions, the auditor:
  a. May limit the evidence obtained to management's responses to inquiries.
  b. Is expected to determine whether a particular transaction would have occurred if the parties had not been related.
  c. Should obtain an understanding of the business purpose of the transaction.
  d. Should determine what the exchange price and terms would have been had the transaction been with an unrelated party.

_____ 17. Auditing procedures performed in the third, or testing, phase of the audit include the following two major classes of tests:
  a. Procedures to obtain an understanding of the internal control structure and tests of controls.
  b. Analytical procedures and tests of controls.
  c. Analytical procedures and substantive tests.
  d. Tests of controls and substantive tests.

_____ 18. The primary purpose of substantive tests is to:
  a. Determine the fairness of significant financial statement assertions.
  b. Determine the effectiveness of design and operation of internal control structure policies and procedures.
  c. Obtain an understanding of the internal control structure.
  d. Provide the auditor with a basis for assessing audit risk.

_____ 19. The nature of the test measurement in substantive tests is:
  a. The frequency of deviations from control structure policies and procedures.
  b. The level of detection risk associated with the procedures.
  c. Monetary errors in transactions and balances.
  d. The probability that the account balance contains a material misstatement.

_____ 20. Substantive tests relate primarily to:
  a. The general standards of GAAS.
  b. The third standard of field work.
  c. The fourth standard of reporting.
  d. The second standard of field work.

SOLUTIONS

TRUE OR FALSE STATEMENTS

1. True	10. False	18. True
2. False	11. False	19. True
3. False	12. False	20. True
4. False	13. True	21. False
5. True	14. True	22. True
6. True	15. False	23. False
7. True	16. False	24. False
8. False	17. False	25. True
9. False		

COMPLETION STATEMENTS

1. actual control risk assessment, planned level of substantive tests
2. cash receipts, existence or occurrence
3. judgmentally weigh, most conservative (highest)
4. nature, timing, extent, detection risk
5. transactions, balances
6. analytical procedures, high
7. tracing, vouching
8. external, direct personal knowledge
9. added audit risk, reduce the cost
10. extent, items
11. initials of individuals, dates, cross-references
12. analytical procedures, tests of details
13. approximation, exact measurement
14. planning, arm's length basis
15. monetary errors in transactions and balances, detection risk

MULTIPLE CHOICE QUESTIONS

1. b	5. c	9. b	13. b	17. d
2. c	6. d	10. c	14. b	18. a
3. b	7. a	11. d	15. c	19. c
4. a	8. b	12. b	16. c	20. b

Chapter 11

Audit Sampling in Tests of Controls

A. CHAPTER OUTLINE

I. Basic Audit Sampling Concepts

A. Nature and Purpose of Audit Sampling

B. Uncertainty and Audit Sampling

C. Sampling Risk and Nonsampling Risk

   1. Sampling Risk

   2. Nonsampling Risk

D. Nonstatistical and Statistical Sampling

E. Audit Sampling Techniques

II. Designing Statistical Attribute Samples for Tests of Controls

A. Determine the Audit Objectives

B. Define the Population and Sampling Unit

C. Specify the Attributes of Interest

D. Determine the Sample Size

   1. Sample Size Tables

   2. Risk of Assessing Control Risk Too Low

   3. Tolerable Deviation Rate

   4. Expected Population Deviation Rate

   5. Population Size

E. Determine the Sample Selection Method

   1. Random Number Sampling

   2. Systematic Sampling

III. Executing Statistical Attribute Samples and Evaluating the Results

A. Execute the Sampling Plan

B. Evaluate the Sample Results

1. Calculate the Sample Deviation Rate

2. Determine the Upper Deviation Limit

3. Determine the Allowance for Sampling Risk

4. Consider the Qualitative Aspects of Deviations

5. Reach an Overall Conclusion

C. Illustrative Case Study

IV. Other Considerations

A. Discovery Sampling

B. Nonstatistical Sampling

1. Determine the Sample Size

2. Determine the Sample Selection Method

3. Evaluate the Sample Results

V. SUMMARY

B. CHAPTER HIGHLIGHTS

1. **Audit sampling** is the application of an audit procedure to less than 100 percent of the items within an account balance or class of transactions for the purpose of evaluating some characteristic of the balance or class.

2. Both the second and third standards of field work contain an element of **uncertainty**, which is collectively referred to as audit risk.

3. Audit sampling applies to two components of **audit risk**: (a) control risk and (b) detection risk.

4. When sampling is used, uncertainties may result from:
    a. **Sampling risk** which relates to the possibility that a properly drawn sample may not be representative of the population.
    b. **Nonsampling** risk which relates to the portion of audit risk that is not due to examining only a portion of the data.

5. The types of **sampling risk** that may occur in audit sampling are:
    In Tests of Controls:
    a. **Risk of assessing control risk too low** (sample supports auditor's planned control risk when true deviation rate, if known, would not).
    b. **Risk of assessing control risk too high** (sample does not support planned control risk when true deviation rate, if known, would).
    In Substantive Tests:
    c. **Risk of incorrect acceptance** (sample supports conclusion that recorded balance is not materially misstated when it is).
    d. **Risk of incorrect rejection** (sample supports conclusion recorded balance is materially misstated when it is not).

6. Auditors may use either nonstatistical or statistical sampling; a major benefit of the latter is that it enables the auditor to quantify and control sampling risk.

7. Two major statistical sampling techniques used in auditing are:
    a. **Attribute sampling** which is used in tests of controls to estimate the occurrence rate of deviations from prescribed control procedures.
    b. **Variables sampling** which is used in substantive tests to estimate the total dollar amount of a population or the dollar amount of misstatement.

8. **Attribute sampling** in tests of controls:
    a. May be used if there is a trail of documentary evidence of the performance of control procedures.
    b. Is ordinarily not applicable to controls that depend primarily on segregation of duties or that produce no documentary evidence of performance.

9. The **steps in an attribute sampling plan** are:
   a. Determine the audit objectives.
   b. Define the population and sampling unit.
   c. Specify the attributes of interest.
   d. Determine the sample size.
   e. Determine the sample selection method.
   f. Execute the sampling plan.
   g. Evaluate the sample results.

10. The **objective** of an attribute sampling plan is to evaluate the effectiveness of the design and operation of internal controls for a specific class of transactions. The results are then used to assess the control risk for relevant material financial statement assertions affected by that class of transactions.

11. Factors to be considered in **defining the population** include (a) appropriateness of the physical representation of the population to the objectives of the plan, (b) the homogeneity of the population with respect to the control procedure to be tested, (c) the existence of multiple client locations, and (d) changes in control procedures during the year.

12. The **sampling unit** is an individual element of the population. It may be a document, a line item of a document, or an entry in a journal or register, and must be compatible with the objectives of the sampling plan.

13. **Attributes** must be specified that relate to the effectiveness of the controls being tested. The relative importance of each attribute should be considered in setting desired statistical parameters for determining sample size and evaluating sample results.

14. In **determining sample size**, the factors to be considered and the nature of their relationship to the sample size are:
   a. Acceptable level of risk of assessing control risk too low (inverse).
   b. Tolerable deviation rate (inverse).
   c. Expected population deviation rate (direct).
   d. Population size (little or no direct).

15. The **acceptable level of risk of assessing control risk too low** relates to the **effectiveness** of the audit test and is generally specified at a low level in the range of 5 to 15 percent, varying directly with planned control risk.

16. The **tolerable deviation rate** is the maximum rate of deviations that an auditor will accept and still use the planned control risk. In setting this rate, the auditor should consider the relationships of the deviations to:
   a. The accounting records being tested.
   b. Any related internal controls.
   c. The purpose of the evaluation.

17. The **expected population deviation rate** may be based on:
    a. Last year's sample deviation rate.
    b. The current year's initial assessment of the control.
    c. The rate found in a preliminary sample.

18. **Population size** has a minimal direct effect on the size of samples drawn from populations with 5,000 or fewer sampling units. But populations over 5,000 units are considered as infinite permitting this factor to be ignored in using tables to determine sample size.

19. In **determining the sample selection method**, the auditor desires to select sample items in a manner that (a) results in a sample that is representative of the population, and (b) gives all items in the population a chance of being selected. Two methods commonly used are **random number sampling** and **systematic sampling**.

20. In **random number sampling**, the auditor must (a) have a basis for relating a unique number to each item in the population, and (b) use a table of random numbers or a computer program that generates random numbers. In using a random number table, the same number may be drawn more than once. When the duplicate is ignored (skipped), the auditor is said to be **sampling without replacement**. When the duplicate number is included in the sample, the auditor is **sampling with replacement**. Auditors usually sample without replacement.

21. In **systematic sampling**, every nth item in the population is selected from one or more random starts. When one random start is used, the **skip interval** is found by dividing the population size by the sample size.

22. In **executing the sampling plan**, the auditor uses one of the sample selection methods described above and applies auditing procedures to the sample items.

23. The following steps are performed in evaluating the sample results:
    a. A **sample deviation rate** for each attribute is calculated.
    b. An **upper deviation limit** for each attribute is determined from evaluation tables based on the specified level of risk of assessing control risk too low, the number of deviations found in the sample, and the size of the sample examined.

24. The **allowance for sampling risk** is the difference between the sample deviation rate and the upper deviation limit. It is directly related to the number of deviations found in the sample.

25. **Quantitatively**, sample results support the auditor's planned control risk (at the specified level of risk of assessing control risk too low) whenever the upper deviation limit does not exceed the tolerable deviation rate. The auditor should also consider the qualitative aspects of the deviations such as their nature and cause and their effect on the financial statements.

26. When the auditor reaches an **overall conclusion** that the planned control risk is not supported, he or she must either modify the nature, timing, or extent of substantive tests, or, if applicable, test other compensating controls.

27. **Discovery sampling** is a form of attribute sampling that is designed to locate at least one exception if the rate of deviations in the population is at or above a specified rate. It is useful when the auditor:
   a. Is examining a large population composed of items which contain a very high proportion of control risk.
   b. Suspects that irregularities have occurred.
   c. Seeks additional evidence in a given case to determine whether a known irregularity is an isolated occurrence or part of a recurring pattern.

28. In **nonstatistical sampling**, the auditor should judgmentally recognize the effects of the following factors on **sample size** when other factors are held constant:
   a. Risk of assessing control risk too low (inverse).
   b. Tolerable deviation rate (inverse).
   c. Expected population deviation rate (direct).

29. In addition to random number and systematic sampling, the auditor may use **block sampling** or **haphazard sampling** in selecting sample items in nonstatistical sampling.

30. In **evaluating the results** in nonstatistical sampling, the auditor should:
   a. Realize that it is not possible to determine an upper deviation limit or a statistically derived allowance for sampling risk.
   b. Compare the deviation rate found in the sample with the tolerable rate considered in determining sample size.

C. TRUE OR FALSE STATEMENTS

Indicate in the space provided whether each of the following statements is true or false.

_____ 1. Audit sampling is widely used in performing tests involving vouching and tracing but not confirming.

_____ 2. The auditor is justified in accepting some uncertainty when the cost and time required to make a 100% examination of the data are, in his judgment, greater than the adverse consequences of possibly expressing an erroneous opinion from examining only a sample of the data.

_____ 3. Audit sampling applies to two components of audit risk: (a) detection risk and (b) control risk.

_____ 4. Sampling risk relates to the possibility that a properly drawn sample may not be representative of the population.

_____ 5. The types of sampling risk related to tests of controls are (a) the risk of assessing control risk too low and (b) the risk of assessing control risk too high.

_____ 6. The risk of assessing control risk too high and the risk of incorrect rejection relate to audit effectiveness.

_____ 7. An advantage of statistical sampling is that it allows the auditor to mathematically measure sampling risk and nonsampling risk.

_____ 8. Statistical sampling does not eliminate the need for the auditor to exercise professional judgment in planning and executing a sampling plan.

_____ 9. Attribute sampling is used primarily in tests of controls to estimate the total dollar amount of a population.

_____ 10. Attribute sampling in tests of controls generally is used only if there is a trail of documentary evidence of the performance of controls.

_____ 11. The steps in an attribute sampling plan involving audit planning for tests of controls include determining the sample size, executing the sampling plan, and evaluating the sample results.

_____ 12. In attribute sampling, it is necessary to know the exact size of the population when the population is larger than 5,000 units.

_____ 13. Auditors may specify an acceptable level of risk of assessing control risk too low ranging from 5 to 15 percent for each control tested.

_____ 14. The expected population deviation rate is the maximum rate of deviations from a prescribed control that an auditor is willing to accept and still rely on the control.

_____ 15. The expected population deviation rate has a direct effect on sample size.

_____ 16. In attribute sampling, the auditor is concerned that the actual population deviation rate does not exceed the tolerable deviation rate.

_____ 17. When the same random number is drawn more than once and the duplicate number is ignored (skipped), the auditor is sampling without replacement.

_____ 18. A disadvantage of systematic sampling is that items in the population must be numbered.

_____ 19. In executing an attribute sampling plan, a sample item that cannot be located should not be counted as a deviation.

_____ 20. The upper deviation limit is the auditor's best estimate of the true deviation rate in the population.

_____ 21. In attribute sampling, the difference between the sample deviation rate and the upper deviation limit is the allowance for sampling risk.

_____ 22. Generally, if the upper deviation limit is less than or equal to the tolerable deviation rate, the sample results support planned control risk.

_____ 23. Discovery sampling is useful in searching for a single occurrence of a fraudulent transaction.

_____ 24. The factors to be considered in determining sample size are the same in nonstatistical sampling as in statistical sampling.

_____ 25. Selection of a single block from a whole year's transactions is generally considered to be unacceptable in nonstatistical sampling.

D. COMPLETION STATEMENTS

Fill in the blanks with the word or words that correctly complete the following statements.

1. The components of audit risk that relate to audit sampling are _____ and _____ .

2. The risk that a properly drawn sample may not be representative of the population is known as _____ while the portion of audit risk not due to examining only a portion of the data is known as _____ .

3. In tests of controls and substantive tests, audit effectiveness relates to the risk of _____ and incorrect _____ , while audit efficiency relates to the risk of _____ and incorrect _____ .

4. Under GAAS, an auditor may use either _____ or _____ sampling.

5. The audit sampling technique used to estimate a deviation rate is known as _____ sampling while the technique used to estimate a dollar amount is known as _____ sampling.

6. In tests of controls, the population is the _____ being tested while an individual element in the population is the _____ .

7. The auditor should recognize that deviations from prescribed controls increase the _____ , but not necessarily the _____ , of errors in the accounting records.

8. The risk of assessing control risk too low and tolerable deviation rate have a(n) _____ effect on sample size while the expected population deviation rate has a(n) _____ effect.

9. The principal random selection methods used in attribute sampling are _____ sampling and _____ sampling.

10. In random number sampling, the inclusion of duplicate numbers in the sample is referred to as _____ while skipping duplicate numbers is referred to as _____ .

11. Whenever the auditor considers using systematic selection, he or she must be alert to the possibility of any _____ within the population coinciding with the _____ .

12. A sample deviation rate for each control tested is found by dividing the _____ by the _____ .

13. To use tables to determine the upper deviation limit, the auditor must specify the _____ , _____ , and _____ .

14. If sample results do not support planned control risk, the auditor will have to modify the nature, extent, or timing of _____ or, if applicable, test other _____ .

15. In evaluating both nonstatistical and statistical samples, the auditor should consider the _____ of deviations as well as the _____ of deviations.

E. MULTIPLE CHOICE

Choose the best answer for each of the following questions and enter the identifying letter in the space provided.

_____ 1. The application of statistical sampling techniques is least related to which of the following generally accepted auditing standards?
   a. The work is to be adequately planned and assistants, if any, are to be properly supervised.
   b. In all matters relating to the assignment, an independence in mental attitude is to be maintained by the auditor or auditors.
   c. A sufficient understanding of the internal control structure is to be obtained to plan the audit and to determine the nature, timing, and extent of tests to be performed.
   d. Sufficient competent evidential matter is to be obtained through inspection, observation, inquiries, and confirmations to afford a reasonable basis for an opinion regarding the financial statements under audit.

_____ 2. Statistical sampling provides a technique for:
   a. Exactly defining materiality.
   b. Greatly reducing the amount of substantive testing.
   c. Eliminating judgment in testing.
   d. Measuring the sufficiency of evidential matter.

_____ 3. The tolerable rate of deviations for a test of controls is generally:
   a. Lower than the expected rate of deviations in the related accounting records.
   b. Higher than the expected rate of deviations in the related accounting records.
   c. Identical to the expected rate of deviations in the related accounting records.
   d. Unrelated to the expected rate of deviations in the related accounting records.

_____ 4. At times, a sample may indicate that the auditor's planned control risk for a given control is reasonable when, in fact, the true deviation rate does not justify such an assessment. This situation illustrates the risk of:
   a. Assessing control risk too low.
   b. Assessing control risk too high.
   c. Incorrect acceptance.
   d. Incorrect rejection.

_____ 5. Which of the following best illustrates the concept of sampling risk?
   a. A randomly chosen sample may not be representative of the population as a whole on the characteristic of interest.
   b. An auditor may select audit procedures that are not appropriate to achieve the specific objective.
   c. An auditor may fail to recognize errors in the documents examined for the chosen sample.
   d. The documents related to the chosen sample may not be available for inspection.

_____ 6. In assessing sampling risk, the risk of incorrect rejection and the risk of assessing control risk too high relate to the:
   a. Efficiency of the audit.
   b. Effectiveness of the audit.
   c. Selection of the sample.
   d. Audit quality controls.

_____ 7. Audit sampling is ordinarily not used in performing which of the following auditing procedures?
   a. Vouching.
   b. Confirming.
   c. Inquiring.
   d. Tracing.

_____ 8. Which of the following best describes the distinguishing feature of statistical sampling?
   a. It requires the examination of a smaller number of supporting documents.
   b. It provides a means for measuring mathematically the degree of uncertainty that results from examining only part of a population.
   c. It reduces the problems associated with the auditor's judgment concerning materiality.
   d. It is evaluated in terms of two parameters--statistical mean and random selection.

_____ 9. Statistical sampling generally may be applied to test the effectiveness of internal controls when the controls:
   a. Depend primarily on appropriate segregation of duties.
   b. Are carefully reduced to writing and are included in client accounting manuals.
   c. Leave an audit trail in the form of documentary evidence of compliance.
   d. Enable the detection of material irregularities in the accounting records.

_____ 10. The sampling method most often used by auditors to estimate the rate of deviations from prescribed control procedures is:
   a. Attribute sampling.
   b. Discovery sampling.
   c. Variables sampling.
   d. Systematic random sampling with replacement.

_____ 11. Which of the following is not a factor in determining sample size in an attribute sampling plan?
   a. Expected population deviation rate.
   b. Risk of assessing control risk too low.
   c. Tolerable deviation rate.
   d. Risk of incorrect acceptance.

_____ 12. If all factors specified in a sampling plan remain constant, changing the acceptable level of risk of assessing control risk too low from 10 to 5 percent would cause the required sample size to:
   a. Increase.
   b. Remain the same.
   c. Decrease.
   d. Become indeterminate.

_____ 13. If all other factors specified in an attribute sampling plan remain constant, changing the tolerable deviation rate from 5% to 10%, and changing the acceptable risk of assessing control risk too low from 5% to 10% would cause the required sample size to:
   a. Increase.
   b. Remain the same.
   c. Decrease.
   d. Become indeterminate.

_____ 14. The tolerable deviation rate for tests of controls depends primarily on which of the following?
   a. The cause of errors.
   b. The level of planned control risk.
   c. The amount of any substantive errors.
   d. The limit used in audits of similar clients.

_____ 15. For a large population of cash disbursement transactions, Smith, CPA, is performing tests of controls by using attribute sampling techniques. Anticipating a deviation rate of 2 percent, Smith found from a table that the required sample size is 181, with a tolerable deviation rate and an acceptable risk of assessing control risk too low of 5 percent each. If Smith anticipated a deviation rate of only one percent and wanted to maintain the same tolerable deviation rate and risk of assessing control risk too low, the sample size would be closest to:
   a. 101.
   b. 181.
   c. 400.
   d. 600.

_____ 16. Which of the following factors is not required to use tables to determine an upper deviation limit?
   a. Sample size used.
   b. Risk of assessing control risk too low.
   c. Number of deviations found.
   d. Expected population deviation rate.

_____ 17. Generally, the sample results support planned control risk when:
   a. The sample deviation rate plus an allowance for sampling risk is less than or equal to the expected population deviation rate.
   b. The tolerable deviation rate plus an allowance for sampling risk is less than or equal to the upper deviation limit.
   c. The expected population deviation rate is less than or equal to the sample deviation rate.
   d. The upper deviation limit is less than or equal to the tolerable deviation rate.

_____ 18. Qualitative aspects of deviations to be considered in evaluating sample results include all of the following except:
   a. The nature and cause of deviations.
   b. Whether deviations may have a direct effect on the financial statements.
   c. Whether the allowance for sampling risk is adequate.
   d. Whether the deviations constitute an irregularity.

_____ 19. Discovery sampling may be useful except when the auditor:
   a. Is examining a large population composed of items that contain a very high proportion of control risk.
   b. Is trying to locate a single incidence of fraud.
   c. Suspects that irregularities have occurred.
   d. Seeks additional evidence in a given case to determine whether a known irregularity is an isolated occurrence or part of a recurring pattern.

_____ 20. In determining the sample size for a nonstatistical sample for a test of controls, the auditor should recognize that:
   a. The risk of assessing control risk too low has a direct effect on sample size.
   b. The expected population deviation rate has an inverse effect on sample size.
   c. The tolerable deviation rate has an inverse effect on sample size.
   d. The risk of incorrect acceptance has a direct effect on sample size.

SOLUTIONS

TRUE OR FALSE STATEMENTS

1. False
2. True
3. True
4. True
5. True
6. False
7. False
8. True
9. False

10. True
11. False
12. False
13. True
14. False
15. True
16. True
17. True

18. False
19. False
20. False
21. True
22. True
23. False
24. True
25. True

COMPLETION STATEMENTS

1. control risk, detection risk
2. sampling risk, nonsampling risk
3. assessing control risk too low, acceptance, assessing control risk too high, rejection
4. statistical, nonstatistical
5. attribute, variables
6. class of transactions, sampling unit
7. risk, number
8. inverse, direct
9. random number, systematic
10. sampling with replacement, sampling without replacement
11. cyclical pattern, skip interval
12. number of deviations found, sample size
13. risk of assessing control risk too low, sample size used, number of deviations found
14. substantive tests, compensating controls
15. qualitative aspects, frequency

MULTIPLE CHOICE QUESTIONS

1. b	5. a	9. c	13. c	17. d
2. d	6. a	10. a	14. b	18. c
3. c	7. c	11. d	15. a	19. b
4. a	8. b	12. a	16. d	20. c

Chapter 12

Audit Sampling in Substantive Tests

A. CHAPTER OUTLINE

I. Basic Concepts

   A. Nature and Purpose

   B. Uncertainty, Sampling Risks, and Audit Risk

   C. Statistical Sampling Approaches

II. Probability-Proportional-to-Size Sampling

   A. Sampling Plan

   B. Determine the Objectives of the Plan

   C. Define the Population and Sampling Unit

   D. Determine Sample Size

      1. Book Value of Population Tested

      2. Reliability Factor for Specified Risk of Incorrect Acceptance

      3. Tolerable Misstatement

      4. Anticipated Misstatement and Expansion Factor

      5. Calculation of Sample Size

   E. Determine the Sample Selection Method

   F. Execute the Sampling Plan

   G. Evaluate the Sample Results

      1. No Misstatements

      2. Some Misstatements

   H. Advantages and Disadvantages of PPS Sampling

III. Classical Variables Sampling

   A. Types of Classical Variables Sampling Techniques

   B. Mean-Per-Unit (MPU) Estimation

      1. Determine the Objectives of the Plan

B. CHAPTER HIGHLIGHTS

1. **Sampling plans for substantive tests** may be designed to (a) obtain evidence that an account balance is not materially misstated, or (b) make an independent estimate of some amount.

2. Audit sampling in substantive tests is subject to both **sampling risk** and **nonsampling risk** The sampling risks are:
   a. The **risk of incorrect acceptance** (sample supports conclusion that the recorded account balance is not materially misstated when it is).
   b. The **risk of incorrect rejection** (sample supports the conclusion that the recorded account balance is materially misstated when it is not).

3. Two statistical sampling approaches used by auditors in substantive testing are (a) **probability-proportional-to-size (PPS)** sampling and (b) **classical variables sampling**.

4. **Conditions favoring the use of PPS sampling** include (a) the number of units in a population and/or the variability of the population are unknown and (b) no misstatements or few overstatements only are expected. **Conditions favoring the use of classical variables sampling** include (a) book values for sampling units are not available, (b) it is desirable to define the population to include zero or credit balances, and (c) many misstatements or misstatements of both under and overstatement are expected.

5. The following **steps** pertain to both PPS and classical variables sampling plans:
   a. Determine the objectives of the plan.
   b. Define the population and sampling unit.
   c. Determine the sample size.
   d. Determine the sample selection method.
   e. Execute the sampling plan.
   f. Evaluate the sample results.

6. In PPS sampling the **population** is considered to be the **number of dollars** comprising the balance to be tested and the **sampling unit** is the **individual dollar**.

7. For each dollar sampling unit selected for the sample, the auditor examines the account, transaction, or document (known as the **logical sampling unit**) with which it is associated. Thus, the probability of a given logical unit being examined is proportional to its size.

8. In **determining sample size** in PPS sampling, the formula is:

$$n = \frac{BV \times RF}{TM - (AM \times EF)}$$

where:
BV = book value of population tested
RF = reliability factor for the specified risk of incorrect acceptance
TM = tolerable misstatement
AM = anticipated misstatement
EF = expansion factor for anticipated misstatement

9. Considerations in specifying the **risk of incorrect acceptance** include (a) the level of audit risk the auditor is willing to take that a material misstatement in the account will go undetected, (b) the assessed level of control risk, and (c) the results of other tests of details and analytical procedures.

10. **Tolerable misstatement** is the maximum misstatement that can exist in an account balance before it is considered to be materially misstated. This factor has an inverse effect on sample size.

11. **Anticipated misstatement** provides a means to indirectly control the risk of incorrect rejection with which it is inversely related. An expansion factor is used only when misstatements are anticipated. It is determined from tables based on the auditor's specified risk of incorrect acceptance.

12. The most common **sample selection method** used in PPS sampling is **systematic selection** in which a **sampling interval** is calculated by dividing the book value by the sample size.

13. In **executing a PPS sampling plan**, the auditor applies appropriate auditing procedures to **determine an audit value** for each logical unit included in the sample.

14. In **evaluating sample results** the auditor calculates from the sample (a) the projected misstatement, (b) the allowance for sampling risk, and (c) the upper misstatement limit which is the sum of (a) and (b), all expressed in terms of dollar amounts. The **upper misstatement limit** is compared to the **tolerable misstatement** and together with qualitative considerations forms the basis for **reaching an overall conclusion**.

15. For logical sampling units with book values smaller than the sampling interval, a **tainting percentage** is used in calculating the projected misstatement. The allowance for sampling risk has two components: (a) **basic precision** and (b) an **incremental allowance** related to misstatements found.

16. Three classical variables sampling techniques used in auditing are (a) **mean-per-unit (MPU)**, (b) **difference**, and (c) **ratio estimation**. Factors relevant to choosing among these techniques include the following:
    a. The ability to design a stratified sample.
    b. The expected number of differences between audit and book values.
    c. The available information.

17. The factors used in **determining sample size** in MPU sampling and their effect on sample size are:
    a. Population size (number of units) (direct).
    b. Estimated population standard deviation (direct).
    c. Tolerable misstatement (inverse).
    d. Risk of incorrect rejection (inverse).
    e. Risk of incorrect acceptance (inverse).
    f. Planned allowance for sampling risk (inverse).

18. The **estimated population standard deviation** may be based on (a) the standard deviation found in the preceding audit, (b) available book values in the current year's population, or (c) the audit values of a presample of 30 to 50 items from the current year's population.

19. The factors considered by the auditor in specifying **tolerable misstatement and risk of incorrect acceptance** are the same as in PPS sampling. The **risk of incorrect rejection** is controlled by determining an appropriate U_R factor from a table.

20. The **planned allowance for sampling risk** is determined by first obtaining **a ratio of planned allowance for sampling risk to tolerable misstatement** from a table based on the auditor's specified risks of incorrect rejection and acceptance. This ratio is then **multiplied by tolerable misstatement**.

21. The formula for determining sample size with replacement is

$$n = \left(\frac{N \cdot U_R \cdot S_{x_j}}{A} \right)^2$$

where:
N is the population size, S_{x_j} is the estimated population standard deviation, U_R is the factor corresponding to the specified risk of incorrect rejection, and A is the planned allowance for sampling risk.

22. In **determining the sample selection method** in MPU sampling, the auditor may choose either random number selection or systematic selection.

23. In **executing the sampling plan**, the auditor performs appropriate auditing procedures to determine an audit value for each sample item. The average and the standard deviation of the audit sample values are then calculated.

24. In evaluating the sample results of a MPU sampling plan with replacement, the auditor calculates:
    a. The **estimated total population value** equal to the number of units in the population times the average audit sample value.
    b. The **achieved allowance for sampling risk** based on the formula

$$A' = N \cdot U_R \cdot \frac{S_{x_j}}{\sqrt{n}}$$

    c. A **range** equal to the estimated total population value plus and minus achieved allowance for sampling risk.

25. If the **recorded value falls within the range**, the sample supports the conclusion that the book value is not materially misstated. When the sample results do not support this conclusion, the auditor may (a) expand the sample and reevaluate the results or (b) have the client investigate and, if warranted, adjust the book value and then reevaluate the sample results.

26. If sampling without replacement is used and the ratio n/N is greater than .05, a **finite correction factor** is recommended for determining sample size as follows:

$$n' = n/(1 + n/N)$$

In this case, the formula for computing A' is modified as follows:

$$A' = N \cdot U_R \cdot \frac{S_{x_j} \sqrt{1 - \dfrac{n'}{N}}}{\sqrt{n'}}$$

27. If the achieved allowance for sampling risk is greater than the planned allowance specified in determining sample size, an **adjusted achieved allowance** is calculated as follows:

$$A'' = A' + TM(1 - A'/A)$$

A'' is then used in calculating the range for the estimated population value in order to hold the risk of incorrect acceptance to the level specified in determining sample size.

28. **Difference estimation sampling** is similar to MPU sampling except that:
    a. For each sample item, in addition to determining an audit value, the auditor calculates the **difference** between the audit and book value.
    b. The **average difference** of the sample items is calculated and multiplied by the number of units in the population to get a total difference. This total is added algebraically to the total recorded book value to arrive at the estimated total population value.
    c. The **estimated standard deviation** of the differences is substituted for the estimated population standard deviation in the formulas for sample size and achieved allowance for sampling risk.

29. **Ratio estimation** is also similar to MPU sampling except that:
    a. In addition to determining an audit value for each sample item, the auditor calculates the **ratio of the sum of the audit values to the sum of the book values** for the sample items. This ratio is multiplied by the total recorded book value to obtain the estimated total population value.

b. The **estimated standard deviation of the ratios** is substituted for the estimated population standard deviation in the formulas for sample size and achieved allowance for sampling risk.

30. In **nonstatistical sampling** in substantive tests, while working outside the framework of a mathematical model, the auditor should:
    a. Judgmentally consider the same factors in determining sample size as used in statistical sampling.
    b. Project any misstatement found in the sample to the population.
    c. Consider sampling risk in evaluating sample results.

C. TRUE OR FALSE STATEMENTS

Indicate in the space provided whether each of the following statements is true or false.

_____ 1. Audit sampling in substantive tests may be designed to determine that an account balance is not materially misstated.

_____ 2. Audit sampling in substantive tests is subject to sampling risk but not nonsampling risk.

_____ 3. The risk of incorrect acceptance refers to the risk that the sample supports the conclusion that the recorded amount is not materially misstated when it is materially misstated.

_____ 4. PPS sampling is based on attribute sampling theory while classical variables sampling is based on normal distribution theory.

_____ 5. PPS sampling is primarily used in testing transactions and balances for understatement.

_____ 6. Book values for sampling units must be known in order to use PPS sampling.

_____ 7. The logical sampling unit in PPS sampling is the individual dollar.

_____ 8. Tolerable misstatement reflects the auditor's judgement about the minimum misstatement that may occur in an account balance without causing the financial statements to be materially misstated.

_____ 9. In PPS sampling, the auditor does not quantify the risk of incorrect rejection.

_____10. When no misstatements are found in a PPS sample, the projected misstatement is zero and the allowance for sampling risk consists of only one component which is equal to the upper misstatement limit.

_____11. The tainting percentage is found by dividing the difference between the book value and audit value by the book value.

_____12. For PPS samples containing misstatements, the upper misstatement limit is the sum of basic precision and the incremental allowance resulting from the misstatements.

_____13. Classical variables sampling may be useful to the auditor when the audit objective relates to either the possible under- or overstatement of an account balance.

_____14. A change in the variability of a population affects sample size by the square of the relative change.

_____15. The U_R factor in the sample size formula for MPU sampling is the standard normal deviate for the desired risk of incorrect rejection.

_____16. When sampling with replacement, a finite correction factor is recommended when the ratio of sample size to population size is greater than .05.

_____17. The misstatement or planned allowance for sampling risk for an MPU sample is equal to tolerable misstatement.

_____18. In MPU sampling, sample size is inversely related to tolerable misstatement.

_____19. In evaluating sample results in a MPU sample, the auditor calculates a range equal to the estimated total population value plus and minus the achieved allowance for sampling risk.

_____20. In order to use difference or ratio estimation, the total book value for the population must be known and correspond to the sum of the book values of the individual items.

_____21. When the differences between audit and book values are closely proportional to the book values, difference estimation will yield a smaller sample size than ratio estimation.

_____22. To use either difference or ratio estimation, the auditor must expect more than a few differences between the audit and book values of sample items.

_____23. In nonstatistical sampling, the auditor may, but is not required to, consult statistical tables or models to evaluate the appropriateness of judgmentally determined sample sizes.

_____24. Sampling risk can be considered in evaluating the results of nonstatistical samples.

_____25. Statistical samples can provide the auditor with sufficient evidence to have a reasonable basis for an opinion but not nonstatistical samples.

D. COMPLETION STATEMENTS

Fill in the blanks with the word or words that correctly complete the following statements.

1. Sampling plans for substantive tests may be designed to test that an account balance is _____ or to make an _____ of some amount.

2. The sampling risks associated with substantive tests are _____ and _____.

3. Two statistical sampling approaches may be used in substantive tests: _____ and _____.

4. In PPS sampling, the individual dollar is the _____ while the account, transaction, document, or line item associated with the dollar selected is known as the _____.

5. Basic precision is calculated by multiplying the reliability factor for the _____ by the _____.

6. When misstatements are found in a PPS sample, the allowance for sampling risk is the sum of _____ and an _____ related to the misstatements.

7. In evaluating a PPS sample, _____ is compared to the _____ which is the sum of _____ and an allowance for sampling risk.

8. Three techniques that may be used in classical variables sampling are _____, _____, and _____.

9. In MPU sampling, _____ and estimated _____ are directly related to sample size, while _____ misstatement and the risks of _____ are inversely related.

10. The planned allowance for sampling risk in MPU sampling is calculated by multiplying a _____ based on the risk of incorrect acceptance and rejection by the _____.

11. The range used to evaluate the results of a MPU sample is equal to the estimated _____ plus and minus the _____.

12. An adjusted achieved allowance for sampling risk is calculated when the achieved allowance is _____ than the _____.

13. In difference estimation, a difference is calculated for each sample item equal to the item's _____ minus its _____.

14. In ratio estimation, an estimate of the total population value is obtained by multiplying the _____ of the population by the ratio of the sum of the _____ of the sample items to the sum of the book values of the sample items.

15. In evaluating nonstatistical samples, the auditor should project the _____ found in the sample to the population and consider the _____.

E. MULTIPLE CHOICE

Choose the best answer for each of the following questions and enter the identifying letter in the space provided.

_____ 1. Auditors who prefer statistical sampling to nonstatistical sampling may do so because the statistical sampling helps the auditor:
   a. Measure the sufficiency of the evidential matter obtained.
   b. Eliminate subjectivity in the evaluation of sampling results.
   c. Reduce the level of tolerable misstatement to a relatively low amount.
   d. Minimize the failure to detect a material misstatement due to nonsampling risk.

_____ 2. The risk of incorrect acceptance and of assessing control risk too low relate to the:
   a. Preliminary estimates of materiality levels.
   b. Allowable risk of tolerable misstatement.
   c. Efficiency of the audit.
   d. Effectiveness of the audit.

_____ 3. Hill has decided to use probability-proportional-to-size (PPS) sampling, sometimes called dollar-unit sampling, in the audit of a client's accounts receivable balances. Hill plans to use the following PPS sampling table:

TABLE
Reliability Factors for Errors of Overstatement

Risk of Incorrect Appearance

Number of over- statement errors	1%	5%	10%	15%	20%
0	4.61	3.00	2.31	1.90	1.61
1	6.64	4.75	3.89	3.38	3.00
2	8.41	6.30	5.33	4.72	4.28
3	10.05	7.76	6.69	6.02	5.52
4	11.61	9.16	8.00	7.27	6.73

Additional Information

Tolerable misstatement
    (net of effect of expected misstatement) $24,000
Risk of incorrect acceptance 5%
Recorded amount of accounts receivable $240,000
Number of accounts 360

    What sample size should Hill use?
    a. 120
    b. 108
    c. 60
    d. 30

_____ 4. A number of factors influence the sample size for a substantive test of details of an account balance. All other factors being equal, which of the following would lead to a larger sample size?
    a. Greater detection risk.
    b. Greater reliance on analytical procedures.
    c. Smaller expected frequency of misstatements.
    d. Smaller measure of tolerable misstatement.

_____ 5. Which of the following statements is correct concerning the auditor's use of statistical sampling?
    a. An auditor needs to estimate the dollar amount of the standard deviation of the population to use classical variables sampling.
    b. An assumption of PPS sampling is that the underlying accounting population is normally distributed.
    c. A classical variables sample needs to be designed with special considerations to include negative balances in the sample.
    d. The selection of zero balances usually requires using PPS sampling.

_____ 6. Audit sampling in substantive tests may be used for each of the following purposes except:
    a. Obtain information about the correctness of monetary amounts.
    b. Test whether an account balance is fairly stated.
    c. Make an independent estimate of some amount.
    d. Estimate a deviation rate from a prescribed control procedure.

_____ 7. The sampling approach best suited to estimating the dollar amount of misstatement in a population when few errors of overstatement are expected is:
    a. Attribute sampling.
    b. PPS sampling.
    c. Mean-per-unit sampling.
    d. Difference estimation sampling.

_____ 8. PPS sampling is best suited to testing the reasonableness of the recorded balance for:
  a. Accounts receivable when unapplied credits are not significant.
  b. Inventory price tests when the auditor anticipates many differences.
  c. Accounts payable, excluding accounts with zero balances.
  d. Fixed assets for which recorded book values are unavailable for additions during the year.

_____ 9. Factors relevant to choosing among mean-per-unit, difference, and ratio estimation sampling include all of the following except:
  a. The ability to design a stratified sample.
  b. The expected number of differences between audit and book values.
  c. The availability of an estimate of an appropriate standard deviation.
  d. The ability to obtain a book value for each sample item.

_____ 10. In classical variables sampling, determination of the planned allowance for sampling risk involves all of the following except:
  a. The specified risk of incorrect rejection.
  b. The specified risk of incorrect acceptance.
  c. Tolerable misstatement.
  d. The estimated population standard deviation.

_____ 11. In specifying the risk of incorrect rejection in a MPU sampling plan, the auditor should realize that:
  a. Specification of a low risk will result in a smaller initial sample size.
  b. The level of risk specified should balance the costs associated with the initial sample and the potential costs of later expanding the sample.
  c. The risk may be specified as low as desired because auditing procedures should ultimately result in the conclusion the balance is not materially misstated.
  d. This is the most important risk for the auditor to control.

_____ 12. The risk of incorrect acceptance in classical variables sampling plans is:
  a. Directly, as opposed to inversely, related to sample size.
  b. Ordinarily specified in the range of from 5 to 30 percent.
  c. Unrelated to the auditor's assessed control risk.
  d. Inversely related to the risk that the sample results will support the conclusion that the recorded book value is not materially misstated when it is.

_____ 13. In classical variables sampling, which of the following must be known in order to determine the appropriate sample size required to meet the auditor's needs in a given situation?
  a. The total amount of the population.
  b. The desired standard deviation.
  c. The desired risk of incorrect acceptance.
  d. The estimated population deviation rate.

_____ 14. The risk that statistical evidence from a sample will fail to support the conclusion that an account balance is not materially misstated when the account is fairly stated is known as:
   a. The risk of incorrect acceptance.
   b. The risk of incorrect rejection.
   c. Ultimate risk.
   d. Sampling risk.

Questions 15 through 17 are based on the following information:

An audit partner is developing an office training program to familiarize the professional staff with statistical decision models applicable to the audit of dollar-value balances. The partner wishes to demonstrate the relationship of sample sizes to population size and variability and the auditors specifications as to sampling risk. The partner prepared the following table to show comparative population characteristics and audit specifications of two populations.

Characteristics of population 1 relative to population 2		**Audit Specifications as to a sample from population 1 relative to a sample from population 2**	
		Desired allowance for sampling risk	**Specified risk of incorrect rejection**
Size	**Variability**		
Case 1 Equal	Equal	Equal	Lower
Case 2 Equal	Larger	Larger	Equal
Case 3 Larger	Equal	Smaller	Higher

In each item 15 through 17 you are to indicate for the specified case from the above table the required sample size to be selected from population 1 relative to the sample from population 2. Your answer should be selected from the following responses:
   a. Larger than the required sample size from population 2.
   b. Equal to the required sample size from population 2.
   c. Smaller than the required sample size from population 2.
   d. Indeterminate relative to the required sample size from population 2.

_____ 15. In case 1 the required sample size from population 1 is:
   a. Larger than the required sample size from population 2.
   b. Equal to the required sample size from population 2.
   c. Smaller than the required sample size from population 2.
   d. Indeterminate relative to the required sample size from population 2.

_____ 16. In case 2 the required sample size from population 1 is:
   a. Larger than the required sample size from population 2.
   b. Equal to the required sample size from population 2.
   c. Smaller than the required sample size from population 2.
   d. Indeterminate relative to the required sample size from population 2.

_____ 17. In case 3 the required sample size from population 1 is:
   a. Larger than the required sample size from population 2.
   b. Equal to the required sample size from population 2.
   c. Smaller than the required sample size from population 2.
   d. Indeterminate relative to the required sample size from population 2.

_____ 18. In difference estimation, the sample results support the conclusion that the book value is not materially misstated when the book value falls within the range of the estimated total population value plus and minus:
   a. The estimated total difference.
   b. Tolerable misstatement.
   c. Planned allowance for sampling risk.
   d. Achieved allowance for sampling risk.

_____ 19. Use of the ratio estimation sampling technique to estimate dollar amounts is inappropriate when:
   a. The total book value is known and corresponds to the sum of all the individual book values.
   b. A book value for each sample item is unknown.
   c. There are some observed differences between audited values and book values.
   d. The differences between the audit and book values of sample items are nearly proportional to the book values.

_____ 20. When evaluating the results of a nonstatistical sample, the auditor may do all of the following except:
   a. Project the misstatement found in the sample to the population.
   b. Consider the number and size of misstatements found relative to expected misstatements.
   c. Quantify the sampling risk associated with the results.
   d. View the difference between the projected misstatement and the tolerable misstatement as an allowance for sampling risk.

SOLUTIONS

TRUE OR FALSE STATEMENTS

1. True	10. True	18. True
2. False	11. True	19. True
3. True	12. False	20. True
4. True	13. True	21. False
5. False	14. True	22. True
6. True	15. True	23. True
7. False	16. False	24. True
8. False	17. False	25. False
9. True		

COMPLETION STATEMENTS

1. not materially misstated, independent estimate
2. risk of incorrect acceptance, risk of incorrect rejection
3. probability-proportional-to-size, classical variables
4. sampling unit, logical sampling unit
5. risk of incorrect acceptance, sampling interval
6. basic precision, incremental allowance
7. tolerable misstatement, upper misstatement limit, projected misstatement
8. mean-per-unit, difference, ratio
9. population size, standard deviation, tolerable, incorrect acceptance and rejection
10. ratio, tolerable misstatement
11. total population value, achieved allowance for sampling risk
12. greater, planned allowance
13. audit value, book value
14. total book value, audit values
15. misstatements, sampling risk

MULTIPLE CHOICE QUESTIONS

1. a	5. a	9. c	13. c	17. d
2. d	6. d	10. d	14. b	18. d
3. d	7. b	11. b	15. a	19. b
4. d	8. a	12. b	16. d	20. c

Chapter 13

Auditing Electronic Data Processing Systems

A. CHAPTER OUTLINE

I. **EDP System Components**

   A. Computer Hardware

   B. Computer Software

      1. Systems Programs

      2. Application Programs

   C. Data Organization and Processing Methods

      1. Data Organization Methods

      2. Data Processing Methods

II. **Effects of EDP on the Internal Control Structure**

   A. Differences Between Computer and Manual Processing

   B. General Controls

      1. Organization and Operation Controls

      2. Systems Development and Documentation Controls

      3. Hardware and Systems Software Controls

      4. Access Controls

      5. Data and Procedural Controls

   C. Application Controls

      1. Input Controls

      2. Processing Controls

      3. Output Controls

III. **Methodology for Meeting the Second Standard of Fieldwork**

   A. Obtaining an Understanding of the ICS

   B. Assessing Control Risk

   C. Tests of Controls without the Computer

    D. Tests of Controls with the Computer

        1. Parallel Simulation

        2. Test Data

        3. Integrated Test Facility

        4. Comparison of Approaches

    E. Tests of Controls in On-Line Entry/On-Line Processing

        1. Tagging Transactions

        2. Audit Log

IV. Other Considerations

    A. Generalized Audit Software

        1. Selecting and Printing Audit Samples

        2. Testing Calculations and Making Computations

        3. Summarizing Data and Performing Analyses

        4. Comparing Audit Data with Computer Records

    B. Microcomputer-Based Audit Software

    C. Expert Systems

    D. Small Computer Systems

        1. Internal Control Structure Considerations

        2. Meeting the Second Standard of Field Work

    E. Computer Service Organizations

VI. Summary

B. CHAPTER HIGHLIGHTS

1. The auditor should be familiar with the following components of an EDP system: **hardware, software,** and **data organization and processing methods.**

2. The **basic hardware configuration** consists of **the central processing unit** (CPU) and peripheral input and output devices.

3. **Computer software** consists of the programs and routines that facilitate the programming and operation of a computer. Of particular interest to auditors are (a) **systems programs**, which perform generalized functions, and (b) **application programs**, which enable the user to perform specific data processing tasks with the computer.

4. **Data organization** refers to the method(s) used to organize data within files; **data processing methods** refer to entering data into the computer and processing the data by the computer. Collectively, these activities are referred to as **data management**.

5. There are two principal methods of data organization:
   a. **Traditional file method** that consists of master files and transaction files that may be organized for sequential or direct access processing.
   b. **Database method** that consists of a single common file for all applications using common data.   Under this method, file organization is based on either logical or physical relationships among data.

6. The three principal data processing methods are:
   a. **Batch entry/batch processing** in which data are entered and processed in batches.
   b. **On-line entry/batch processing** in which data are entered directly into the computer via a terminal and are then processed periodically in batches.
   c. **On-line entry/on-line processing** in which data are entered directly into the computer and the master files are updated concurrently with data entry.

7. There are both similarities and differences in **internal control structures** between manual and EDP systems. A critical difference is that the **concentration of functions** in EDP tends to combine duties that would be incompatible in manual systems.

8. There are two categories of EDP controls:
   a. **General controls** which pertain to the EDP environment and all EDP activities.
   b. **Application controls** which are designed to provide reasonable assurance that the recording, processing, and reporting of data by EDP for individual specific applications are properly performed.

9. **General controls** include:
   a. Organization and operation controls.
   b. Systems development and documentation controls.
   c. Hardware and systems software controls.
   d. Access controls.
   e. Data and procedural controls.

10. **Organization and operation** controls pertain to segregation of duties within the EDP department and between EDP and user departments.

11. In order to have proper **systems development and documentation controls**,
    a. Systems design should include representatives of user departments, and, as appropriate, the accounting department and internal auditors.
    b. Each system should have written specifications that are reviewed and approved by management and the user department.
    c. Systems testing should be a cooperative effort of users and EDP personnel.
    d. The EDP manager, user personnel, and the appropriate level of management should give final approval to a new system before it is placed in normal operation.
    e. Program changes should be approved before implementation to determine whether they have been authorized, tested, and documented.

12. The primary purpose of **hardware and systems software controls** is to detect any malfunctioning of computer equipment.

13. **Access controls** are designed to prevent unauthorized use of EDP equipment, data files, and computer programs.

14. **Data and procedural controls** include a control function that is often performed by a data control group, and controls that assure the continuity of operations in the event of a physical disaster or computer failure.

15. **Application controls** consist of (a) input, (b) processing, and (c) output controls.

16. **Input controls** are of vital importance because most errors occur at this point. These controls are designed to provide reasonable assurance that data received for processing have been (a) properly authorized, and (b) converted into machine-sensible form.

17. **Processing controls** are designed to provide reasonable assurance that data are not lost, added, duplicated, or altered during processing.

18. **Output controls** relate to the accuracy of the processing result and to assuring that only authorized personnel receive the output.

19. **GAAS** apply in a financial statement audit regardless of the method of data processing used by the client. EDP systems have a significant impact on the second standard of field work, dealing with the auditor's understanding of client controls.

20. When **EDP is used in significant accounting applications**, the auditor should obtain an understanding of the EDP control structure sufficient to plan the audit. The understanding should include knowledge of:
    a. The classes of transactions in the entity's operations processed by the EDP system that are significant to the financial statements.
    b. The accounting records, supporting documents, machine-readable information, and specific accounts in the financial statements involved in the EDP processing and reporting of these significant classes of transactions.
    c. The types of potential misstatements that could occur.

21. The process of **assessing control risk** is the same for an EDP control structure as in a manual structure. Because of their pervasive nature, general controls should be assessed before application controls.

22. **Tests of controls** may be made **without the computer** when the processing applications are well documented and sufficient printed output exists. This method of testing offers the following advantages:
    a. The auditor can use familiar auditing procedures in performing the tests.
    b. Recourse to the complexities of computer programs is unnecessary.

23. **Tests of controls with the computer** involve the use of computer-assisted audit techniques. This method of testing is advantageous when:
    a. Significant internal controls are embodied in a computer program.
    b. There are significant gaps in the visible transaction trail.
    c. There are large volumes of records to be tested.

24. The three common **computer-assisted audit techniques** for testing application controls are:
    a. **Parallel simulation** which involves creating a model of the system to be tested and processing actual data through the model.
    b. **Test data** which involves the processing of dummy transactions through the client's system using actual client programs.
    c. **Integrated test facility** which involves the creation of a small system (a mini-company) within the regular EDP system and the processing of test data using actual client programs.

25. In an on-line entry/on-line processing system, the auditor often uses **continuous monitoring** of the system in lieu of traditional tests of controls.

26. **Generalized audit software** enables the auditor to deal effectively with large quantities of data in both tests of controls and substantive tests. Examples of substantive test applications include:
    a. Selecting and printing audit samples.
    b. Testing calculations and making computations.
    c. Summarizing data and performing analyses.
    d. Comparing audit data with computer records.

27. **Microcomputer-based audit software** is useful in both the execution and administration of the audit. Common applications include
    a. Preparation of a trial balance and financial statements.
    b. Preparation of lead schedules and working papers.
    c. Generation of audit programs for tests of controls and substantive tests.
    d. Performance of analytical procedures.
    e. Preparation of standardized audit correspondence such as engagement letters, confirmations, and audit reports.
    f. Performance of engagement administrative tasks such as preparation of the time budget, recording time worked, and tabulating observance of audit deadlines.

28. Both of the two categories of EDP controls are relevant to **small computer systems**. Because of the following possible weaknesses in general controls, it may be more cost efficient in an audit to concentrate on application controls:
    a. Lack of segregation of duties between the EDP department and users.
    b. Location of the computer.
    c. Lack of segregation of duties within the EDP department.
    d. Limited knowledge of EDP.

29. Computer service organizations provide EDP services for other entities. The organization may be:
    a. A **computer service center** that records transactions and processes related data for small companies.
    b. A **trust department of a bank** or similar entity that invests and holds assets for a company's employee benefit or pension plan.

30. At a **minimum**, the auditor must (1) obtain an understanding of the computer service organization's control structure and (2) make an initial assessment of control risk. If the auditor plans to assess control risk below the maximum, evidence of the effectiveness of controls must be obtained by either:
    a. Performing tests of controls at the service organization.
    b. Relying on an internal control report prepared by the service organization's auditors for customers of the service organization.

C. TRUE OR FALSE STATEMENTS

Indicate in the space provided whether each of the following statements is true or false.

_____ 1. The basic hardware configuration in an EDP system consists of the central processing unit, data files, and processing methods.

_____ 2. Auditors are interested in two types of computer software: systems programs and utility programs.

_____ 3. The activities of entering data into the computer and processing the data by the computer are collectively referred to as data management.

_____ 4. The traditional file method consists of two types of files: master and transaction.

_____ 5. The principal alternative to the traditional file method is the database method.

_____ 6. The processing method that concurrently updates the master file with data entry is on-line/batch processing.

_____ 7. On-line entry/ on-line processing may result in either immediate or memo updating of the master file.

_____ 8. The objectives of internal control in an EDP system are different than in a manual system.

_____ 9. A major difference between computer processing and manual processing is that an EDP system may produce a transaction trail for only a short period of time.

_____ 10. General controls pertain to the EDP environment and are pervasive in their effect on other EDP controls.

_____ 11. Application controls are designed to provide reasonable assurance that the recording, processing, and reporting of data by EDP are properly performed.

_____ 12. The primary responsibilities of the EDP manager and the database administrator are essentially the same.

_____ 13. Hardware and systems software controls include parity check, echo check, and sequence tests.

_____ 14. Access controls are designed to prevent unauthorized use of EDP equipment but not the unauthorized use of data files and computer files.

_____ 15. Input controls focus on whether data received for processing have been properly authorized and converted into machine-sensible form.

_____ 16. Processing controls include control totals, file identification labels, and limit and reasonableness checks.

_____ 17. Output controls include reconciliation of totals and comparison to source documents.

_____ 18. The methodology for making a study and evaluation of internal controls in an EDP system is conceptually different than in a manual system.

_____ 19. The auditor's understanding of the EDP control structure should include both general controls and application controls.

_____ 20. Tests of general EDP controls should precede the testing of application controls.

_____ 21. The computer-assisted techniques of parallel simulation and integrated test facility both use test data.

_____ 22. Generalized audit software is only usable in substantive testing.

_____ 23. An expert system is a computer model that incorporates the knowledge of human experts in order to assist others in performing functions or making decisions.

_____ 24. In some computer systems it may be more cost-efficient to concentrate on application controls.

_____ 25. When the auditor plans to use an assessed level of control risk below the maximum in a service organization, he or she must personally test the controls.

D. COMPLETION STATEMENTS

Fill in the blanks with the word or words that correctly complete the following statements.

1. Three components of an EDP system are _____, _____, and _____.

2. The principal methods of data organization are the _____ method and the _____ method.

3. Three widely used methods of data processing are _____, _____, and _____.

4. Organization and operation controls are a type of _____ control; input controls are a type of _____ control.

5. Systems development and documentation controls relate to the review, testing, and approval of _____, control of _____, and _____ procedures.

6. Access controls include both _____ and _____ safeguards.

7. Other data and procedural controls include a control function that is often assumed by the _____ group and ability to reconstruct _____.

8. Controls over the conversion of input data include _____, _____, and _____.

9. Output controls are designed to assure that the processing result is _____ and that only _____ receive the output.

10. The auditor should obtain sufficient knowledge of the EDP system to understand the classes of _____, how the computer is used to _____, and the types of _____ that could occur.

11. Tests of controls without the computer may be possible when the processing applications are _____ and sufficient _____ exists.

12. The three common computer-assisted audit techniques for testing application controls are _____, _____, and _____.

13. The most common type of audit software is _____ which enables the auditor to deal effectively with large _____.

14. Because _____ may be weak in small computer systems, it may be cost-effective for the auditor to concentrate on _____ in reviewing the system.

15. A computer service organization may be a computer _____ or a _____ of a bank.

E. MULTIPLE CHOICE

Choose the best answer for each of the following questions and enter the identifying letter in the space provided.

_____ 1. Which of the following activities would most likely be performed in the EDP department?
   a. Initiation of changes to master records.
   b. Conversion of information to machine-readable form.
   c. Correction of transaction errors.
   d. Initiation of changes to existing applications.

_____ 2. For control purposes, which of the following should be organizationally segregated from the computer operations function?
   a. Data conversion.
   b. Surveillance of CRT messages.
   c. Systems development.
   d. Minor maintenance according to a schedule.

_____ 3. Which of the following is an example of a check digit?
   a. An arrangement of the total number of employees to the total number of checks printed by the computer.
   b. An algebraically determined number produced by the other digits of the employee number.
   c. A logic test that ensures all employee numbers are nine digits.
   d. A limit check that an employee's hours do not exceed 50 hours per work week.

_____ 4. Totals of amounts in computer-record data fields which are not usually added for other purposes but are used only for data processing purposes are called:
   a. Record totals.
   b. Hash totals.
   c. Processing data totals.
   d. Field totals.

_____ 5. When an on-line, real-time (OLRT) electronic data processing system is in use, internal control can be strengthened by:
   a. Providing for the separation of duties between keypunching and error listing operations.
   b. Attaching plastic file protection rings to reels of magnetic tape before new data can be entered in the file.

    c. Making a validity check of an identification number before a user can obtain access to the computer files.

    d. Preparing batch totals to provide assurance that file updates are made for the entire input.

6. Which of the following would most likely be a weakness in the internal control structure of a client that utilized microcomputers rather than a larger computer system?

    a. Employee collusion possibilities are increased because microcomputers from one vendor can process the programs of a system from a different vendor.

    b. The microcomputer operators may be able to remove hardware and software components and modify them at home.

    c. Programming errors result in all similar transactions being processed incorrectly when those transactions are processed under the same conditions.

    d. Certain transactions may be automatically initiated by the microcomputers and management's authorization of these transactions may be implicit in its acceptance of the system design.

7. Which of the following characteristics distinguishes computer processing from manual processing?

    a. Computer processing virtually eliminates the occurrence of computational error normally associated with manual processing.

    b. Errors or irregularities in computer processing will be detected soon after their occurrences.

    c. The potential for systematic error is ordinarily greater in manual processing than in computerized processing.

    d. Most computer systems are designed so that transaction trails useful for audit purposes do not exist.

Item 8 is based on the following flowchart:

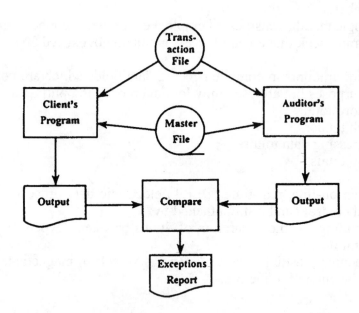

_____ 8. The above flowchart depicts
   a. Program code checking.
   b. Parallel simulation.
   c. Integrated test facility.
   d. Controlled reprocessing.

_____ 9. A primary advantage of using generalized audit software packages to audit the financial statements of a client that uses an EDP system is that the auditor may:
   a. Consider increasing the use of substantive tests of transactions in place of analytical procedures.
   b. Substantiate the accuracy of data through self-checking digits and hash totals.
   c. Reduce the level of required tests of controls to a relatively small amount.
   d. Access information stored on computer files while having a limited understanding of the client's hardware and software features.

_____ 10. In auditing through a computer, the test data method is used by auditors to test the:
   a. Accuracy of input data.
   b. Validity of the output.
   c. Procedures contained within the program.
   d. Normalcy of distribution of test data.

_____ 11. When an auditor tests a computerized accounting system, which of the following is true of the test data approach?
   a. Test data are processed by the client's computer programs under the auditor's control.
   b. Test data must consist of all possible valid and invalid conditions.
   c. Testing a program at year end provides assurance that the client's processing was accurate for the full year.
   d. Several transactions of each type must be tested.

_____ 12. Which of the following is an advantage of generalized computer audit packages?
   a. They are all written in one identical computer language.
   b. They can be used for audits of clients that use differing EDP equipment and file formats.
   c. They have reduced the need for the auditor to study input controls for EDP related procedures.
   d. Their use can be substituted for a relatively large part of the required tests of controls.

_____ 13. When erroneous data are detected by computer program controls, such data may be excluded from processing and printed on an error report. The error report should most probably be reviewed and followed up by the
   a. EDP data control group.
   b. Database administrator.
   c. Supervisor of computer operations.
   d. Computer programmer.

_____ 14. Auditors often make use of computer programs that perform routine processing functions such as sorting and merging. These programs are made available by electronic data processing companies and others and are specifically referred to as:
   a. Compiler programs.
   b. Supervisory programs.
   c. Utility programs.
   d. User programs.

_____ 15. The use of a header label in conjunction with magnetic tape is most likely to prevent errors by the:
   a. Computer operator.
   b. Keypunch operator.
   c. Computer programmer.
   d. Maintenance technician.

_____ 16. Where computers are used, the effectiveness of internal control depends, in part, upon whether the organizational structure includes any incompatible combinations. Such a combination would exist when there is no separation of the duties between:
   a. Documentation librarian and manager of programming.
   b. Programmer and console operator.
   c. Systems analyst and programmer.
   d. Processing control clerk and keypunch supervisor.

_____ 17. Which of the following would not be a valid reason for choosing to omit tests of an EDP application control?
   a. The controls duplicate operative controls existing elsewhere in the system.
   b. There appear to be major weaknesses that would preclude reliance on the stated procedure.
   c. The time and dollar costs of testing exceed the time and dollar savings in substantive tests if the tests of controls show the controls to be operative.
   d. The controls appear adequate enough to be relied upon.

_____ 18. The two requirements crucial to achieving audit efficiency and effectiveness with a microcomputer are selecting:
   a. The appropriate audit tasks for microcomputer applications and the appropriate software to perform the selected audit tasks.
   b. The appropriate software to perform the selected audit tasks and client data that can be accessed by the auditor's microcomputer.
   c. Client data that can be accessed by the auditor's microcomputer and audit procedures that are generally applicable to several clients in a specific industry.
   d. Audit procedures that are generally applicable to several clients in a specific industry and the appropriate audit tasks for microcomputer applications.

_____ 19. Which of the following would lessen internal control in an electronic data processing system?
   a. The computer librarian maintains custody of computer program instructions and detailed listings.
   b. Computer operators have access to operator instructions and detailed program listings.
   c. The control group is solely responsible for the distribution of all computer output.
   d. Computer programmers write and debug programs which perform routines designed by the systems analyst.

_____ 20. Which of the following client electronic data processing (EDP) systems generally can be audited without examining or directly testing the EDP computer programs of the system?
   a. A system that performs relatively uncomplicated processes and produces detailed output.
   b. A system that affects a number of essential master files and produces a limited output.
   c. A system that updates a few essential master files and produces no printed output other than final balances.
   d. A system that performs relatively complicated processing and produces very little detailed output.

SOLUTIONS

TRUE OR FALSE STATEMENTS

1. False	10. True	18. False
2. False	11. True	19. True
3. True	12. False	20. True
4. True	13. False	21. False
5. True	14. False	22. False
6. False	15. True	23. True
7. True	16. True	24. True
8. False	17. True	25. False
9. True		

COMPLETION STATEMENTS

1. hardware, software, and data organization and processing methods
2. traditional file, database
3. batch entry/batch processing, on-line entry/batch processing, on-line entry/on-line processing
4. general, application
5. new systems, program changes, documentation
6. physical, procedural
7. data control, data files
8. verification controls, computer editing, control totals
9. correct, authorized personnel
10. transactions, process data, potential misstatements
11. well documented, printed output
12. parallel simulation, test data, integrated test facility
13. generalized audit software, quantities of data
14. general controls, application controls
15. service center, trust department

MULTIPLE CHOICE QUESTIONS

1. b	5. c	9. d	13. a	17. d
2. c	6. b	10. c	14. c	18. a
3. b	7. a	11. a	15. a	19. b
4. b	8. b	12. b	16. b	20. a

Chapter 14

Auditing the Revenue Cycle

A. CHAPTER OUTLINE

I. **Nature of the Revenue Cycle**

   A. Audit Objectives

   B. Materiality, Risk, and Audit Strategy

     1. Materiality

     2. Inherent and Control Risks

     3. Audit Strategy

II. **Consideration of Internal Control Structure Components**

   A. Control Environment

   B. Risk Assessment

   C. Information and Communication (Accounting System)

   D. Monitoring

   E. Initial Assessment of Control Risk

III. **Control Activitiess - Credit Sales Transactions**

   A. Common Documents and Records

   B. Functions

     1. Accepting Customer Orders

     2. Approving Credit

     3. Filling Sales Orders

     4. Shipping Sales Orders

     5. Billing Customers

     6. Recording the Sales

     7. Illustrative System for Processing Credit Sales

   C. Obtaining the Understanding and Assessing Control Risk

        1. Computer-Assisted Tests of Controls

IV. **Control Activities - Cash Receipts Transactions**

    A. Common Documents and Records

    B. Functions

        1. Receiving Cash Receipts

        2. Depositing Cash in Bank

        3. Recording the Receipts

        4. Illustrative System for Processing Cash Receipts

    C. Obtaining the Understanding and Assessing Control Risk

V. **Control Activities - Sales Adjustments Transactions**

VI. **Substantive Tests of Accounts Receivable**

    A. Determining Detection Risk

    B. Designing Substantive Tests

    C. Initial Procedures

    D. Analytical Procedures

    E. Tests of Details of Transactions

        1. Vouch Recorded Receivables to Supporting Transactions

        2. Perform Cutoff Tests for Sales and Sales Returns

        3. Perform Cash Receipts Cutoff Test

    F. Tests of Details of Balances

        1. Confirm Accounts Receivable

        2. Evaluate Adequacy of Allowance for Uncollectible Accounts

    G. Comparison of Statement Presentation with GAAP

VI. **Summary**

B. CHAPTER HIGHLIGHTS

1. An entity's **revenue cycle** consists of the activities relating to the exchange of goods and services with customers and the collection of the revenue in cash. For a merchandising company, the classes of transactions in this cycle include:
   a. Credit sales,
   b. Cash receipts (collections on account and cash sales), and
   c. Sales adjustments (discounts, returns and allowances, and uncollectible accounts).

2. The **audit objectives** for the revenue cycle and the related assertions are:
   a. **Existence or occurrence**:
      - Recorded sales transactions represent goods shipped during the period under audit.
      - Recorded cash receipts transactions represent cash received during the period from cash and credit sales.
      - Recorded sales adjustment transactions during the period represent authorized discounts, returns and allowances, and uncollectible accounts.
      - Recorded accounts receivable balances represent amounts owed by customers at the balance sheet date.
   b. **Completeness**:
      - All credit sales, cash receipts, and sales adjustment transactions that occurred during the period have been recorded.
      - Accounts receivable include all claims on customers at the balance sheet date.
   c. **Rights and obligations**:
      - Accounts receivable represent legal claims on customers for payment.
   d. **Valuation or allocation**:
      - All sales, cash receipts, and sales adjustment transactions are correctly journalized. The accounts receivable balance represents gross claims on customers and agrees with the sum of the accounts receivable subsidiary ledger.
      - The allowance for uncollectible accounts represents a reasonable estimate of the difference between gross receivables and their net realizable value.
   e. **Presentation and disclosure**:
      - Accounts receivable are properly identified and classified in the balance sheet. Appropriate disclosures have been made concerning accounts receivable that have been assigned or pledged.
      - Sales, sales discounts, sales returns and allowances, and bad debts expense are correctly identified and classified in the income statement.

3. Sales transactions are a principle source of operating revenue and accounts receivable are **nearly always material** to the balance sheet.
   a. Because of the **high inherent risk** associated with receivables, it is often appropriate to **allocate a proportionately larger share of financial statement materiality** (i.e., tolerable misstatement) to this account, thus reducing the overall cost of evidence accumulation.
   b. To enhance effectiveness and efficiency, **careful consideration** should be given to inherent and control risks and **choosing the audit strategy** (primarily substantive or lower assessed control risk) appropriate to each audit objective (i.e., assertion). Normally, due to high transaction volume affecting receivables and sales, a lower assessed control risk approach is appropriate. However, if transaction volume is low, or controls are ineffective, a primarily substantive approach would be more appropriate.

4. **Inherent and control risk considerations** include:
   a. Factors that might **motivate management to misstate revenue cycle assertions**, including:
      • Pressure to overstate revenues.
      • Pressure to overstate cash and receivables, while understating the allowance for uncollectibles.
   b. **Other factors** that contribute to misstatements include:
      • High transaction volume for affected accounts.
      • Complex calculations, estimates, ambiguous accounting standards, and the purchaser's right of return, and contentious treatment of factoring arrangements done with recourse.
      • Difficulty in classifying receivables as current or not due to uncertainty of collection.
      • Cash receipts generated in this cycle are susceptible to misappropriation.
      • Sales adjustment methods (returns, discounts, or allowances) can be used to conceal theft.

5. **Internal control structure considerations** for revenue cycle transactions include the following:
   a. **Control environment factors** include adherence to high standards of integrity and ethical values, including eliminating incentives to dishonest reporting (e.g., undue emphasis on unrealistic profit targets), management's philosophy, operating style, and commitment to competence, clear assignment of authority through written assignments, the **bonding of employees who handle cash**, making these employees take vacations, and rotating their assigned duties periodically.
   b. **Risk assessment** factors including evidence of management's identification and assessment of risk areas.
   c. **Information and communication or accounting system** factors such as the existence of an audit trail, documentation of significant systems (both manual and computerized) including flowcharts, chart of accounts, policy and reporting manuals, understanding of EDP general and application controls.
   d. **Monitoring** by management to ensure that control policies and procedures are operating as intended. Feedback sources include customer inquiries, regulatory agency scrutiny, follow-up on reportable conditions identified by independent auditors.

6. **Common documents and records** generated in the revenue cycle are:
   • Customer order (i.e., customer's purchase order)
   • Sales order specifying description and quantities of goods
   • Shipping documents (e.g., bill of lading)
   • Sales invoice specifying prices, amount owed and credit terms
   • Authorized price list for goods offered for sale
   • Accounts receivable subsidiary ledger or master file showing customer balances and activity
   • Sales transaction file or sales journal
   • Customer statements sent monthly showing balance owed

7. The **credit sales functions** are (a) accepting customer orders, (b) approving credit, (c) filling sales orders, (d) shipping sales orders, (e) billing customers, and (f) recording the sales.

8. **Accepting customer orders** involves approval of the order by the sales order department by:
   a. Tracing the order to an approved customer list, or
   b. Using a computer terminal to determine whether the customer is in the accounts receivable master file, and
   c. Having a supervisor approve new customers.

9. **Approving credit** is the responsibility of the credit department in accordance with management's credit policies and authorized credit limits.
   a. For a new customer, a credit check may be made with an agency such as Dunn & Bradstreet.
   b. Controls over approving credit relate to the valuation or allocation assertion for accounts receivable.

10. A copy of the **approved sales order** is normally the **authorization to the warehouse** for filling sales orders. The shipping of sales orders involves:
    a. Independent checks by shipping clerks to determine that (1) goods received from the warehouse are accompanied by an approved sales order and (2) the order was properly filled.
    b. Preparation of a multicopy shipping document that provides evidence for the existence or occurrence assertion for sales transactions.

11. **Billing of customers** involves preparing and sending prenumbered sales invoices to customers. Controls pertaining to this function include:
    a. An independent check by billing department personnel of the existence of a shipping document and matching approved sales order before each invoice is prepared.
    b. Use of an authorized price list or computerized master price file in preparing the sales invoices.
    c. Manual independent checks or computer programmed checks on the mathematical accuracy of sales invoices.
    d. Comparison of control totals for shipping documents with corresponding totals for sales invoices.

    These controls relate to the existence or occurrence, completeness, and valuation or allocation assertions.

12. The auditor's primary concerns in **recording sales** are that sales invoices are recorded accurately and in the proper period. Controls over this function include:
    a. Recording sales only on the basis of a sales invoice with a matching shipping document and sales order evidencing the sale and transaction date.
    b. Accounting for all prenumbered sales invoices.
    c. Manual or computer programmed checks on agreement of control totals for invoices processed and recorded amounts.
    d. Segregating the responsibility for recording from the previous functions in processing sales transactions.
    e. Restricting access to records and computer programs involved in the recording process to reduce the risk of unauthorized entries.
    f. Performing periodic independent checks on the agreement of the accounts receivable subsidiary ledger or accounts receivable master file with the general ledger control account.

g. Mailing monthly statements to customers with instructions to report any exceptions to a designated accounting supervisor not otherwise involved in the execution or recording of revenue cycle transactions.

These controls pertain to the existence or occurrence, completeness, and valuation or allocation assertions.

13. **Common potential misstatements and (necessary controls)** include:
   a. Sales to unauthorized customers (approved customer lists and approved sales orders prior to shipping)
   b. Sales made without credit approval (credit department check of new customers and credit limits for all customers)
   c. Goods shipped on unauthorized orders or for wrong quantities (approved sales order required to ship and independent counts by shipping clerk)
   d. Billings for fictitious transactions or duplicate billings (match sales order and shipping documents to every invoice sent)
   e. Invoices priced incorrectly (independent check of prices and computations)
   f. Sales not recorded correctly or posted to wrong customer (independent check of control totals in sales journal and subsidiary ledgers; monthly statements sent to customers)

14. Based on evidence obtained from the procedures to obtain an understanding of relevant portions of all five components of the ICS and based on the results of the related tests of controls through inquiry, observation, inspection, and reperformance, **a final assessment of control risk** is made and documented for each significant assertion affecting credit sales transactions.

15. The auditor may use **computer-assisted tests of controls** when **credit** sales transactions are processed on the computer. They may include edit routines and the following tests:
   • Using **generalized audit software** or a utility program to perform sequence checks to detect missing sales order, shipping document, and sales invoice numbers in **computer** files.
   • Designing, selecting, and evaluating an **attribute sample** of shipping documents.
   • Selecting and printing a sample of sales prices from the sales price master file for manual comparison with authorized prices established by management.

16. **Common documents and records** in the cash receipts transaction cycle are:
   a. Remittance advice (i.e., portion of the sales invoice returned by customers with payment).
   b. Prelist of mail receipts
   c. Cash count sheets for cash registers
   d. Daily cash summary of mail and counter receipts
   e. Validated bank deposit slip
   f. Cash receipts transaction file (journal)

17. **Cash receipts transactions** in the revenue cycle include the following cash receipts functions: (a) receiving cash receipts, (b) depositing cash in bank, and (c) recording the receipts.

18. Control procedures over **receiving cash receipts** should provide reasonable assurance that documentation establishing accountability is created at the moment cash is received, and that the cash is subsequently safeguarded.
   a. A **cash register or point-of-sale terminal** is indispensable for over-the-counter receipts.
   b. A **lockbox system** is useful for mail receipts.
   c. When a company processes its own mail receipts, mail clerks should immediately restrictively endorse checks **for deposit only.**
   d. List the checks on a multicopy **prelist.**

19. An important control in **depositing cash receipts** is that all receipts should be **deposited intact daily.** Documentation for this function includes **a daily cash summary** and **a validated deposit slip.**

20. **Recording the receipts** involves journalizing the receipts and posting mail receipts to customer accounts. Controls pertaining to this function should ensure that:
   a. Only valid receipts are entered (existence or occurrence assertion).
   b. All actual receipts are entered (completeness assertion).
   c. All receipts are entered at the correct amounts (valuation or allocation assertion).

21. The auditor's responsibilities for **meeting the second standard of field work** for cash receipts transactions is the same as described previously for credit sales transactions.

22. Common **potential misstatements and (necessary controls)** include:
   a. Cash sales not registered or mail receipts lost or stolen (use of cash registers and periodic surveillance, prelist of mail receipts and immediate restrictive endorsement of checks).
   b. Access to cash inadequate (cash deposited daily).
   c. Receipts not recorded or posted to wrong customer (independent reconciliation of prelist, deposit slip, cash receipts journal; monthly statements sent to customers).

23. Controls over **sales adjustments transactions** include:
   a. **Proper authorization** of all sales adjustments transactions. For example, all write-offs of uncollectible accounts should be authorized by the treasurer's office.
   b. The use of appropriate **documents and records,** particularly the use of an approved **credit memo** for granting credit for returned or damaged goods, and an approved **writeoff authorization memo** for writing off uncollectible customer accounts.
   c. **Segregation of duties** for authorizing sales adjustments transactions and handling and recording cash receipts.

24. **Determining detection risk** for accounts receivable balance assertions involves a consideration of the audit risk model and assessments of inherent and control risk for revenue cycle transactions that affect the assertions.
   a. Planned detection risk for each assertion may be determined in the planning phase using a planned assessed level of control risk.
   b. The actual assessed level of control risk for each assertion is subsequently used to determine whether planned detection risk and the planned level of substantive tests are supported.
   c. Either the planned level, if supported, or a revised level of detection risk is used in completing the design of appropriate substantive tests for each assertion.

25. An **audit program for accounts receivable balances** is designed from possible substantive tests.
    a. The auditor's primary concern is about the overstatement of accounts receivable.
    b. Four possible tests apply to three or more assertions.
    c. In performing substantive tests, the auditor relies primarily on two types of evidential matter: confirmations and review of documentation originating within the client organization.

26. The **starting point for substantive tests of accounts receivable** balances is to verify the accuracy of the accounts receivable **trial balance** and agreement with general ledger control. This test relates to the valuation or allocation assertion.

27. **Analytical procedures** for accounts receivable may include the following:

Ratio	Formula
Accounts receivable turnover	Net sales ÷ Average accounts receivable
Accounts receivable to total current assets	Accounts receivable ÷ Total current assets
Rate of return on net sales	Net income ÷ Net sales
Uncollectible accounts expense to net credit sales	Uncollectible accounts expense ÷ Net sales
Uncollectible accounts expense to actual uncollectibles	Uncollectible accounts expense ÷ Actual uncollectibles

This test provides evidence about three assertions: existence or occurrence, completeness, and valuation or allocation.

28. The **sales cutoff test** relates to the existence or occurrence and completeness assertions. The test involves:
    a. Examining shipping documents for several days before and after the cutoff date to determine the date and terms of shipment.
    b. Tracing shipping documents to the sales and inventory records to establish that the entries were made in the correct accounting period.
    c. Inspecting invoices for a period of time before and after the cutoff date to ascertain the validity and propriety of the shipments and corresponding entries.
    d. Inquiring of management about any direct shipments by outside suppliers to customers and determining the appropriateness of related entries.

29. The **sales return cutoff test** is directed at the possibility that sales return activity prior to year end will not be recorded until after year end. Unusually heavy returns after year end may indicate inflated sales for the prior year through unauthorized shipments to customers.

30. **Cash receipts cutoff tests** attempt to determine whether receipts are recorded in the period received. The auditor's presence on the last day of the year is helpful in verifying cutoff through observation and review of cash receipts documentation.

31. The **confirmation of accounts receivable** is the primary test of details of balances.
    a. There is a presumption that accounts receivable will be confirmed unless (1) accounts receivable are immaterial, (2) confirmation would be ineffective, or (3) the auditor's combined assessment of inherent and control risk is low, and that assessment, in conjunction with the evidence expected to be provided by analytical procedures or other substantive tests of details, is sufficient to reduce audit risk to an acceptably low level for the applicable financial statement assertions.
    b. There are **two forms of confirmation** request: (1) the **positive** form which requires the debtor to respond and (2) the **negative** form which requires the debtor to respond only when the amount shown is incorrect. A variation of the positive form is the **"blank form"** where the customer's balance is not provided on the confirmation but must be written in by the customer. This form provides high assurance, but may result in lower response rates for confirmation requests.
    c. The confirmation date and the number of requests are decisions made by the auditor on the basis of detection risk.

32. The auditor should **control the confirmation** of accounts receivable by:
    a. Ascertaining that the **amount and name and address** on the confirmation **agree with the corresponding data in the customer's account**.
    b. **Maintaining custody** of the confirmations until they are mailed.
    c. Using the **CPA firm's own return address envelopes** for the confirmations.
    d. **Personally depositing** the requests in the mail.
    e. Insisting that the **returns be sent directly to the auditor.**

33. Confirmation of accounts receivable is the **primary source of evidence** for the **existence or occurrence** assertion but it also provides evidence about each of the **other assertions except presentation and disclosure.**

34. All **customer exceptions** noted in returned confirmations **must be addressed** by the auditor. In addition, for positive confirmations not returned, **alternative procedures** must be performed. These consist of examining **subsequent collections and vouching open invoices** included in the balance.

35. The **best evidence of collectibility** is the **receipt of payment** from the customer. The test of examining subsequent collections provides evidence about the existence or occurrence, completeness, and valuation or allocation assertions. In the absence of subsequent payment, the vouching of invoices comprising balances for confirmations not returned is normally done.

36. The vouching of the **aged trial balance** relates to the valuation or allocation assertion. In determining the **adequacy of the allowance for uncollectible accounts**, the auditor should:
    a. Examine correspondence in the debtor's file.
    b. Review debtor's published annual financial statements.
    c. Make inquiries of outside agencies, such as Dun & Bradstreet, about the customer's credit rating.

     d. Review correspondence between the client and outside collection agencies about the status of accounts turned over for collection.

     e. Discuss the collectibility of the account with appropriate management personnel.

37. Two widely used **computer assisted applications** in testing accounts receivable balances are (a) verifying the accuracy of the aged trial balance and (b) preparing confirmation requests.

C. TRUE OR FALSE STATEMENTS

Indicate in the space provided whether each of the following statements is true or false.

_____   1. Inherent risk is usually high in the revenue cycle and thus a smaller portion of financial statement materiality is assigned to this cycle.

_____   2. A specific audit objective for the completeness assertion is: Accounts receivable include all claims on customers at the balance sheet date.

_____   3. The audit strategy for the revenue cycle generally is to use the lower assessed level of control risk approach for all assertions.

_____   4. The first two credit sales functions are accepting customer orders and filling sales orders.

_____   5. Controls over approving credit relate to the valuation or allocation assertion.

_____   6. The key document in filling sales orders is the approved sales order.

_____   7. Billing of customers involves preparing prenumbered shipping documents and sending sales invoices to customers.

_____   8. The auditor's primary concern in recording sales is that sales invoices are recorded accurately and in the proper period.

_____   9. Controls over billing customers and recording sales relate to the same financial statement assertions.

_____ 10. The final step in assessing control risk is to make the assessment for each significant assertion for sales transactions.

_____ 11. Computer-assisted tests of controls may include edit routines to detect incorrect or missing data on sales orders.

_____ 12. A cash register or point-of-sale terminal is indispensable for mail receipts.

_____ 13. An important control in depositing cash receipts is that all receipts should be deposited intact daily.

_____ 14. Controls over sales adjustments transactions include proper authorization, documents and records, and segregation of duties.

_____ 15. In completing the design of substantive tests, the auditor may use either the planned or actual assessed level of control risk.

_____ 16. The auditor's primary concern is about the understatement (completeness) assertion for accounts receivable.

_____ 17. Verifying the accuracy of the accounts receivable trial balance relates to the existence or occurrence and valuation or allocation assertions.

_____ 18. The confirmation of accounts receivable is always a required procedure.

_____ 19. Confirming accounts receivable is the primary source of evidence for the existence or occurrence assertion.

_____ 20. A blank form confirmation provides higher assurance than other forms, but may result in lower response rate by customers.

_____ 21. The auditor may use both the positive and negative forms of confirmation on the same audit engagement.

_____ 22. The sales cutoff test provides evidence about the existence or occurrence and valuation or allocation assertions.

_____ 23. The best evidence of collectibility is a positive confirmation from a customer as to the correctness of the balance due.

_____ 24. The vouching of the aged trial balance relates to the valuation or allocation assertion.

_____ 25. Making inquiries of the credit manager provides important evidence concerning the collectibility of accounts receivable.

D. COMPLETION STATEMENTS

Fill in the blanks with the word or words that correctly complete the following statements.

1. The classes of transactions in the revenue cycle are _____ , and _____ , and _____ .

2. A specific audit objective for the rights and obligations assertion is: Accounts receivable represent _____ on _____ for payment.

3. Inherent risk for revenue cycle transactions is usually _____ because of the volume of transactions and because _____ is very susceptible to misappropriation.

4. One control environment factor is the _____ of employees who handle cash, which is the purchase of an _____ against losses from _____.

5. Controls over the recording of sales relate to three assertions: _____, _____, and _____.

6. The first three steps in assessing control risk for sales transactions are identifying _____ that could occur, identifying _____ to prevent or detect the misstatements, and obtaining evidence from _____ as to the effectiveness of the controls.

7. The cash receipts functions are _____ , _____ , and _____.

8. When a company processes its own mail receipts, mail clerks should immediately _____ checks for _____ and list the checks on a multicopy _____.

9. Controls over the recording of receipts should ensure that (a) only _____ are entered, (b) all _____ are entered, and (c) all receipts are entered at the _____.

10. Determining detection risk for accounts receivable balances involves consideration of _____ and assessments of _____ and _____ risk for revenue cycle transactions that affect the balance.

11. For accounts receivable, the auditor relies primarily on two types of evidential matter: _____ and review of _____ originating within the _____.

12. Two ratios that may be used in applying analytical procedures to accounts receivable are (a) accounts _____ and (b) rate of _____.

13. Two circumstances that may preclude the confirmation of accounts receivable are: (a) accounts receivable are _____ to the financial statements and (b) use of confirmations would be _____.

14. The confirmation of accounts receivable relates to the assertions of _____, _____, _____, and _____.

15. Two widely-used computer-assisted applications in testing accounts receivable are (a) verifying the accuracy of the _____ and (b) preparing _____.

E. MULTIPLE CHOICE

Choose the best answer for each of the following questions and enter the identifying letter in the space provided.

_____ 1. Sound internal control procedures dictate that defective merchandise returned by customers should be presented initially to the:
a. Sales clerk.
b. Purchasing clerk.
c. Receiving clerk.
d. Inventory control clerk.

_____ 2. To determine whether internal controls operated effectively to minimize errors of failure to invoice a shipment, the auditor would select a sample of transactions from the population represented by the:
a. Customer order file.
b. Bill of lading file.
c. Open invoice file.
d. Sales invoice file.

_____ 3. Smith Corporation has numerous customers. A customer file is kept on disk storage. Each customer file contains name, address, credit limit, and account balance. The auditor wishes to test this file to determine whether credit limits are being exceeded. The best procedure for the auditor to follow would be to:
a. Develop test data that would cause some account balances to exceed the credit limit and determine if the system properly detects such situations.
b. Develop a program to compare credit limits with account balances and print out the details of any account with a balance exceeding its credit limit.
c. Request a printout of all account balances so they can be manually checked against the credit limits.
d. Request a printout of a sample of account balances so they can be individually checked against the credit limits.

_____ 4. During the study of a small business client's internal control structure, the auditor discovered that the accounts receivable clerk approves credit memos and has access to cash. Which of the following controls would be most effective in offsetting this weakness?
a. The owner reviews errors in billings to customers and postings to the subsidiary ledger.
b. The controller receives the monthly bank statement directly and reconciles the checking accounts.
c. The owner reviews credit memos after they are recorded.
d. The controller reconciles the total of the detail accounts receivable accounts to the amount shown in the ledger.

_____ 5. A sales clerk at Schackne Company correctly prepared a sales invoice for $5,200 but the invoice was entered as $2,500 in the sales journal and similarly posted to the general ledger and accounts receivable ledger. The customer remitted only $2,500, the amount on his monthly statement. The most effective procedure for preventing this type of error is to:
   a. Use predetermined totals to control posting routines.
   b. Have an independent check of sales invoice serial numbers, prices, discounts, extensions, and footings.
   c. Have the bookkeeper prepare monthly statements which are verified and mailed by a responsible person other than the bookkeeper.
   d. Have a responsible person who is independent of the accounts receivable department promptly investigate unauthorized remittance deductions made by customers or other matters in dispute.

_____ 6. The CPA tests sales transactions. One step is tracing a sample of sales invoices to debits in the accounts receivable subsidiary ledger. Based upon this step, he will form an opinion as to whether:
   a. Each sales invoice represents a bona fide sale.
   b. All sales have been recorded.
   c. All debit entries in the accounts receivable subsidiary ledger are properly supported by sales invoices.
   d. Recorded sales invoices have been properly posted to customer accounts.

_____ 7. Which of the following is not a control environment factor affecting the revenue cycle?
   a. Eliminating incentives to dishonest reporting.
   b. Monitoring by management to ensure that control policies and procedures are operating.
   c. Bonding of employees who handle cash.
   d. Commitment to competence.

_____ 8. Data Corporation has just completely computerized its billing and accounts receivable record keeping. You want to make maximum use of the new computer in your audit of Data Corporation. Which of the following audit procedures could not be performed through a computer program?
   a. Tracing audited cash receipts to accounts receivable credits.
   b. On a random number basis selecting accounts to be confirmed.
   c. Examining sales invoices for completeness, consistency between different items, valid conditions, and reasonable amounts.
   d. Resolving differences reported by customers on confirmation requests.

_____ 9. A lockbox system for cash receipts is:
   a. A locked company controlled box for storing cash until it can be deposited.
   b. A post office box for mail receipts that is controlled by the company's bank.
   c. A safety deposit vault at the bank for the deposit of daily receipts.
   d. A post office box for over-the-counter receipts controlled by the company's bank.

_____ 10. Which of the following would be an incompatible operation for a cashier who handles over-the-counter receipts?
a. Register cash received on a cash register.
b. Restrictively endorse checks received from customers.
c. Read cash register daily and reconcile the total to cash on hand.
d. Transfer daily receipts to head cashier for deposit.

_____ 11. At which point in an ordinary sales transaction of a wholesaling business would a lack of specific authorization least concern the auditor conducting an audit?
a. Determining discounts.
b. Selling goods for cash.
c. Granting credit.
d. Shipping goods.

Item 12 is based on the following flowchart:

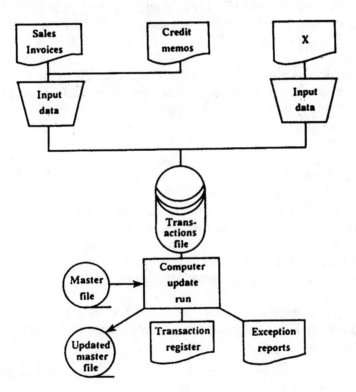

_____ 12. In a credit sales and cash receipts system flowchart, symbol X could represent:
a. Auditor's test data.
b. Remittance advices.
c. Error reports.
d. Credit authorization forms.

_____ 13. When there are a large number of relatively small account balances, negative confirmation of accounts receivable is feasible if internal control is:
   a. Strong, and the individuals receiving the confirmation requests are unlikely to give them adequate consideration.
   b. Weak, and the individuals receiving the confirmation requests are likely to give them adequate consideration.
   c. Weak, and the individuals receiving the confirmation requests are unlikely to give them adequate consideration.
   d. Strong, and the individuals receiving the confirmation requests are likely to give them adequate consideration.

_____ 14. In the confirmation of accounts receivable, the auditor would most likely:
   a. Request confirmation of a sample of the inactive accounts.
   b. Seek to obtain positive confirmations for at least 50% of the total dollar amount of the receivables.
   c. Require confirmation of all receivables from agencies of the federal government.
   d. Require that confirmation requests be sent within one month of the fiscal year end.

_____ 15. Confirmation is most likely to be a relevant form of evidence with regard to assertions about accounts receivable when the auditor has concerns about which assertion?
   a. Valuation.
   b. Classification.
   c. Existence.
   d. Completeness.

_____ 16. An aged trial balance of accounts receivable is usually used by the auditor to:
   a. Verify the validity of recorded receivables.
   b. Ensure that all accounts are promptly credited.
   c. Evaluate the results of tests of controls.
   d. Evaluate the provision for bad debt expense.

_____ 17. An auditor is reviewing sales cutoff as of March 31. All sales are shipped FOB destination, and the company records sales three days after shipment. The auditor notes the following items:

(Amounts in thousands)

Date Shipped	Month Recorded	Selling Price	Cost
March 28	March	$192	$200
March 29	March	44	40
March 30	April	77	81
April 2	March	208	220
April 5	April	92	84

If the client records the required adjustment, the net effect on income in thousands of dollars for the period ended March 31 is:
   a. An increase of 12.
   b. An increase of 8.
   c. A decrease of 12.
   d. A decrease of 8.

_____ 18. Confirmation of individual accounts receivable balances directly with debtors will, of itself, normally provide evidence concerning the:
   a. Collectibility of the balances confirmed.
   b. Ownership of the balances confirmed.
   c. Existence of the balances confirmed.
   d. Internal control over balances confirmed.

_____ 19. In determining the adequacy of the allowance for uncollectible accounts, the least reliance should be placed upon which of the following?
   a. The credit manager's opinion.
   b. An aging schedule of past due accounts.
   c. Collection experience of the client's collection agency.
   d. Ratios calculated showing the past relationship of the valuation allowance to net credit sales.

_____ 20. In connection with his examination of the Beke Supply Company for the year ended August 31, Derek Lowe, CPA, has mailed accounts receivable confirmations to three groups as follows:

Group Number	Type of Customer	Type of Confirmation
1	Wholesale	Positive
2	Current retail	Negative
3	Past-due retail	Positive

The confirmation responses from each group vary from 10 to 90 percent. The most likely response percentages are:

   a. Group 1, 90%; Group 2, 50%; Group 3, 10%.
   b. Group 1, 90%; Group 2, 10%; Group 3, 50%.
   c. Group 1, 50%; Group 2, 90%; Group 3, 10%.
   d. Group 1, 10%; Group 2, 50%; Group 3, 90%.

SOLUTIONS

TRUE OR FALSE STATEMENTS

1. False	10. False	18. False
2. True	11. True	19. True
3. False	12. False	20. True
4. False	13. True	21. True
5. True	14. True	22. False
6. True	15. False	23. False
7. False	16. False	24. True
8. True	17. False	25. False
9. True		

COMPLETION STATEMENTS

1. credit sales, cash receipts, sales adjustments
2. legal claims, customers
3. high, cash
4. bonding, insurance policy, theft
5. existence or occurrence, completeness, valuation or allocation
6. potential misstatements, necessary controls, tests of controls
7. receiving cash receipts, depositing cash in bank, recording the receipts
8. restrictively endorse, deposit only, prelist
9. valid receipts, actual receipts, correct amounts
10. audit risk, inherent, control
11. confirmations, documentation, client's organization
12. receivable turnover, return on sales
13. immaterial, ineffective
14. existence or occurrence, completeness, rights and obligations, valuation or allocation
15. aged trial balance, confirmation requests

MULTIPLE CHOICE QUESTIONS

1. c	5. a	9. b	13. d	17. b
2. b	6. d	10. c	14. a	18. c
3. b	7. c	11. b	15. c	19. a
4. c	8. d	12. b	16. d	20. b

Chapter 15

Auditing the Expenditure Cycle

A. CHAPTER OUTLINE

I. Nature of the Expenditure Cycle

A. Audit Objectives

B. Materiality, Risk, and Audit Strategy

    1. Materiality

    2. Inherent and Control Risks

    3. Audit Strategy

C. Consideration of Internal Control Structure Components

    1. Control Environment

    2. Risk Assessment

    3. Information and Communication (Accounting System)

    4. Monitoring

    5. Initial Assessment of Control Risk

II. Control Activities - Purchases Transactions

A. Common Documents and Records

B. Functions

    1. Requisitioning Goods and Services

    2. Preparing Purchase Orders

    3. Receiving the Goods

    4. Storing Goods Received for Inventory

    5. Preparing the Payment Voucher

    6. Recording the Liability

    7. Illustrative System for Purchases Transactions

C. Obtaining the Understanding and Assessing Control Risk

    1. Computer-Assisted Tests of Controls

B. CHAPTER HIGHLIGHTS

1. The **expenditure cycle** consists of the activities related to the **acquisition of and payment for plant assets and goods and services**. The major classes of transactions in this cycle are (a) **purchases** and (b) **cash disbursements**.

2. The **audit objectives are derived from management's assertions** for the expenditure cycle (i.e., existence or occurrence, completeness, rights and obligations, valuation or allocation, and disclosure).

3. Transactions in this cycle **affect more accounts than all other cycles combined**. Therefore, the auditor seeks to **achieve a low level of risk** that expenditure cycle transaction will cause material misstatements in the financial statements. The **allocation of financial statement materiality to accounts affected by this cycle will vary** based on the nature of the account. For example, the materiality threshold for accounts payable will be relatively small, while the materiality threshold for plant assets will be larger.

4. **Inherent and control risk factors** for the expenditure cycle include:
    a. Pressures to understate expenses and payables
    b. Usually a high volume of transactions
    c. Potential for unauthorized purchases or cash disbursements
    d. Potential for misappropriated assets through purchasing
    e. Contentious accounting issues such as capitalization vs. expense treatment for leases or repairs and maintenance

5. **Control environment considerations** include:
    a. Numerous employee fraud opportunities, including "kickback" possibilities for the purchasing agent.
    b. Management's commitment to competence and assignment of authority and responsibility.
    c. Bonding of employees who process disbursements.

6. **Management's risk assessments** related to the expenditure cycle include:
    a. Ability to meet cash flow requirements
    b. Contingencies such as purchase commitments
    c. Availability of important supplies
    d. Cost increases
    e. Realizability of plant assets

7. Periodic, ongoing **monitoring of the ICS** causes considerations such as:
    a. Feedback about supplier delivery problems or payment problems
    b. Reportable conditions noted by independent auditors
    c. Periodic assessment of ICS operation by internal auditors

8. **Selected specific audit objectives** related to financial statement assertions include:
    a. **Existence or occurrence**:
        • Recorded accounts payable represent amounts owed by the entity at the balance sheet date.

- Recorded plant assets represent assets that are in use at the balance sheet date.
- Recorded purchase transactions represent goods, productive assets, and services received during the period under audit.
- Recorded cash disbursements transactions represent payments made during the period to suppliers and creditors.

b. **Completeness**:
- Accounts payable include all amounts owed by the entity to suppliers of goods and services at the balance sheet date.
- Property, plant, and equipment balances include the effects of all transactions and events that occurred during the period.
- Recorded purchases and cash disbursements include all transactions that occurred during the period.

c. **Rights and obligations**:
- Accounts payable are legal obligations of the entity at the balance sheet date.
- The entity owns or has rights to all property, plant, and equipment at the balance sheet date.

d. **Valuation or allocation**:
- Accounts payable are stated at the correct amount owed.
- Property, plant, and equipment are stated at cost less accumulated depreciation.
- Recorded expense balances are in conformity with GAAP.

e. **Presentation and disclosure**:
- Accounts payable and plant assets are properly identified and classified in the balance sheet.
- Disclosure is properly made of the depreciation methods used by the entity, the major conditions of capital lease contracts, and the pledging of plant assets as collateral for loans.

9. **Common documents and records** include:
   a. Purchase requisition (PR)
   b. Purchase order (PO)
   c. Receiving Report
   d. Vendor's invoice (including remittance advice)
   e. Voucher and voucher summary
   f. Voucher Register or purchase transaction file (journal)
   g. Open purchase order file
   h. Unpaid voucher file
   I. Paid voucher file
   j. Accounts payable master file (subsidiary ledger)

10. The **processing of purchases** transactions involves the following purchasing functions: (a) requisitioning goods and services, (b) preparing purchase orders, (c) receiving the goods, (d) storing goods received for inventory, (e) preparing the payment voucher, and (f) recording the liability.

11. **Requisitioning** goods and services should be evidenced by purchase requisition forms.
    a. The forms may be prepared manually or electronically.
    b. Each form should be signed by a supervisor who has budgetary responsibility for the expenditure.
    c. Requisitions may originate in any department.
    d. Requisitions are rarely prenumbered.

12. The purchasing department should have the responsibility for preparing **purchase orders.**
    a. Purchase orders should only be issued on receipt of properly approved purchase requisitions.
    b. Purchase orders should be prenumbered.
    c. Prenumbering contributes to the completeness assertion for purchasing transactions.

13. A valid purchase order is the **receiving department's authorization** for receiving the goods. Controls over this function include:
    a. Comparing the goods received with the goods ordered, counting the goods, and inspecting the goods for damage.
    b. Preparing prenumbered receiving reports. Often a blind copy of the P.O. serves as a receiving report.
    c. Obtaining a signed receipt upon delivering the goods to stores or other department.

14. In **storing goods received for inventory**, there should be:
    a. Separation of custody of the goods from the other purchasing functions.
    b. Locked storage areas with limited access and proper surveillance by security personnel.

    These controls pertain to the existence or occurrence assertion for the goods.

15. Controls over the function of **preparing the payment voucher** include:
    a. Establishing the agreement of the details of vendor's invoices with the related receiving reports and purchase orders.
    b. Determining the mathematical accuracy of the vendor's invoices.
    c. Preparing prenumbered vouchers and attaching the supporting documents (purchase orders, receiving reports, and vendor's invoices).
    d. Performing an independent check on the mathematical accuracy of the vouchers.
    e. Coding the account distributions on the vouchers (i.e., indicating the asset and expense accounts to be debited).
    f. Approving the vouchers for payment by having an authorized person sign the vouchers.

16. The **recording of the liability** may be done manually or electronically.
    a. In manual systems, (1) source documents include the approved unpaid vouchers and the daily voucher summary, and (2) there should be an independent check of the agreement of the two documents.
    b. In computerized systems, (1) the purchases transaction file is used to update master files and (2) an accounting supervisor determines the agreement of printouts with the daily voucher summary.

17. In meeting the second standard of field work for purchasing transactions, the auditor:
    a. Must obtain and document the understanding of the internal control structure and determine if these controls have been placed in operation.
    b. Must assess and document the assessment of control risk.
    c. May employ statistical attribute sampling techniques if tests of controls are done.
    d. May use computer-assisted tests of controls including test data or generalized audit software.

18. There are two **cash disbursements functions**: paying the liability and recording the cash disbursements.

19. Controls over the **paying the liability** include the following:
    a. **An independent check** of the agreement of the total of the checks issued (usually reported on a check summary) with a batch total of the vouchers processed for payment.
    b. **Authorized personnel in the treasurer's department** should be responsible for **signing the checks.**
    c. **Authorized check signers** should determine that **each check is accompanied by a properly approved unpaid voucher** and that the name of the **payee and amount** on the check **agree with the voucher**.
    d. The **voucher and supporting documents** should be stamped, perforated, or otherwise **canceled** when the check is signed.
    e. The **check signer** should **control the mailing** of the checks.
    f. **No checks** should be made **payable to "cash" or "bearer"** and **no blank** checks should be issued.
    g. **Prenumbered checks** should be used.
    h. **Access to blank checks and to signature plates should be limited** to authorized personnel.

20. In **recording the disbursements,** there should be:
    a. An **independent check** by an accounting supervisor of **the agreement of the amounts** journalized and posted to accounts payable with the **check summary** received from the treasurer.
    b. An **independent check** on the **timeliness of recording** by periodic comparisons of the dates of cash disbursements entries with the dates on copies of the checks.
    c. Independently prepared **bank reconciliations.**

21. **Substantive testing considerations** for **accounts payable** balances include the following:
    a. The rights and obligations assertion pertains to obligations.
    b. Most of the possible substantive tests pertain to the completeness assertion.

c. The starting point is tracing the beginning balance to prior year workpapers, reviewing the ledger account for unusual items throughout the year, and obtaining and footing a list of year end payables.

22. In determining **detection risk**, the auditor should recognize that **accounts payable** is usually the largest liability on the balance sheet, having high transaction volume from both purchases and cash disbursements, and high susceptibility to misstatements. Evidence about the **completeness assertion (i.e., potential understatement)** is the primary audit concern.

23. The application of **analytical procedures** to accounts payable involves financial relationships that are similar to those described in Chapter 14 for accounts receivable.
   a. An abnormal increase in accounts payable turnover may be due to unrecorded accounts payable.
   b. This test relates to all assertions, but its applicability to completeness is limited.

24. The substantive tests of performing **purchases and cash disbursements cutoff tests** are obtained by personal observation and review of internal documentation (obtaining information about the last purchase and last check for the year). Being present on the balance sheet date adds to the reliability of the tests. The auditor then traces the cutoff information to the accounting records to verify whether transactions were recorded in the proper period.

25. The **search for unrecorded payables** may include the following procedures:
   a. Examine documentation and checks written for vouchers paid after year end to determine if any should have been recorded as a payable at year end.
   b. Inquire of accounting and purchasing personnel concerning unrecorded invoices that are being held for approval or further information such as a requested allowance for damaged goods.
   b. Investigate unmatched purchase orders, receiving reports, and invoices that may indicate the incurrence of a liability as of the balance sheet date.
   c. Review capital budgets, work orders, and construction contracts for unrecorded amounts.

26. The test of **examining subsequent payments** consists of tracing "paid" vouchers or checks issued after the statement date to the list of payables at the balance sheet date. The test should enable the auditor to identify:
   a. Large disbursements that clearly relate to the list of payables or to liabilities incurred subsequent to the statement date.
   b. Large disbursements pertaining to the prior period not included in the list of payables.
   c. Significant listed balances that remain unpaid.

27. Unlike the confirmation of accounts receivable, the **confirmation of accounts payable** is not required because the test offers no assurance that unrecorded payables will be discovered, and external evidence in the form of invoices and vendor monthly statements should be available to substantiate the balances. Confirmation of accounts payable is **recommended** when:
   a. Detection risk is low.
   b. There are individual creditors with relatively **large balances,** or
   c. The client is experiencing **difficulties in meeting its obligations.**

28. When confirmation of accounts payable is to be undertaken:
    a. Accounts with **zero or small balances** should be among those selected.
    b. Confirmations should be sent to **major vendors** who (1) were used in prior years but not in the current year and (2) do not send monthly statements.
    c. The test provides evidence primarily for the existence or occurrence and rights and obligations assertions.
    d. The test provides some evidence concerning the completeness and valuation or allocation assertions.

29. **Reconciling unconfirmed payables to vendors' monthly statements** provides additional evidence, but is less reliable that confirmations sent directly to the auditor.

30. Plant assets normally are the largest dollar balance assets, and transactions are normally material. However, **auditing plant assets typically involves less time** and cost due to the low volume of activity.

31. In **determining detection risk,** there may be significant variations in the **inherent and control risk** assessments for assertions pertaining to different plant asset accounts.
    a. For the **existence or occurrence assertion,** inherent risk may be (1) low for a merchandising company because fixed assets are not normally vulnerable to theft and (2) moderate or high for a manufacturing company because of the likelihood that scrapped or retired equipment may not be written off the books.
    b. For **the valuation or allocation assertion,** inherent risk may be (1) low for plant assets purchased for cash or on account and (2) high for major construction.
    c. **Control risk assessments** are usually less dependent on controls over major transaction classes.
    d. When expenditures for plant assets are processed as routine purchase transactions, the auditor may elect to use a lower assessed level of control risk approach for some assertions.

32. **Substantive testing considerations** for plant assets include the following:
    a. Substantive tests will be much more **extensive in an initial audit** than in a repeat engagement.
    b. Heavy reliance is placed on **documentary evidence** in verifying current year **additions and retirements**.
    c. **Mathematical evidence** is important in verifying accumulated depreciation.
    d. Substantive tests do not have to be performed at or near the balance sheet date.
    e. **Risk** considerations usually result in greater emphasis being placed on the **existence or occurrence** and **valuation or allocation** assertions.

33. In **applying analytical procedures to plant assets,** the following financial **ratios** are often used:

Ratio	Formula
Plant asset turnover	Net sales ÷ Average plant assets
Rate of return on plant assets	Net income ÷ Average plant assets
Plant assets to stockholders' equity	Plant assets ÷ Stockholders' equity
Repairs expenses to net sales	Repairs expense ÷ Net sales

34. Tests of details of transactions involve testing both additions and disposals.   **Substantive tests of plant asset additions** include:
   a. **Inspecting plant additions** provides the auditor with direct personal knowledge of their existence or occurrence and may also pertain to the valuation or allocation assertion.
   b. **Examining title documents and lease contracts** provides evidence of the existence or occurrence, rights and obligations, and presentation and disclosure assertions.
   c. **Vouching plant asset additions** provides evidence about the existence or occurrence, rights and obligations, and valuation or allocation assertions.

35. The **vouching of plant asset disposals** relates to the existence or occurrence and valuation or allocation assertions. The following procedures may also be useful to the auditor in determining whether all retirements have been recorded.
   a. Analyze the miscellaneous revenue account for proceeds from sales of plant assets.
   b. Investigate the disposition of facilities associated with discontinued product lines and operation.
   c. Trace retirement work orders and authorizations for retirements to the accounting records.
   d. Review insurance policies for termination or reductions of coverage.
   e. Make inquiry of management as to retirements.

36. In reviewing entries to **repairs and maintenance expense**, the auditor considers whether the client has made appropriate distinctions between capital and revenue expenditures.

37. For **tests of details of account balances**, the major procedures are inspecting plant assets, examining title documents and contracts, and reviewing provisions for depreciation.

38. In **reviewing entries to accumulated depreciation,** the auditor seeks evidence on the reasonableness, consistency, and accuracy of depreciation charges. This test relates to all assertions except the rights and obligations assertion.

C. TRUE OR FALSE STATEMENTS

Indicate in the space provided whether each of the following statements is true or false.

_____ 1. The expenditure cycle consists of the activities related to the acquisition of and payment for plant assets, goods, and services.

_____ 2. A specific audit objective pertaining to the completeness assertion is: Accounts payable are legal obligations of the entity at the balance sheet date.

_____ 3. Transactions in the expenditure cycle often affect more financial statement accounts than the other cycles combined.

_____ 4. Inherent risk factors do not include contentious accounting issues for purchases transactions.

_____ 5. Each of the control environment factors and categories of control procedures applies to transactions in this cycle.

_____ 6. The key documents in ordering goods are purchase requisition forms and purchase orders.

_____ 7. A valid purchase requisition form is the receiving department's authorization for receiving the goods.

_____ 8. The control procedures of segregation of duties, access controls, and independent checks are applicable to storing goods received for inventory.

_____ 9. The control procedures of documents and records and independent checks are important in preparing the payment voucher.

_____ 10. In computerized accounting systems, the purchases transaction file is used to update master files.

_____ 11. Computer-assisted tests of controls should not be used for purchase transactions.

_____ 12. All of the categories of control procedures except independent checks apply to the function of paying the liability.

_____ 13. The control procedure of independent checks is important in recording disbursements.

_____ 14. Risk considerations usually result in emphasizing the existence or occurrence and completeness assertions for plant assets.

_____ 15. Examining title documents and lease contracts provides evidence about the existence or occurrence, rights and obligations, and presentation and disclosure assertions.

_____ 16. Vouching plant asset additions does not provide evidence about the completeness assertion.

_____ 17. The substantive test of reviewing entries to accumulated depreciation relates to all financial statement assertions.

_____ 18. Inherent risk for the accounts payable balance is affected by the high volume of two classes of transactions: purchases and cash disbursements.

_____ 19. The auditor's primary concern about accounts payable is with the existence or occurrence assertion.

_____ 20. Like the confirmation of accounts receivable, the confirmation of accounts payable is a required substantive test.

_____ 21. Confirming accounts payable is a primary source of evidence for the completeness assertion.

_____ 22. When accounts payable are confirmed, accounts with zero or small balances should be among those selected.

_____ 23. Performing purchases and cash disbursements cutoff tests provide evidence about the completeness assertion for accounts payable.

_____ 24. The test of examining subsequent payments should be performed shortly after the balance sheet date.

_____ 25. The test of searching for unrecorded accounts payable includes investigating unmatched purchase orders, receiving reports, and invoices.

D. COMPLETION STATEMENTS

Fill in the blanks with the word or words that correctly complete the following statements.

1. The major classes of transactions in the expenditure cycle are _____ and _____.

2. For the valuation or allocation assertion, two specific audit objectives are (a) accounts payable are stated at the correct _____ and (b) plant assets are stated at _____, less _____.

3. A major control environment concern in the purchasing function is the possibility of _____ to the _____ agent.

4. Two purchasing functions involved in placing purchase orders are _____ and _____.

5. Controls over receiving the goods include preparing prenumbered _____ and obtaining a _____ upon delivering the goods to stores.

6. The two cash disbursements functions are _____ and _____.

7. Important controls in paying the liability are prohibiting checks payable to _____ or _____ and the signing of checks by _____ in the treasurer's department.

8. When expenditures for plant assets are processed as routine _____, the auditor may elect to use the _____ audit strategy.

9. Two ratios that may be used in applying analytical procedures to plant assets are _____ turnover and _____ on plant assets.

10. Inspecting plant additions provides the auditor with direct _____ concerning the _____ assertion.

11. The vouching of plant asset disposals relates to the _____ and _____ assertions.

12. Confirmation of accounts payable is recommended when _____ risk is low, there are individual creditors with _____ and the client is having difficulty in meeting its _____.

13. When accounts payable are confirmed, accounts selected should include those with _____ balances and _____ who do not send monthly statements.

14. The test of examining subsequent payments consists of tracing _____ issued after the statement date to the list of _____ at the _____.

15. Two substantive tests that provide evidence for all assertions except presentation and disclosure are examining _____ and searching for _____.

E. MULTIPLE CHOICE

Choose the best answer for each of the following questions and enter the identifying letter in the space provided.

_____ 1. In a properly designed accounts payable system, a voucher is prepared after the invoice, purchase order, requisition, and receiving report are verified. The next step in the system is to:
   a. Cancel the supporting documents.
   b. Enter the check amount in the check register.
   c. Approve the voucher for payment.
   d. Post the voucher amount to the expense ledger.

_____ 2. When an auditor selects a sample of items from the vouchers payable register for the last month of the period under audit and traces these items to underlying documents, the auditor is gathering evidence primarily in support of the assertion that:
   a. Recorded obligations were paid.
   b. Incurred obligations were recorded in the correct period.
   c. Recorded obligations were valid.
   d. Cash disbursements were recorded as incurred obligations.

_____ 3. Which of the following is the most effective control procedure to detect vouchers that were prepared for the payment of goods that were not received?
   a. Count goods upon receipt in storeroom.
   b. Match purchase order, receiving report, and vendor's invoice for each voucher in accounts payable department.
   c. Compare goods received with goods requisitioned in receiving department.
   d. Verify vouchers for accuracy and approval in internal audit department.

_____ 4. For effective internal control, the accounts payable department should compare the information on each vendor's invoice with the:
   a. Receiving report and the purchase order.
   b. Receiving report and the voucher.
   c. Vendor's packing slip and the purchase order.
   d. Vendor's packing slip and the voucher.

_____ 5. A major control environment factor for the expenditure cycle is the threat of:
   a. Lapping
   b. Kickbacks
   c. Kiting
   d. Pyramiding

_____ 6. A client erroneously recorded a large purchase twice. Which of the following internal control measures would be most likely to detect this error in a timely and efficient manner?
   a. Footing the purchases journal.
   b. Reconciling vendors' monthly statements with subsidiary accounts payable ledger.
   c. Tracing totals from the purchases journal to the ledger accounts.
   d. Sending written quarterly confirmations to all vendors.

_____ 7. To avoid potential misstatements, a well-designed internal control structure in the accounts payable area should include a separation of which of the following functions?
   a. Cash disbursements and invoice verification.
   b. Invoice verification and merchandise ordering.
   c. Physical handling of merchandise received and preparation of receiving reports.
   d. Check signing and cancellation of payment documentation.

_____ 8. An effective internal control measure that protects against the preparation of improper or inaccurate disbursements would be to require that all checks be:
   a. Signed by an officer after necessary supporting evidence has been examined.
   b. Reviewed by the treasurer before mailing.
   c. Sequentially numbered and accounted for by internal auditors.
   d. Perforated or otherwise effectively canceled when they are returned with the bank statement.

_____ 9. To strengthen the internal control structure over merchandise purchases, a company's receiving department should:
   a. Accept merchandise only if a purchase order or approval granted by the purchasing department is on hand.
   b. Accept and count all merchandise received from the usual company vendors.
   c. Rely on shipping documents for the preparation of receiving reports.
   d. Be responsible for the physical handling of merchandise but not the preparation of receiving reports.

_____ 10. Which of the following is an effective internal control measure that encourages receiving department personnel to count and inspect all merchandise received?
   a. Quantities ordered are excluded from the receiving department copy of the purchase order.
   b. Vouchers are prepared by accounts payable department personnel only after they match item counts on the receiving report with the purchase order.
   c. Receiving department personnel are expected to match and reconcile the receiving report with the purchase order.
   d. Internal auditors periodically examine, on a surprise basis, the receiving department copies of receiving reports.

_____ 11. Which of the following internal control procedures is effective in preventing duplicate payment of vendors' invoices?
   a. The invoices should be stamped, perforated or otherwise effectively cancelled before submission for approval of the voucher.
   b. Unused voucher forms should be prenumbered and accounted for.
   c. Cancelled checks should be sent to persons other than the cashier or accounting department personnel.
   d. Properly authorized and approved vouchers with appropriate documentation should be the basis for check preparation.

_____ 12. Which of the following is an effective internal control over cash payments?
   a. Signed checks should be mailed under the supervision of the check signer.
   b. Spoiled checks which have been voided should be disposed of immediately.
   c. Checks should be prepared only by persons responsible for cash receipts and cash disbursements.
   d. A check-signing machine with two signatures should be utilized.

_____ 13. An auditor compares information on cancelled checks with information contained in the cash disbursement journal. The objective of this test of controls is to determine that:
   a. Recorded cash disbursement transactions are properly authorized.
   b. Proper cash purchase discounts have been recorded.
   c. Cash disbursements are for goods and services actually received.
   d. No discrepancies exist between the data on the check and the data in the journal.

_____ 14. Which of the following audit procedures would be least likely to lead the auditor to find unrecorded fixed asset disposals?
   a. Examination of insurance policies.
   b. Review of repairs and maintenance expense.
   c. Review of property tax files.
   d. Scanning of invoices for fixed assets additions.

_____ 15. The auditor may conclude that depreciation charges are insufficient by noting:
   a. Insured values greatly in excess of book values.
   b. Large amounts of fully depreciated assets.
   c. Continuous trade-ins of relatively new assets.
   d. Excessive recurring losses on assets retired.

_____ 16. Which of the following is a customary audit procedure for the verification of the legal ownership of real property?
   a. Examination of correspondence with the corporate counsel concerning acquisition matters.
   b. Examination of ownership documents registered and on file at a public hall of records.
   c. Examination of corporate minutes and resolutions concerning the approval to acquire property, plant, and equipment.
   d. Examination of deeds and title guaranty policies on hand.

_____ 17. An examination of the balance in the accounts payable account is ordinarily not designed to:
   a. Detect accounts payable which are substantially past due.
   b. Verify that accounts payable were properly authorized.
   c. Ascertain the reasonableness of recorded liabilities.
   d. Determine that all existing liabilities at the balance sheet date have been recorded.

_____ 18. In order to efficiently establish the correctness of the accounts payable cutoff, an auditor will be most likely to:
   a. Coordinate cutoff tests with physical inventory observation.
   b. Compare cutoff reports with purchase orders.
   c. Compare vendors' invoices with vendors' statements.
   d. Coordinate mailing of confirmations with cutoff tests.

_____ 19. Only one of the following four statements, which compare confirmation of accounts payable with suppliers and confirmation of accounts receivable with debtors, is true. The true statement is that:
   a. Confirmation of accounts payable with suppliers is a more widely accepted auditing procedure than is confirmation of accounts receivable with debtors.
   b. Statistical sampling techniques are more widely accepted in the confirmation of accounts payable than in the confirmation of accounts receivable.
   c. As compared to the confirmation of accounts payable, the confirmation of accounts receivable will tend to emphasize accounts with zero balances at balance sheet date.
   d. It is less likely that the confirmation request sent to the supplier will show the amount owed him than the request sent to the debtor will show the amount due from him.

_____ 20. Under which of the following circumstances would it be advisable for the auditor to confirm accounts payable with creditors?
   a. Internal control over accounts payable is adequate and there is sufficient evidence on hand to minimize the risk of a material misstatement.
   b. Confirmation response is expected to be favorable and accounts payable balances are of immaterial amounts.
   c. Creditor statements are not available and internal control over accounts payable is unsatisfactory.
   d. The majority of accounts payable balances are with associated companies.

SOLUTIONS

TRUE OR FALSE STATEMENTS

1. True		10. True		18. True	
2. False		11. False		19. False	
3. True		12. False		20. False	
4. False		13. True		21. False	
5. True		14. False		22. True	
6. True		15. True		23. True	
7. False		16. True		24. False	
8. False		17. False		25. True	
9. True					

COMPLETION STATEMENTS

1. purchases, cash disbursements
2. amount owed, cost, accumulated depreciation
3. kickbacks, purchasing
4. requisitioning goods and services, preparing purchase orders
5. receiving report, signed receipt
6. paying the liability, recording the cash disbursement
7. cash, bearer, authorized personnel
8. purchases transactions, lower assessed level of control risk
9. plant asset, rate of return
10. personal knowledge, existence or occurrence
11. existence or occurrence, valuation or allocation
12. detection, large balances, obligations
13. zero or small, major vendors
14. "paid" checks or vouchers, payables, balance sheet date
15. subsequent payments, unrecorded accounts payable

MULTIPLE CHOICE QUESTIONS

1. c	5. c	9. a	13. d	17. b
2. c	6. b	10. a	14. b	18. a
3. b	7. a	11. d	15. d	19. d
4. a	8. a	12. a	16. d	20. c

Chapter 16

Auditing the Production and Personnel Services Cycles

A. CHAPTER OUTLINE

F. Tests of Details of Balances

1. Observe Client's Physical Inventory Count

2. Test Clerical Accuracy of Inventory Listings

3. Test Inventory Pricing

4. Confirm Inventories at Locations Outside the Entity

5. Examine Consignment Agreements and Contracts

G. Compare Statement Presentation with GAAP

IV. **The Personal Services Cycle**

A. Audit Objectives

B. Materiality, Risk, and Audit Strategy

C. Consideration of Internal Control Structure Components

V. **Control Activities - Payroll Transactions**

A. Common Documents and Records

B. Functions and Related Controls

1. Hiring Employees

2. Authorizing Payroll Changes

3. Preparing Attendance and Timekeeping Data

4. Preparing the Payroll

5. Recording the Payroll

6. Paying the Payroll and Protecting Unclaimed Wages

7. Filing Payroll Tax Returns

C. Obtaining the Understanding and Assessing Control Risk

VI. **Substantive Tests of Payroll Balances**

A. Determining Detection Risk

B. Designing Substantive Tests

1. Apply Analytical Procedures

2. Recalculate Accrued Payroll Liabilities

3. Verify Officers' Compensation

VII. **Summary**

B. CHAPTER HIGHLIGHTS

1. The **production cycle** relates to the conversion of raw materials into finished goods.
    a. The transactions in this cycle are called manufacturing transactions.
    b. This cycle interfaces with the personnel services, expenditure, and revenue cycles.

2. The **primary audit objectives** for the production cycle relate to (1) transaction class audit objectives for manufacturing transactions and (2) account balance audit objectives pertaining to inventory accounts and the cost of goods sold.

3. **Transaction class audit objectives** are:
    a. **Existence or Occurrence**: Recorded manufacturing transactions represent valid materials, labor, and overhead transferred to production and the movement of completed production to finished goods.
    b. **Completeness**: All manufacturing transactions have been recorded for the period.
    c. **Rights and Obligations**: The client has ownership rights to manufactured inventory.
    d. **Valuation or allocation**: Manufacturing transactions are correctly journalized, summarized and posted.
    e. **Presentation and Disclosure**: Manufacturing transactions support their presentation in the financial statements.

4. **Account balance audit objectives** are:
    a. **Existence or Occurrence**: Inventories physically exist. Cost of goods sold represents the cost of goods shipped (sold) during the period.
    b. **Completeness**: Inventories include all materials, products and supplies on hand at year end. Cost of goods sold includes the effects of all sales transactions during the period.
    c. **Rights and Obligations**: The client has legal title to all inventories.
    d. **Valuation or Allocation**: Inventories are properly stated at lower of cost or market. Cost of goods sold is based on the consistent application of an acceptable cost flow method or methods.
    e. **Presentation and Disclosure**: Inventories and cost of goods sold are properly classified in the income statement, and the cost flow method or methods used are disclosed.

5. Each of the **control structure components** applies to manufacturing transactions in the production cycle. For example, in the **control environment component**, an officer, the vice president of operations, manufacturing and production, has line authority over all manufacturing activities. **Accounting systems** for inventory include the use of control accounts and supporting records (e.g., perpetual inventories), job order and process costing systems, budgeting, and performance reviews.

6. **Common documents and records** for this cycle are:
    a. Production order to order a job or batch.
    b. Materials requisition report to order raw materials to production.
    c. Materials issue slip to authorize release of raw materials from inventory.
    d. Time ticket for labor costs.
    e. Move ticket for documenting work in process movement between departments.
    f. Daily production activity report and completed production report.

g. Inventory subsidiary ledgers or master files (perpetual inventory records).

7. The **manufacturing functions** are:
    a. Planning and controlling production.
    b. Issuing raw materials.
    c. Processing goods in production.
    d. Transferring completed work to finished goods.
    e. Protecting manufacturing inventories.
    f. Determining and recording manufacturing costs.
    g. Maintaining the correctness of inventory balances.

8. The procedures for **obtaining and documenting the understanding of the internal control structure and assessing control risk** for manufacturing transactions are the same as for other major classes of transactions.

9. Determining **detection risk** involves consideration of the classes of transactions that affect each inventory account. Of particular concern to the auditor is the risk of misstatements in the existence or occurrence and valuation or allocation assertions.

10. **Initial substantive procedures** include tracing beginning year balances to prior year workpapers, scanning current year ledger entries for unusual items, and determining whether perpetual inventory records tie in with general ledger balances.

11. The application of **analytical procedures** to inventories involves the following ratios:

Ratio	Formula
Rate of gross profit	Gross profit ÷ Net sales
Inventory turnover	Cost of goods sold ÷ Average inventory
Number of days sales in inventory	365 ÷ Inventory turnover
Inventory to total current assets	Inventory ÷ Total current assets

12. **Tests of details of transactions** include vouching:
    a. Increases in raw materials to vendors' invoices, receiving reports and purchase orders.
    b. Increases in work in process or finished goods to manufacturing.
    c. Decreases in finished goods to sales documents and records.
    d. Decreases in raw materials and work in process to manufacturing records or production reports.

13. **Cutoff tests** include:
    a. Auditing **shipping terms** (F.O.B.) for shipments and receipts near year end.
    b. Ascertaining **proper cutoff of last shipments and receipts** at year end. Physical presence at the balance sheet date to obtain the last shipping document and last receiving report adds to the reliability of the tests. Cutoff information is then traced to appropriate journals to determine if transactions are appropriately included or excluded from the year under audit.

14. The **timing of inventory observation** depends on the quality of the client's inventory system and the effectiveness of internal controls. Periodic systems require complete counts at a designated date, while perpetual systems may employ periodic cycle counting procedures or

apply statistical sampling techniques to parts of the inventory.

15. **Client instructions** for inventory counts should include:
    a. Names of responsible client employees.
    b. Date and locations of counts.
    c. Detailed instructions on how counts are done.
    d. Use and control of prenumbered count tags and summary sheet.
    e. Provisions for handling shipments, movements, and receipts during counts if this activity cannot be avoided.
    f. Segregation of goods not owned (e.g., consignment).

16. **Observing the client's inventory taking** is a generally accepted auditing procedure whenever inventories are material to a company's financial statements and it is practicable and reasonable. In performing this test, the auditor should:
    a. Scrutinize the care with which client employees are following the inventory plan.
    b. See that all merchandise is tagged and no items are double-tagged.
    c. Determine that prenumbered inventory tags and compilation sheets are properly controlled.
    d. Make some test counts and trace quantities to compilation sheets.
    e. Be alert for empty containers and hollow squares (empty spaces) that may exist when goods are stacked in solid formations.
    f. Watch for damaged and obsolete inventory.
    g. Appraise the general condition of the inventory.
    h. Identify the last receiving and shipping documents used and determine that goods received during the count are properly segregated.
    i. Inquire about and observe evidence of the existence of slow-moving items.

17. When inventories are material and the **auditor does not observe the inventory at or near the year-end**:
    a. Tests of the accounting records alone will not be sufficient as to quantities.
    b. It will always be necessary for the auditor to make, or observe, some physical counts of the inventory and to apply appropriate tests of intervening transactions.

18. To express an unqualified opinion on the income statement, the auditor must observe both the beginning and ending inventories. In an **initial audit**, the auditor may rely on the predecessor auditor's beginning inventory observation (after appropriate review of the working papers) or, if the client has never been audited, the auditor may be able to obtain sufficient evidence by reviewing summaries of client counts, vouching prior inventory transactions and applying analytical procedures (gross profit reasonableness tests).

19. The **observation of client inventory** procedures provides evidence regarding **existence, completeness, and some evidence for valuation and allocation** (since physical quantities are one component of computing price extensions). **Observation does not provide evidence for the rights and obligations** assertion since goods on hand may be held on consignment for other parties.

20. The testing of **inventory pricing** consists of the following steps: (1) determining the propriety and consistency of the client's pricing (costing) of inventory quantities and (2) comparing unit

costs used by the client to supporting documentation.
   a. For purchased inventories, costs should be vouched to vendor invoices, and when the lower of cost or market method is used, both cost and market (i.e., replacement cost) must be verified. Reviewing purchase prices at and after year end and inquiries of suppliers provides evidence on replacement costs.
   b. For manufactured inventories, the costing methods should be reviewed for propriety and for the accuracy and consistency of application.

This test relates to the valuation or allocation assertion.

21. The auditor's responsibility for **inventory quality** is limited to that of a reasonably informed observer. The auditor obtains evidence of general condition or obsolescence by:
   a. Observing the client's inventory taking.
   b. Scanning perpetual inventory records for slow-moving items.
   c. Reviewing quality control production reports.
   d. Making inquires of client.

This test relates to the valuation or allocation assertion.

22. **Confirmation of inventories in public warehouses** is sufficient except when the amounts involved represent a significant proportion of a client's current assets or total assets. When this is the case, the auditor must obtain additional evidence through one or more of the following procedures:
   a. Test the owner's procedures for investigating the warehouseman and evaluating the warehouseman's performance.
   b. Obtain an independent accountant's report on the warehouseman's control procedures relevant to custody of goods and, if applicable, pledging receipts, or apply alternative procedures at the warehouse to gain reasonable assurance that information received from the warehouseman is reliable.
   c. Observe physical counts of the goods, if practicable and reasonable.
   d. If warehouse receipts have been pledged as collateral, confirm with lenders pertinent details of the pledged receipts (on a test basis, if appropriate).

23. The auditor should inquire of management as to **goods held on consignment** and consignment agreements should be examined for terms and conditions. Goods held by the client on consignment should be segregated and not counted during inventory taking procedures. Also client goods held by third parties on consignment should be confirmed.

24. **GAAP presentation issues** include:
   a. Disclosure of inventory costing methods.
   b. Assignment or pledging agreements.
   c. Major purchase commitment contingencies.

Evidence regarding disclosure issues may be obtained in the course of performing the previously-described substantive tests, through inquiry of management, or by reviewing the minutes of board of directors' meetings.

25. An entity's **personnel services cycle** involves the events and activities that pertain to executive and employee compensation.
    a. The major class of transactions in this cycle is payroll transactions.
    b. This cycle interfaces with two other cycles: the expenditure cycle and the production cycle.

26. The **audit objectives** for payroll transactions and balances and related assertions are:
    a. **Existence or occurrence**:
       • Recorded payroll transactions represent compensation for services rendered during the period covered by the income statement.
       • Recorded payroll tax expenses represent taxes applicable to compensation earned during the period.
       • Accrued payroll and payroll tax liability balances represent amounts owed at the balance sheet date.
    b. **Completeness**:
       • Recorded payroll and payroll tax expenses include all expenses incurred for personnel services during the year.
       • Accrued payroll and payroll tax balances include all amounts owed to personnel and governmental agencies at the balance sheet date.
    c. **Rights and obligations**:
       • Accrued payroll and payroll tax liabilities are legal obligations of the entity at the balance sheet date.
    d. **Valuation or allocation**:
       • Payroll expenses are accurate summarizations of correctly computed gross earnings for each pay period.
       • Payroll tax expenses are correctly computed using applicable tax rates.
       • Accrued payroll and payroll taxes payable at the balance sheet date are correctly determined.
       • Factory labor is correctly classified as direct or indirect labor.
    e. **Presentation and disclosure**:
       • Payroll and payroll tax expenses are properly identified and classified in the income statement.
       • Accrued payroll and payroll tax liability accounts are correctly classified as current liabilities in the balance sheet.

27. **Audit risk considerations** include:
    a. Gross earnings of personnel is generally the largest operating expense in merchandising companies and service enterprises.
    b. Factory labor is often a significant component in costing work in process.
    c. Payroll fraud is a major concern for the auditor.
    d. Most auditors adopt the lower assessed level of control risk audit strategy for payroll transactions.

28. **Internal control structure** considerations include each of the three elements.
    a. The control environment factors include delegating overall responsibility to a vice president of labor relations and the use of management control methods and personnel policies and practices.
    b. Accounting systems are almost always computerized, generally in a batch processing environment.

29. **Common documents and records** include:
    a. Personnel authorization to document the hiring and firing process.
    b. Clock cards or time tickets to document hours worked.
    c. Payroll register (journal) showing net payroll calculations for the period.
    d. Imprest payroll bank account from which all wages and salaries are paid.
    e. Payroll checks.
    f. Labor cost distributions showing account classifications for gross earnings for the period.
    g. Payroll tax returns for withheld taxes from employees' checks and employer matching contributions (FICA) and other taxes (unemployment insurance).
    h. Personnel files for each employee.
    i. Personnel data or employee earnings master file showing job classification, withholding status, wage rate, etc.

30. The processing of payroll transactions involves the following **payroll functions**:
    a. Hiring employees.
    b. Authorizing payroll changes.
    c. Preparing attendance and timekeeping data.
    d. Preparing the payroll.
    e. Recording the payroll.
    f. Paying the payroll and protecting unclaimed wages.
    g. Filing payroll tax returns.

31. The functions of **hiring employees and authorizing payroll changes** are the responsibility of the personnel department.
    a. All hires and changes should be documented on a personnel authorization form.
    b. Controls over hiring relate to the existence or occurrence assertion for payroll transactions.
    c. Controls over payroll changes apply to the existence or occurrence and valuation or allocation assertions.

32. The timekeeping department is responsible for preparing **attendance and timekeeping data.**
    a. Time clocks are frequently used to record time worked.
    b. For factory employees, clock card hours must be supported by time tickets.
    c. Controls over this function relate to the existence or occurrence, completeness, and valuation or allocation assertions.

33. The function of **preparing the payroll** is the responsibility of the payroll and EDP departments (if not performed by an outside service agency).
    a. Controls include (1) the use of batch totals of hours worked, (2) data control verification of information on the batch transmittal form, and (3) an edit check routine of input data by the computer.
    b. These controls provide evidence concerning the assertions of existence or occurrence, completeness, and valuation or allocation.

34. The **function of recording the payroll** involves:
    a. Updating the employee earnings master file, and
    b. Accumulating totals for journalizing and posting the general ledger.

35. **Paying the payroll and protecting unclaimed wages** is the responsibility of the treasurer's office. Applicable controls for this function include the following:
    a. An independent check by treasurer's office personnel should be made of the agreement of names and amounts on checks with payroll register entries.
    b. Payroll checks should be signed and distributed by authorized treasurer's office personnel not involved in preparing or recording the payroll.
    c. Access to check signing machines and signature plates should be restricted to authorized individuals.
    d. Payroll checks should be distributed only on proper identification of employees.
    e. Unclaimed payroll checks should be stored in a safe or vault in the treasurer's office.

36. The auditor is required to **obtain and document his or her understanding of the internal control structure.** Of particular concern is the risk of overstatement of payroll through fictitious employees, payment for hours not worked, or higher payment rates than authorized.

37. In **assessing control risk** the auditor should assess potential misstatements, and (necessary controls). Among these are:
    a. Fictitious employees (separate personnel department authorization).
    b. Unauthorized rate increases (personnel department rate authorization and notification of all changes).
    c. Payment for hours not worked (time clocks and supervisor approval of hours).
    d. Payroll entry or processing errors (batch control totals, keypunch verification, exception reports reviewed by data control group).
    e. Checks distributed to unauthorized recipients (segregation of payroll preparation and input from distribution of checks, employee identification required for check distribution).

38. Two tests of controls for the existence or occurrence assertion are **tests for terminated employees** and **witnessing a payroll distribution (i.e., a "payoff").**

39. **Substantive tests of payroll balances** are normally performed at or near the balance sheet date.
    a. Low assessments of control risk often permit a moderate or high acceptable level of detection risk.
    b. Tests of payroll balances are often limited to applying analytical procedures to payroll expenses and related accruals and performing limited tests of details.

40. The application of **analytical procedures** to payroll balances may involve the following:
    a. Compare payroll expenses (salaries and wages, commissions, bonuses, employee benefits, etc.) with prior year balances (adjusted for known differences in wage rates or contractual terms) and with budgeted amounts.
    b. Compare accrued payroll liability balances with prior year (adjusted for differences in lengths of accrual periods).
    c. Compute ratio of total payroll expense to net sales and compare with prior year.
    d. Compute ratio of payroll tax expense to total payroll and compare with prior year (adjusted for changes in tax rates).
    e. Reconcile total payroll expense with amounts reported on payroll tax returns.

41. The auditor is also concerned with the **possible understatement of accrued payroll liabilities** (bonus, pension, commissions, and vacation/sick pay). In obtaining evidence, the auditor reviews client computations or makes independent computations. Examining subsequent payments also helps verify the accrued amounts.

42. **Officers' compensation** is audit sensitive due to SEC disclosure requirements and susceptibility for override of controls by officers.

C.   TRUE OR FALSE STATEMENTS

Indicate in the space provided whether each of the following statements is true or false.

_____   1.   The production cycle relates to the conversion of raw materials into work in process.

_____   2.   Audit objectives for the production cycle relate to manufacturing inventories and cost of goods sold.

_____   3.   An officer with the title of factory manager or foreman usually has overall responsibility for production.

_____   4.   The manufacturing functions include (a) determining and recording manufacturing costs and (b) maintaining the correctness of inventory balances.

_____   5.   The procedures for meeting the second standard of field work for the production cycle are different than for other cycles.

_____   6.   There are a minimum of three possible substantive tests for inventories that apply to each assertion.

_____   7.   The observation of the client's inventory taking is a generally accepted auditing standard (GAAS).

_____   8.   To comply with GAAS, the auditor must obtain some physical evidence pertaining to ending inventories.

_____   9.   To maximize the reliability of the audit evidence, the auditor should take or supervise the taking of the physical inventory.

_____10.   Tests of the accounting records alone will not be sufficient as to ending inventory quantities.

_____11.   For inventories in public warehouses, the auditor must both confirm the inventories and observe the warehouse inventory taking.

_____12.   The auditor's responsibility for inventory quality is limited to that of a reasonably informed observer.

_____13. The testing of inventory pricing relates to the valuation or allocation assertion.

_____14. The auditor is expected to review the costing of manufacturing inventories for propriety and the accuracy and consistency of application.

_____15. An entity's personnel services cycle involves events and activities that pertain to executive and employee compensation.

_____16. An audit objective in meeting the completeness assertion in this cycle is: Payroll expenses are accurate summarizations of gross earnings for each pay period.

_____17. Payroll fraud is seldom a major concern for the auditor.

_____18. In most audits, the lower assessed level of control risk audit strategy is used for some payroll transaction assertions.

_____19. Accounting systems for payroll transactions are almost always computerized.

_____20. Two payroll functions are (a) preparing the payroll and (b) distributing unclaimed wages.

_____21. Computer controls in preparing the payroll include batch totals of hours worked and an edit check routine for input data.

_____22. There should be segregation of duties between preparing the payroll and paying the payroll.

_____23. An important concern of the auditor is the possible overstatement of the payroll.

_____24. Assessing control risk involves identifying potential misstatements, necessary controls, and possible tests of controls.

_____25. The auditor's assessments of control risk for payroll transactions seldom permit a moderate or high acceptable level of detection risk for payroll balances.

D. COMPLETION STATEMENTS

Fill in the blanks with the word or words that correctly complete the following statements.

1. The personnel services cycle interfaces with the _____ and _____ cycles.

2. An audit objective in meeting the valuation or allocation assertion in this cycle is: Factory labor is correctly classified as _____ or _____ labor.

3. The personnel department is responsible for two payroll functions: _____ and _____ .

4. Controls pertaining to preparing attendance and timekeeping data include the use of _____ and _____ to record time worked and _____ to support hours.

5. Recording the payroll involves (a) updating the _____ file and (b) accumulating totals for _____ to the general ledger.

6. The treasurer's department is responsible for two payroll functions: _____ and _____ .

7. Two tests of controls for the existence or occurrence assertion for payroll transactions are tests for _____ and _____ .

8. Substantive tests of payroll balances are often limited to applying _____ and performing limited _____ .

9. The production cycle interfaces with the _____ , _____ and _____ cycles.

10. In determining detection risk for inventory balances, the auditor is primarily concerned with two assertions: _____ and _____ .

11. Two ratios that may be used in applying procedures to inventory balances are rate of _____ and number of _____ .

12. The observation of inventories is the primary source of evidence for the _____ assertion; it also is a source of evidence for the _____ and _____ assertions, but does not provide assurance for the _____ assertion.

13. For inventories in public warehouses, _____ is sufficient except when the amounts involved represent a significant proportion of a client's _____ or _____ .

14. The testing of inventory pricing involves determining the _____ and _____ of the pricing and comparing _____ with supporting documentation.

15. Cutoff tests for inventory involve obtaining the last transactions for _____ and _____ by being present on the balance sheet date.

E. MULTIPLE CHOICE

Choose the best answer for each of the following questions and enter the identifying letter in the space provided.

Items 1 through 3 are based on the section of a system flowchart shown below.

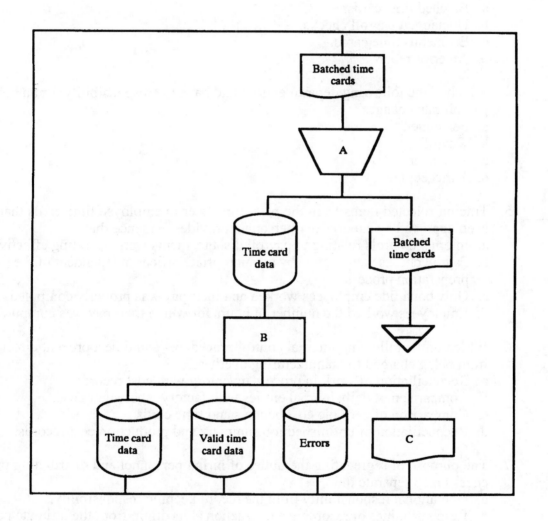

_____   1. Symbol A could represent:
    a. Computation of gross pay.
    b. Input of payroll data.
    c. Preparation of paychecks.
    d. Verification of pay rates.

_____ 2. Symbol B could represent:
   a. Computation of net pay.
   b. Separation of erroneous time cards.
   c. Validation of payroll data.
   d. Preparation of the payroll register.

_____ 3. Symbol C could represent:
   a. Batched time cards.
   b. Unclaimed payroll checks.
   c. Erroneous time cards.
   d. An error report.

_____ 4. Which of the following departments should have the responsibility for authorizing payroll rate changes?
   a. Personnel.
   b. Payroll.
   c. Treasurer.
   d. Timekeeping.

_____ 5. Tracing selected items from the payroll register to employee time cards that have been approved by supervisory personnel provides evidence that:
   a. Internal controls relating to payroll disbursements were operating effectively.
   b. Payroll checks were signed by an appropriate officer independent of the payroll preparation process.
   c. Only bona fide employees worked and their pay was properly computed.
   d. Employees worked the number of hours for which their pay was computed.

_____ 6. Which of the following internal control procedures could best prevent direct labor from being charged to manufacturing overhead?
   a. Reconciliation of work in process inventory with cost records.
   b. Comparison of daily journal entries with factory labor summary.
   c. Comparison of periodic cost budgets and time cards.
   d. Reconciliation of unfinished job summary and production cost records.

_____ 7. The purpose of segregating the duties of hiring personnel and distributing payroll checks is to separate the:
   a. Operational responsibility from the record keeping responsibility.
   b. Responsibilities of recording a transaction at its origin from the ultimate posting in the general ledger.
   c. Authorization of transactions from the custody of related assets.
   d. Human resources function from the controllership function.

_____ 8. An auditor would consider internal control over a client's payroll procedures to be ineffective if the payroll department supervisor is responsible for:
   a. Hiring subordinate payroll department employees.
   b. Having custody over unclaimed paychecks.
   c. Updating employee earnings records.
   d. Applying pay rates to time tickets.

_____ 9. The auditor may observe the distribution of paychecks to ascertain whether:
   a. Pay rate authorization is properly separated from the operating function.
   b. Deductions from gross pay are calculated correctly and are properly authorized.
   c. Employees of record actually exist and are employed by the client.
   d. Paychecks agree with the payroll register and the time cards.

_____ 10. If a control total were to be computed on each of the following data items, which would best be identified as a hash total for a payroll EDP application?
   a. Hours worked.
   b. Total debits and total credits.
   c. Net pay.
   d. Department numbers.

_____ 11. When an auditor tests a client's cost accounting system, the auditor's tests are primarily designed to determine that:
   a. Quantities on hand have been computed based on acceptable cost accounting techniques that reasonably approximate actual quantities on hand.
   b. Physical inventories are in substantial agreement with book inventories.
   c. The system is in accordance with generally accepted accounting principles and is functioning as planned.
   d. Costs have been properly assigned to finished goods, work in process, and cost of goods sold.

_____ 12. A well functioning internal control structure over the inventory/production functions would provide that finished goods are to be accepted for stock only after presentation of a completed production order and a(n):
   a. Shipping order.
   b. Material requisition.
   c. Bill of lading.
   d. Inspection report.

_____ 13. Which of the following is a question that the auditor would expect to find on the production cycle section of an internal control questionnaire?
   a. Are vendors' invoices for raw materials approved for payment by an employee who is independent of the cash disbursements function?
   b. Are signed checks for the purchase of raw materials mailed directly after signing without being returned to the person who authorized the invoice processing?
   c. Are all releases by storekeepers of raw materials from storage based on approved requisition documents?
   d. Are details of individual disbursements for raw materials balanced with the total to be posted to the appropriate general ledger account?

_____ 14. The auditor tests the quantity of material charged to work in process by tracing these quantities to:
   a. Cost ledgers.
   b. Perpetual inventory records.
   c. Receiving reports.
   d. Material requisitions.

_____ 15. Instead of taking a physical inventory count on the balance sheet date the client may take physical counts prior to the year-end if internal controls are adequate and:
a. Computerized records of perpetual inventory are maintained.
b. Inventory is slow-moving.
c. EDP error reports are generated for missing prenumbered inventory tickets.
d. Obsolete inventory items are segregated and excluded.

_____ 16. When auditing merchandise inventory at year-end, the auditor performs a purchase cutoff test to obtain evidence that:
a. All goods purchased before year-end are received before the physical inventory count.
b. No goods held on consignment for customers are included in the inventory balance.
c. No goods observed during the physical count are pledged or sold.
d. All goods owned at year-end are included in the inventory balance.

_____ 17. Which of the following audit procedures would an auditor be least likely to perform using a generalized computer audit program?
a. Searching records of accounts receivable balances for credit balances.
b. Investigating inventory balances for possible obsolescence.
c. Selecting accounts receivable for positive and negative confirmation.
d. Listing of unusually large inventory balances.

_____ 18. An auditor examining inventory may appropriately apply sampling for variables in order to estimate the:
a. Average price of inventory items.
b. Percentage of slow-moving inventory items.
c. Dollar value of inventory.
d. Physical quantity of inventory items.

_____ 19. An auditor will usually trace the details of the test counts made during the observation of the physical inventory taking to a final inventory schedule. This audit procedure is undertaken to provide evidence that items physically present and observed by the auditor at the time of the physical inventory count are:
a. Owned by the client.
b. Not obsolete.
c. Physically present at the time of the preparation of the final inventory schedule.
d. Included in the final inventory schedule.

_____ 20. An auditor would be most likely to learn of slow-moving inventory through:
a. Inquiry of sales personnel.
b. Inquiry of stores personnel.
c. Physical observation of inventory.
d. Review of perpetual inventory records.

SOLUTIONS

TRUE OR FALSE STATEMENTS

1. False	10. True	18. True
2. True	11. False	19. True
3. False	12. True	20. False
4. True	13. True	21. True
5. False	14. True	22. True
6. False	15. False	23. True
7. False	16. False	24. True
8. True	17. False	25. False
9. False		

COMPLETION STATEMENTS

1. expenditure, production
2. direct, indirect
3. hiring employees, authorizing payroll changes
4. time clocks, time tickets, clock card
5. employee earnings, journalizing and posting
6. paying the payroll, safeguarding unclaimed wages
7. terminated employees, witnessing a payroll distribution
8. analytical procedures, tests of details
9. personnel services, expenditure, revenue
10. existence or occurrence, valuation or allocation
11. gross profit, days sales in inventory
12. existence or occurrence, completeness, valuation or allocation, rights or obligations
13. confirmation, current assets, total assets
14. propriety, consistency, unit costs
15. test counts, inventory pricing

MULTIPLE CHOICE QUESTIONS

1. b	5. d	9. c	13. c	17. b
2. c	6. b	10. d	14. d	18. c
3. d	7. c	11. d	15. a	19. d
4. a	8. b	12. d	16. d	20. d

Chapter 17

Auditing the Investing and Financing Cycles

A. CHAPTER OUTLINE

I. The Investing Cycle

   A. Audit Objectives

   B. Materiality, Risk, and Audit Strategy

   C. Consideration of Internal Control Structure Components

      1. Common Documents and Records

      2. Functions and Related Controls

II. Substantive Tests of Investment Balances

   A. Determining Detection Risk

   B. Designing Substantive Tests

   C. Initial Procedures

   D. Analytical Procedures

   E. Tests of Details of Transactions

   F. Tests of Details of Balances

      1. Inspect and Count Securities on Hand

      2. Confirm Securities Held by Others

      3. Recalculate Investment Revenue Earned

      4. Review Documentation Concerning Fair Values

   G. Comparison of Statement Presentation with GAAP

III. The Financing Cycle

   A. Audit Objectives

   B. Materiality, Risk, and Audit Strategy

   C. Consideration of Internal Control Structure Components

      1. Common Documents and Records

      2. Functions and Related Controls

IV. Substantive Tests of Long-term Debt Balances

    A. Determining Detection Risk

    B. Designing Substantive Tests

    C. Initial Procedures

    D. Analytical Procedures

    E. Tests of Details of Transactions

    F. Tests of Details of Balances

        1. Review Authorizations and Contracts

        2. Confirm Debt

        3. Recalculate Interest Expense

    G. Comparison of Statement Presentation with GAAP

V. Substantive Tests of Stockholders' Equity Balances

    A Determining Detection Risk

    B. Designing Substantive Tests

    C. Initial Procedures

    D. Analytical Procedures

    E. Tests of Details of Transactions

        1. Vouch Entries to Paid-in Capital Accounts

        2. Vouch Entries to Retained Earnings

    F. Tests of Details of Balances

        1. Review Articles of Incorporation and Bylaws

        2. Review Authorizations and Terms of Stock Issues

        3. Confirm Shares Outstanding with Registrar and Transfer Agent

        4. Inspect Stock Certificate Book

        5. Inspect Certificates of Shares Held in Treasury

    G. Comparison of Statement Presentation with GAAP

VI. Summary

B. CHAPTER HIGHLIGHTS

1. An entity's **investing cycle** pertains to the activities relating to the ownership of securities issued by other entities.
   a. The investing cycle interfaces with the revenue cycle when interest and dividends are received, and the expenditure cycle through cash disbursements for the purchase of securities.
   b. Investing transactions are usually classified as either short- or long-term.

2. The audit objectives and related assertions for investing cycle transactions and balances are:
   a. **Existence or occurrence**:
      • Recorded investment asset balances represent investments that exist at the balance sheet date.
      • Investment revenues, gains, and losses resulted from investment transactions and events that occurred during the period.
   b. **Completeness**:
      • All investments are included in recorded investment asset balances.
      • The income statement effects of all investment transactions and events during the period are included in investment revenues, gains, and losses.
   c. **Rights and obligations**:
      • All recorded investments are owned by the client.
   d. **Valuation or allocation**:
      • Investments are reported on the balance sheet at cost, equity, or market value, as appropriate. Investment revenues, gains, and losses are reported at proper amounts.
   e. **Presentation and disclosure**:
      • Investment balances are properly identified and classified in the financial statements.
      • The bases for valuing investments and investments pledged as collateral are adequately disclosed.

3. Both short-and long-term investments may be **material to the balance sheet** and long-term investments may also be material to the income statement.
   a. The risk of misstatements in investing transactions is usually low because of infrequent transactions.
   b. Internal control is generally effective because company officers (primarily the Treasurer) has authority and responsibility for the transactions and have custody of the securities.
   c. The Treasurer should be a person of unquestioned integrity, possess appropriate knowledge and skills, realize the importance of controls, and be able to assist other management members in assessing ongoing risks associated with investments.

4. **Common documents and records** include:
   a. Stock and bond certificates
   b. Bond indenture
   c. Broker's advice
   d. Books of original entry (general journal)
   e. Investment subsidiary ledger

5. The **functions and control objectives** in the investing cycle are:
   a. Purchasing securities. Purchases are made in accordance with management's authorizations.
   b. Receiving periodic income. Dividend and interest checks are promptly deposited intact.
   c. Selling securities. Sales are made in accordance with management's authorizations and cash receipts are deposited intact.
   d. Recording transactions. Transactions and events are correctly recorded as to amount, classification, and accounting period.
   e. Safeguarding securities. Securities are stored in safes or vaults and access is restricted to authorized personnel.
   f. Recording market adjustments and reclassifications. Changes in fair values are periodically analyzed and recorded.
   g. Assessing investment performance and reporting. Performance reviews are conducted by management to detect poor investment performance and/or erroneous reporting.

6. It is common in substantive testing in this cycle to **test balance sheet accounts** (investments) **and the related income statement accounts** (interest and dividend income) **at the same time.**

7. The acceptable level of **detection risk** for investment balance assertions is determined from the audit risk model.
   a. Because relevant inherent and control risks will vary owing to the variety of types of investments, acceptable detection risk levels will also vary significantly across assertion categories. Inherent risk concerns include such matters as the vulnerability of securities to theft and misappropriation (existence or occurrence assertion), and the complexities of fair valuation methods (valuation or allocation assertion).
   b. Difficulties in designing controls to adequately address risks associated with the use of fair values and the proper classification of investments as long or short term means that acceptable levels of detection risk for the valuation and allocation and presentation assertions must be specified.

8. **Initial substantive procedures** include tracing beginning balances to prior year workpapers, reviewing activity in the investment ledger accounts for unusual items, and checking client-prepared schedules and subsidiary ledgers for mathematical accuracy.

9. The following ratios may be used in applying **analytical procedures** to investment balances:
   a. Investments as a percentage of total assets (investments/ total assets or short term investments/ current assets).
   b. Rate of return on investments (investment revenue/ total investments).

10. **Tests of details of transactions** include vouching additions to investment accounts to brokers' advices and cancelled checks, vouching reductions to investments to bank or brokers' advices and documenting adjustments in fair values of securities. For investments accounted for using the equity method, increases can be vouched to the investee's financial statements while decreases (dividends) can be vouched to appropriate cash receipts records or brokers' advices.

11. **Tests of details of balances** are as follows:
    a. Inspect and count securities.
    b. Confirm securities held by others.
    c. Recalculate investment revenue.
    d. Review fair-value documentation.

12. In **inspecting and counting securities** on hand,
    a. The custodian of the securities should be present throughout the count.
    b. A receipt should be obtained from the custodian when the securities are returned.
    c. All securities should be controlled by the auditor until the count is completed.
    d. The auditor should observe certificate numbers, owner's name if indicated, number of shares, and name of issuer.

13. **Securities held by others should be confirmed** by the auditor as of the date the securities are counted. This test relates to the existence or occurrence, completeness, and rights and objections assertions.

14. **Income from investments** is verified by documentary evidence (brokers' advices) and through recalculation.

15. **SFAS No. 115 requires most investments** to be accounted for using **fair value**. Exceptions are debt securities qualifying as held-to-maturity securities which are accounted for at cost, investments with no ready fair value, and investments accounted for using the equity method. Generally, fair values can be verified by reference to publicly-available market quotations for various exchanges.

16. **GAAP presentation considerations** include fair value disclosures, current vs. noncurrent classification depending on management's intentions, and correct classification of realized and unrealized gains and losses, depending on short or long term classification.

17. An entity's **financing cycle** consists of transactions pertaining to the acquisition and payback of capital funds.
    a. The two major classes of transactions in this cycle are (1) long-term debt and (2) stockholders' equity.
    b. This cycle interfaces with the expenditure cycle when cash is disbursed for bond interest and cash dividends, the redemption of bonds, and the purchase of treasury stock.

18. The **audit objectives** for financing cycle transactions and balances are derived from management's financial statement assertions. The relationships are as follows:
    a. **Existence or occurrence**:
       • Recorded long-term debt and stockholders' equity balances exist at the balance sheet date.
       • Bond interest expense and dividends paid resulted from transactions and events that occurred during the year.
       • Stockholders' equity balances represent owners' interests that exist at the balance sheet date.
    b. **Completeness**:
       • Long-term debt balances represent all the amounts payable to long-term creditors at the balance sheet date.

- Income statement balances represent the effects of all long term debt transactions and events that occurred during the year.
- Stockholders' equity balances include all owners' claims on assets at the balance sheet date.

  c. **Rights and obligations**:
- Long-tem debt balances represent obligations of the reporting entity at the balance sheet date.
- Stockholders' equity balances represent owners' claims on the reporting entity.

  d. **Valuation or allocation**:
- Long-term debt, the related income statement accounts, and stockholders' equity balances are properly valued in accordance with GAAP.

  e. **Presentation and disclosure**:
- Long-term debt, related income statement accounts, and stockholders' equity balances are properly identified and classified in the financial statements.
- All terms, covenants, commitments, and retirement provisions pertaining to long-term debt are adequately disclosed.
- All facts concerning stock issues such as the par or stated value of the shares, shares authorized and issued, and the number of shares held as treasury stock or subject to options are disclosed.

19. There is considerable variation in the **importance of long-term debt to the fair presentation** of financial position.
    a. While long-term debt may be material or immaterial, stockholders' equity is clearly a material component of a balance sheet.
    b. The income statement effects of financing cycle transactions for a manufacturing company vary widely in size.
    c. The risk of misstatements is usually low because of infrequent transactions. Also board of directors' involvement and authorization, and the use of independent agents to pay bond interest contribute to low risk and make a primarily substantive approach generally most applicable.

20. The **functions and related controls** associated with financing cycle transactions are:
    a. Issuing bonds and capital stock issues are made in accordance with board of directors' authorizations and legal requirements, and proceeds are promptly deposited intact.
    b. Paying bond interest and cash dividends. Payments are made to proper payees in accordance with board of directors' or management authorizations.
    c. Redeeming and reacquiring bonds and capital stock. Transactions are executed in accordance with board of directors' authorizations.
    d. Recording financing transactions. Transactions are correctly recorded as to amount, classification, and accounting period.
    e. Maintaining correctness of bondholder and stockholder ledgers. Recorded balances are periodically verified with bond trustee and transfer agent and agreed with general ledger balances.

21. **Substantive tests of long-term debt** balances:
    a. Rarely present year-end cutoff problems.
    b. May be performed either before or after the balance sheet date.
    c. Normally involve related expense accounts when liability balances are audited.

22. In determining **detection risk** for long-term debt balances, the auditor is primarily concerned with understatement issues. The auditor generally relies on direct communication with outside parties (confirmation), review of documentation, and recomputation.

23. **Analytical procedures** that may be used for **long-term debt balances** include the following ratios:

Ratio	Formula
Debt to total assets	Total liabilities ÷ Total assets
Times bond interest earned	Operating income (income before income taxes and interest expense) ÷ Bond interest expense
Interest expense to debt	Interest expense ÷ Average debt

24. **Tests of details of transactions** include vouching issuances of debt to cash receipts records and brokers' advices, vouching principle and/or interest payments to cancelled checks, vouchers or cancelled bonds or notes when paid in full. For installment notes, repayment or amortization schedules are reviewed or recomputed. When bond interest is paid by an independent agent, the agent's report should be reviewed and tested.

25. **Tests of details of balances** consist of (1) reviewing authorizations and contracts, (2) confirming debt, and (3) recalculating expenses.

26. **Evidence of authorization** for borrowing transactions should be found in the **board of directors minutes**. Also, contracts and the related covenants, and the entity's compliance therewith, should be reviewed and placed in the permanent file along with details of obligations under capital leases.

27. **Confirming long-term debt** and accrued interest directly with the lender or trustee (and returned directly to the auditor) provides evidence for all assertions except presentation and disclosure. Bank loans are usually confirmed on standard bank confirmation requests.

28. **Recalculating interest expense** provides mathematical evidence about all assertions except presentation and disclosure.

29. Inherent risk and control risk may both be low in determining detection risk for **stockholders' equity balances** when there are few transactions and a registrar and transfer agent are used.

30. The following ratios may be used in applying **analytical procedures to stockholders' equity** balances:

Ratio	Formula
Earnings per share	Net income ÷ Weighted average common shares outstanding
Book value per share of stock	Stockholder's equity ÷ Average shares of common stock outstanding
Return on common stockholders' equity	Net income ÷ Average common stockholders' equity
Dividend payout	Cash dividends ÷ Net income

31. **Each change in a capital stock account can be vouched** to supporting documentation including: remittance advices for stock issues, market quotations or appraisals when stock is issued for other than cash, cancelled checks or vouchers for treasury stock purchases. All significant transactions should be authorized in the board minutes.

32. Each **entry to retained earnings**, other than closing income or loss, can be vouched to supporting documents, including board authorization for dividend declarations and retained earnings appropriations and cancelled check for dividend payments. The auditor should also recalculate dividend amounts and determine that all legal and contractual requirements (including restrictions on dividends in loan covenants) have been met.

33. The **review of articles of incorporation and bylaws** and the **review of authorizations and terms of stock issues** provide evidence about the existence or occurrence and rights and obligations assertions.

34. **Confirming shares outstanding with registrar and transfer agent, inspecting stock certificate book, and inspecting certificates of shares in the treasury** pertain to three assertions: existence or occurrence, completeness, and rights and obligations.

35. **GAAP presentation issues** include: details of stock option plans, dividends in arrears, par or stated value, shares authorized, issued and outstanding, dividend and liquidation preferences, commitments for future issuances of stock, dividend payout restrictions, and minimum requirements imposed by loan covenants.

C. TRUE OR FALSE STATEMENTS

Indicate in the space provided whether each of the following statements is true or false.

_____ 1. An entity's investing cycle pertains to the activities relating to ownership of equity securities issued by the client.

_____ 2. A specific audit objective for the existence or occurrence assertion is: all investments are included in recorded investment asset balances.

_____ 3. Internal control is generally effective because company officers often participate in investing transactions.

_____ 4. Two of the functions pertaining to investing transactions are: safeguarding securities and maintaining the correctness of general ledger balances.

_____ 5. In meeting the second standard of field work, the auditor must obtain and document the understanding of the internal control structure pertaining to investing transactions.

_____ 6. When there are few investing transactions, it normally will be cost-efficient to use a lower assessed level of control risk audit strategy.

_____ 7. The acceptable level of detection risk for investment balances is determined from the audit risk model.

_____ 8. Substantive tests of investment balances result in evidential matter that has a low degree of reliability.

_____ 9. The test of inspecting and counting securities on hand should be performed simultaneously with the auditor's count of cash and other negotiable instruments.

_____ 10. The substantive test of confirming securities held by others applies to the existence or occurrence, completeness, and rights and obligations assertions.

_____ 11. The financing cycle interfaces with the revenue cycle.

_____ 12. An audit objective that pertains to the valuation or allocation assertion is: long-term debt and stockholders' equity balances are properly valued in accordance with GAAP.

_____ 13. The auditor's responsibilities for meeting the second standard of field work for financing transactions are basically different than for investing cycle transactions.

_____ 14. In determining detection risk for long-term debt balances, inherent risk is usually low for all assertions.

_____ 15. In performing substantive tests of financing cycle balances the auditor relies primarily on his or her direct personal knowledge.

_____ 16. Confirming long-term debt provides evidence for all assertions except presentation and disclosure.

_____ 17. When a registrar and transfer agent are used, both inherent and control risk may be assessed as low.

_____ 18. The steps in determining the acceptable level of detection risk for tests of stockholders' equity balances is conceptually different from tests of long-term debt balances.

_____ 19. For stockholders' equity balances, it frequently is possible for the auditor to conclude that a high level of detection risk is acceptable.

_____ 20. Audit program considerations for stockholders' equity balances show that there are at least four substantive tests for each assertion.

_____ 21. Applying analytical procedures to stockholders' equity balances provides evidence about the existence or occurrence, completeness, and valuation or allocation assertions.

_____ 22. The review of articles of incorporation and bylaws provides evidence about the rights and obligations assertions.

_____ 23. The test of reviewing authorizations and terms of stock issues provides evidence about the existence or occurrence and completeness assertions.

_____ 24. Confirming shares outstanding with registrar and transfer agent provides evidence about three assertions.

_____ 25. Inspecting certificates of shares held in the treasury does not apply to the completeness assertion.

D. COMPLETION STATEMENTS

Fill in the blanks with the word or words that correctly complete the following statements.

1. An entity's investing cycle pertains to the activities relating to the _____ of _____ issued by other entities.

2. The internal control structure for investing cycle transactions consists of the _____, _____ and _____.

3. SFAS 115 requires that most investments be accounted for at _____, except for securities classified as _____ securities, securities where no_____, or securities accounted for using the _____.

4. Much of the evidence for investment balances is obtained from the auditor's direct _____ and from _____ with outside independent sources.

5. Two ratios that may be used in applying analytical procedures to investment balances are _____ and _____.

6. The test of inspecting and counting securities on hand applies to the assertions of
_____, _____, and _____.

7. Securities held by others should be _____ by the auditor as of the
date other securities are _____.

8. An entity's financing cycle consists of transactions pertaining to the _____ and
_____ of capital funds.

9. Two functions that pertain to financing cycle transactions are issuing _____ and
paying _____.

10. In obtaining evidence for long-term debt balances, the auditor relies primarily on direct
communication with _____, review of _____, and
_____.

11. Two ratios that may be used in applying analytical procedures to long-term debt balances are:
debt to _____ and the times _____.

12. Recalculating interest expense provides _____ evidence about all
assertions except _____.

13. For stockholders' equity balances, it is frequently possible for the auditor to assess both
_____ and _____ risks as _____.

14. Two tests that apply to the existence or occurrence and rights and obligations assertions for
stockholders' equity balances are (a) the review of _____ and bylaws and (b) the
review of _____ and terms of stock issues.

15. The vouching of entries to capital stock accounts provides evidence about the assertions of
_____, _____, and _____.

E. MULTIPLE CHOICE

Choose the best answer for each of the following questions and enter the identifying letter in the
space provided.

_____ 1. When an auditor is unable to inspect and count a client's investment securities until
after the balance sheet date, the bank where the securities are held in a safe deposit
box should be asked to:
a. Verify any differences between the contents of the box and the balances in the
client's subsidiary ledger.
b. Provide a list of securities added and removed from the box between the balance
sheet date and the security count date.
c. Confirm that there has been no access to the box between the balance sheet date
and the security count date.
d. Count the securities in the box so the auditor will have an independent direct
verification.

_____ 2. Which of the following controls would be most effective in assuring that the proper custody of assets in the investing cycle is maintained?
   a. Direct access to securities in the safety deposit box is limited to only one corporate officer.
   b. Personnel who post investment transactions to the general ledger are not permitted to update the investment subsidiary ledger.
   c. The purchase and sale of investments are executed on the specific authorization of the board of directors.
   d. The recorded balances in the investment subsidiary ledger are periodically compared with the contents of the safety deposit box by independent personnel.

_____ 3. An auditor was unable to obtain audited financial statements or other evidence supporting an entity's investment in a foreign subsidiary. Between which of the following opinions should the entity's auditor choose?
   a. Adverse and unqualified with an explanatory paragraph added.
   b. Disclaimer and unqualified with an explanatory paragraph added.
   c. Qualified and adverse.
   d. Qualified and disclaimer.

_____ 4. Which of the following is the most effective audit procedure for verification of dividends earned on investments in marketable equity securities?
   a. Tracing deposit of dividend checks to the cash receipts book.
   b. Reconciling amounts received with published dividend records.
   c. Comparing the amounts received with preceding year dividends received.
   d. Recomputing selected extensions and footings of dividend schedules and comparing totals to the general ledger.

_____ 5. Which of the following would provide the best form of evidential matter pertaining to the annual valuation of a long-term investment in which the independent auditor's client owns a 30% voting interest?
   a. Market quotations of the investee company's stock.
   b. Current fair value of the investee company's assets.
   c. Historical cost of the investee company's assets.
   d. Audited financial statements of the investee company.

_____ 6. Apex Incorporated issued common stock to acquire another company in an acquisition that was accounted for as a pooling of interests. The auditor examining this transaction would be least interested in ascertaining:
   a. The net book value of the acquired company.
   b. The par value of the stock that was issued.
   c. Whether the fair market value of the acquired assets was independently appraised.
   d. Whether or not the acquisition was approved by the board of directors of Apex Incorporated.

_____ 7. Late in December, Tech Products Company sold its marketable securities which had appreciated in value and then repurchased them the same day. The sale and purchase transactions resulted in a large gain. Without the gain the company would have reported a loss for the year. Which of the following statements with respect to the auditor is correct?

    a. If the sale and repurchase are disclosed, an unqualified opinion should be rendered.

    b. The repurchase transaction is a sham and the auditor should insist upon a reversal or issue an adverse opinion.

    c. The auditor should withdraw from the engagement and refuse to be associated with the company.

    d. A disclaimer of opinion should be issued.

_____ 8. When negotiable securities are of considerable volume, planning by the auditor is necessary to guard against:

    a. Unauthorized negotiation of the securities before they are counted.

    b. Unrecorded sales of securities after they are counted.

    c. Substitution of securities already counted for other securities which should be on hand but are not.

    d. Substitution of authentic securities with counterfeit securities.

_____ 9. Jones was engaged to examine the financial statements of Gamma Corporation for the year ended June 30, 19X0. Having completed an examination of the investment securities, which of the following is the best method of verifying the accuracy of recorded dividend income:

    a. Tracing recorded dividend income to cash receipts records and validated deposit slips.

    b. Utilizing analytical procedures and statistical sampling.

    c. Comparing recorded dividends with amounts appearing on federal information form 1099.

    d. Comparing recorded dividends with a standard financial reporting service's record of dividends.

_____ 10. In order to avoid the misappropriation of company-owned marketable securities, which of the following is the best course of action that can be taken by the management of a company with a large portfolio of marketable securities?

    a. Require that the safekeeping function for securities be assigned to a bank that will act as a custodial agent.

    b. Require that employees who enter and leave the safekeeping area sign and record in a log the exact reason for their access.

    c. Require that employees involved in the safekeeping function maintain a subsidiary control ledger for securities on a current basis.

    d. Require that one trustworthy and bonded employee be responsible for access to the safekeeping area where securities are kept.

_____ 11. Grauer, Inc., carries its investment in Salvemini Corporation at equity. Grauer's investment in Salvemini accounts for 45 percent of the total assets of Grauer. Grauer and Salvemini are not audited by the same CPA. In order for Grauer's

auditor to issue an unqualified opinion in regard to the value of Grauer's investment in Salvemini and the income derived therefrom, Grauer's auditor:
a. Needs to obtain only Salvemini's unaudited financial statements.
b. Needs to obtain only Salvemini's audited financial statements.
c. Must obtain Salvemini's audited financial statements and make inquiries concerning the professional reputation and independence of Salvemini's auditor.
d. Must review the working papers of Salvemini's auditor.

_____ 12. During an examination of a publicly-held company, the auditor should obtain written confirmation regarding debenture transactions from the:
a. Debenture holders.
b. Trustee.
c. Internal auditors.
d. Client's attorney.

_____ 13. During the course of an audit, a CPA observes that the recorded interest expense seems to be excessive in relation to the balance in the long-term debt account. This observation could lead the auditor to suspect that:
a. Long-term debt is understated.
b. Discount on bonds payable is overstated.
c. Long-term debt is overstated.
d. Premium on bonds payable is understated.

_____ 14. In connection with the audit of a current issue of long-term bonds payable, the auditor should:
a. Determine whether bondholders are persons other than owners, directors, or officers of the company issuing the bonds.
b. Calculate the effective interest rate to see if it is substantially the same as the rates for similar issues.
c. Decide whether the bond issue was made without violating state or local law.
d. Ascertain that the client has obtained the opinion of counsel on the legality of the issue.

_____ 15. When a company has treasury stock certificates on hand, a year-end count of the certificates by the auditor is:
a. Required when the company classifies treasury stock with other assets.
b. Not required if treasury stock is a deduction from stockholders' equity.
c. Required when the company had treasury stock transactions during the year.
d. Always required.

_____ 16. Which of the following is the most important consideration of an auditor when examining the stockholders' equity section of a client's balance sheet?
a. Changes in the capital stock account are verified by an independent stock transfer agent.
b. Stock dividends and/or stock splits during the year under audit were approved by the stockholders.
c. Stock dividends are capitalized at par or at stated value on the dividend declaration date.

d. Entries in the capital stock account can be traced to a resolution in the minutes of the board of directors meetings.

_____ 17. A company holds bearer bonds as a short-term investment. Responsibility for custody of these bonds and submission of coupons for periodic interest collections probably should be delegated to the:
a. Chief accountant.
b. Treasurer.
c. Cashier.
d. Internal auditor.

_____ 18. Braginetz Corporation acts as its own registrar and transfer agent and has assigned these responsibilities to the company secretary. The CPA primarily will rely upon:
a. Confirmation of shares outstanding at year-end with the company secretary.
b. Review of the corporate minutes for data as to shares outstanding.
c. Confirmation of the number of shares outstanding at year end with the appropriate state official.
d. Inspection of the stock book at year end and accounting for all certificate numbers.

_____ 19. The auditor should insist that a representative of the client be present during the physical examination of securities in order to:
a. Acknowledge the receipt of securities returned.
b. Detect forged securities.
c. Coordinate the return of all securities to proper locations.
d. Lend authority to the auditor's directives.

_____ 20. An audit program for the examination of the retained earnings account should include a step that requires verification of the:
a. Market value used to charge retained earnings to account for a two-for-one stock split.
b. Approval of the adjustment to the beginning balance as a result of a write-down of an account receivable.
c. Authorization for both cash and stock dividends.
d. Gain or loss resulting from disposition of treasury shares.

SOLUTIONS

TRUE OR FALSE STATEMENTS

1. False	10. True	18. False
2. False	11. False	19. True
3. True	12. True	20. False
4. False	13. False	21. True
5. True	14. False	22. True
6. False	15. False	23. False
7. True	16. True	24. True
8. False	17. True	25. False
9. True		

COMPLETION STATEMENTS

1. ownership, securities
2. control environment, accounting system, control procedures
3. fair value, hold-to-maturity, ready fair value, equity method
4. personal knowledge, confirmation
5. investments as a percentage of total assets, rate of return on investments
6. existence or occurrence, completeness, rights and obligations
7. confirmed, counted
8. acquisition, payback
9. bonds and capital stock, bond interest and cash dividends
10. outside independent sources, documentation, recomputations
11. total assets, bond interest earned
12. mathematical, presentation and disclosure
13. inherent, control, low
14. articles of incorporation, authorizations
15. existence or occurrence, rights and obligations, valuation or allocation

MULTIPLE CHOICE QUESTIONS

1. c	5. d	9. d	13. a	17. b
2. d	6. c	10. a	14. d	18. d
3. d	7. a	11. c	15. d	19. a
4. b	8. c	12. b	16. d	20. c

Chapter 18

Auditing Cash Balances

A. CHAPTER OUTLINE

I. General Considerations

   A. Relationship of Cash Balances to Transaction Cycles

   B. Audit Objectives

   C. Materiality, Risk and Audit Strategy

II. Substantive Tests of Cash Balances

   A. Determining Detection Risk

   B. Designing Substantive Tests

   C. Initial Procedures

   D. Analytical Procedures

   E. Tests of Details of Transactions

      1. Perform Cash Cutoff Tests

      2. Trace Bank Transfers

      3. Prepare Proof of Cash

   F. Tests of Details of Balances

      1. Count Cash on Hand

      2. Confirm Bank Deposit and Loan Balances

      3. Confirm Other Arrangements with Banks

      4. Scan, Review, or Prepare Bank Reconciliations

      5. Obtain and Use Bank Cutoff Statements

   G. Comparison Statement Presentation with GAAP

III. Other Considerations

   A. Tests to Detect Lapping

      1. Lapping Illustrated

      2. Auditing Procedures

B. CHAPTER HIGHLIGHTS

1. There are **five transaction cycles that affect cash**. The cycles are revenue, expenditure, personnel services, investing, and financing.

2. The **volume of transactions** in some cycles is **high, which increases the risk** of misstatements. In assessing control risk, it is necessary to consider relevant tests of controls for transactions in all cycles that affect cash.

3. The **audit objectives and related assertions** for cash balances are as follows:
   a. **Existence or occurrence**:
      - Recorded cash balances exist at the balance sheet date.
   b. **Completeness**:
      - Recorded cash balances include the effects of all cash transactions that have occurred.
      - Year-end transfers of cash between banks are recorded in the proper period.
   c. **Rights and obligations**:
      - The client has legal title to all cash balances shown at the balance sheet date.
   d. **Valuation or allocation**:
      - Recorded cash balances are realizable at the amounts stated on the balance sheet and agree with supporting schedules.
   e. **Presentation and disclosure**:
      - Cash balances are properly identified and classified in the balance sheet.
      - Restrictions on the use of cash balances are properly identified and disclosed in the balance sheet.
      - Compensating balances, lines of credit, and loan guarantees are appropriately disclosed.

4. In determining **detection risk**,
   a. Inherent risk is frequently assessed as high for the existence or occurrence and completeness assertions, and lower assessments are usually appropriate for the other assertions.
   b. The assessment of control risk involves a consideration of all components of the internal control structure, and the methodology explained in Chapter 10 for relating control assessments for transactions to related balances.

5. **Initial substantive procedures** include tracing beginning balances to prior year workpapers and reviewing activity in the ledger accounts throughout the year for unusual items.

6. Because cash balances are affected significantly by managements' day to day financing decisions, these balances may not show a stable or predictable relationship with other operating data. Therefore, **analytical procedures are not usually useful**. Despite this, certain analytical procedures such as comparisons with budgets may be helpful.

7. There are **eleven possible substantive tests** of cash balances. Nine of these tests relate to the existence or occurrence assertion because of the auditor's **concerns about possible overstatement of cash**.

8. Tests of details of transactions include:
   a. Cutoff tests for cash receipts and disbursements explained earlier in chapters 14 and 15.
   b. Preparing a **schedule of all transfers between cash accounts** for several days prior to and after year end. This test relates to the possibility of overstatement of cash through an irregularity known as kiting. **Kiting** is the process of recording the deposit in one account in the current year while recording the withdrawal in the other cash account in the following year. It can be prevented by proper segregation of duties between issuing and recording checks, and can be detected by obtaining and using a bank cutoff statement and by tracing bank transfers.
   c. A **proof of cash** is a simultaneous reconciliation of bank transactions and balances with corresponding data per books for a specified period of time. It permits a reconciliation of bank to book for beginning cash balances, cash receipts transactions, cash disbursements transactions, and ending cash balances.

9. **Tests of details of balances** for cash consist of verification of both bank accounts and cash on hand.

10. In **counting cash on hand**, the auditor should:
    a. Control all cash and negotiable instruments held by the client until all funds have been counted.
    b. Insist that the custodian of the cash be present throughout the count.
    c. Obtain a signed receipt from the custodian on return of the funds to the client.
    d. Ascertain that all undeposited checks are payable to the order of the client, either directly or through endorsement.

    The control of all funds at the time of count is designed to prevent double counting of assets through transfers between counted and uncounted funds.

11. **Confirming bank deposit and loan balances** involves three items: (a) deposit balances, (b) loan balances, and (c) other deposit and loan accounts that may have come to the attention of the authorized bank official.

12. **Confirmation requests** should be:
    a. Prepared in duplicate and signed by an authorized check signer.
    b. Personally mailed by the auditor in his or her own return address envelope.
    c. Sent to all banks in which the client has an account including those with a zero balance at the end of the year.

    Confirming bank deposit and loan balances provides evidence concerning all assertions except presentation and disclosure.

13. **Confirming other arrangements with banks** includes such matters as lines of credit, compensating balances, and contingent liabilities.
    a. The required minimum amount to maintain a line of credit is known as a compensating balance.
    b. Preferably, the confirmation request should be sent to the bank official who is in charge of the client's relationship with the bank.

This test provides evidence about all financial statement assertions.

14. **Substantive tests pertaining to bank reconciliations** vary with the acceptable level of detection risk.
    a. When the acceptable detection risk is high, the auditor may scan the client-prepared reconciliation and verify the mathematical accuracy.
    b. When the risk is moderate, the auditor may review the client's reconciliation.
    c. When the risk is low, the auditor may prepare the bank reconciliation using bank data in the client's possession.
    d. When the risk is very low and the auditor suspects possible misstatements, the auditor may obtain the year-end bank statement directly from the bank and prepare the bank reconciliation.

15. **Scanning, reviewing, or preparing a bank reconciliation** is the primary source of evidence concerning the valuation or allocation assertion. This test also provides evidence for the existence or occurrence, completeness, and rights and obligations assertions.

16. In obtaining and using a **bank cutoff statement**,
    a. A bank cutoff statement is a bank statement as of a date subsequent to the balance sheet date (normally less than an entire month's activity).
    b. The cutoff statement should be sent directly by the bank to the auditor.
    c. Two reasons for obtaining a cutoff statement are (1) to increase the reliability of documentary evidence by having the statement sent directly to the auditor, and (2) to allow for a more timely test of the reconciliation, if desired, rather than waiting for the client to receive the next month's full statement.
    d. In using the cutoff statement, the auditor should:
       • Trace all prior-year dated checks to the outstanding checks listed on the bank reconciliation.
       • Trace deposits in transit on the bank reconciliation to deposits on the cutoff statement.
       • Scan the cutoff statement and enclosed data for unusual items.

This test provides evidence about each assertion except presentation and disclosure.

17. When the aggregate effect of uncleared checks is material, it may be indicative of an irregularity known as **window dressing**, which is a deliberate attempt to overstate the entity's short term solvency.

18. The final substantive test of cash balances is to **compare the statement presentation with GAAP.** Major disclosure issues involve the short- vs. long-term classification (e.g., bond sinking funds) and any restrictions on cash balances. The auditor determines the appropriateness of the presentation by:
    a. Reading a draft of the financial statements.
    b. Considering the evidence from other substantive tests.
    c. Reviewing minutes of board of director meetings and inquiring of management about cash restrictions.

19. **Lapping** is an irregularity that results in the deliberate misappropriation of cash receipts. Lapping is usually associated with collections from customers, but it may involve other receipts.

20. **Conditions conducive to lapping** exist when an individual who handles cash receipts also maintains the accounts receivable ledger: i.e., there is **improper segregation of duties**.

21. **Substantive tests for lapping** normally are only performed when control risk for cash receipts transactions is moderate or high. The tests that should detect lapping are
    a.   Confirm accounts receivable.
    b.   Make a surprise cash count.
    c.   Compare details of cash receipts journal entries with the details of corresponding daily deposit slips.

22. The **imprest petty cash account** is unusual in that it is audited even though its balance is almost always immaterial. The reason is that material irregularities may occur in disbursing petty cash and in replenishing the fund throughout the year.

23. The following internal control considerations pertain to a petty cash fund:
    a.   The fund should be maintained at the imprest level. That is, cash in the fund plus receipts for payments should always equal the imprest amount.
    b.   The fund should be in the custody of one individual.
    c.   The fund should be locked and stored in the safe when not in use.
    d.   Disbursements from the fund should be for small amounts and prenumbered receipts and documentation should support each payment.
    e.   The fund should not be mingled with other receipts or other activities.
    f.   Replenishment of the fund should be based on prenumbered receipts and a review of supporting documentation.
    g.   Upon payment, supporting documents should be stamped PAID to prevent their reuse.

24. **Substantive tests of petty cash** involve tests of details of both transactions and balances.
    a.   Tests of transactions pertain to replenishing transactions. The extent of testing depends on the acceptable level of detection risk.
    b.   Tests of balances involve counting cash in the fund.

25. Internal controls over an **imprest payroll bank account** include the following:
    a.   An individual such as a paymaster or assistant treasurer should be authorized to sign checks drawn on the account.
    b.   Only payroll checks should be written against the account.
    c.   Each pay period a check for the total net amount payable to employees should be deposited in the payroll bank account.
    d.   The payroll bank account should be independently reconciled monthly.

26. The **acceptable level of detection risk for a payroll bank account** will often be high. The substantive tests should include (a) confirming the balance, (b) reviewing the client's reconciliation, and (c) obtaining a bank cutoff statement.

C. TRUE OR FALSE STATEMENTS

Indicate in the space provided whether each of the following statements is true or false.

_____ 1. Window dressing is the deliberate attempt to overstate the entity's short term solvency.

_____ 2. An audit objective for the completeness assertion is: Year-end transfers of cash between banks are recorded in the proper period.

_____ 3. To meet the presentation and disclosure assertion for cash balances, restrictions on the use of cash balances should be properly identified and disclosed in the balance sheet.

_____ 4. Inherent risk for the existence or occurrence assertion is frequently assessed as moderate.

_____ 5. Substantive tests of cash balances result in evidential matter that has a high degree of reliability.

_____ 6. Analytical procedures are often a useful audit procedure to verify the reasonableness of cash balances.

_____ 7. In counting cash on hand, all cash and negotiable instruments should be controlled by the auditor until all funds have been counted.

_____ 8. A cutoff bank statement should be obtained from the client to test year end cash balances.

_____ 9. In confirming bank deposit and loan balances, confirmation requests should only be sent to banks where a balance is maintained at year-end.

_____10. The substantive tests of confirming bank balances and confirming other arrangements with banks both relate to all financial statement assertions.

_____11. When the acceptable level of detection risk is high the auditor should test the details of the client's bank reconciliation.

_____12. When the acceptable level of detection risk is low or very low, the auditor should prepare the bank reconciliation.

_____13. A compensating balance is an arrangement in connection with a bank loan to maintain a minimum level in a given cash account.

_____14. In using a bank cutoff statement, the auditor should prepare a reconciliation at the cutoff date.

_____15. A bank transfer schedule is prepared when the client has changed banks.

_____16. The tracing of bank transfers relates to the detection of lapping.

_____17. Kiting is an irregularity that involves unauthorized transfers of checks between banks.

_____18. Preparing a proof of cash is required in most audits.

_____19. In preparing a proof of cash for May, the deposit in transit at April 30 is added to the May 1 bank balance and deducted from the May receipts per the bank.

_____20. Lapping is an irregularity that results in the deliberate misappropriation of cash receipts.

_____21. Lapping can be prevented by the proper application of segregation of duties.

_____22. Petty cash is seldom audited because the amount of the account balance is usually immaterial.

_____23. Substantive tests of petty cash involve tests of details of both transactions and balances.

_____24. A payroll bank account should be kept on an imprest basis.

_____25. The acceptable level of detection risk for a payroll bank account is usually moderate or low.

D. COMPLETION STATEMENTS

Fill in the blanks with the word or words that correctly complete the following statements.

1. All _____ relate directly to cash except the _____ cycle.

2. To meet the existence or occurrence assertion, recorded cash balances must _____ at the _____ date.

3. A properly designed bank confirmation request asks for information about _____, _____, and _____.

4. Major GAAP presentation issues related to cash are _____ of cash and classification of balances as _____ vs. _____.

5. In counting cash on hand, the auditor should control all _____ and insist that the _____ of the cash be present.

6. In confirming bank deposit and loan balances, the confirmation request should be by the auditor in his or her own _____ envelope.

7. Confirming other arrangements with banks includes such matters as _____, _____, and _____.

8. The evidence provided by a bank reconciliation alone is generally not sufficient for two important reconciling items: _____ and _____.

9. A bank cutoff statement should be requested by the _____ and be sent directly by the bank to the _____.

10. Kiting can be prevented by proper _____; it can be detected by tracing _____.

11. A proof of cash is a simultaneous reconciliation of bank _____with corresponding data per _____ for a specified time period.

12. Two tests that may detect lapping are: confirm_____ and make a _____.

13. Petty cash funds are usually audited because material irregularities may occur in _____ and in _____ the fund.

14. Two controls over petty cash funds are: (a) the fund should be maintained at the _____ and (b) the fund should be in the custody of _____.

15. Substantive tests of a payroll bank account should include _____ the balance with the bank and using a _____.

E. MULTIPLE CHOICE

Choose the best answer for each of the following questions and enter the identifying letter in the space provided.

_____ 1. An auditor who is engaged to audit the financial statements of a business enterprise will request a cutoff bank statement primarily in order to:
   a. Verify the cash balance reported on the bank confirmation inquiry form.
   b. Verify reconciling items on the client's bank reconciliation.
   c. Detect lapping.
   d. Detect kiting.

_____ 2. For good internal control, the monthly bank statements should be reconciled by someone under the direction of the:
   a. Credit manager.
   b. Controller.
   c. Cashier.
   d. Treasurer.

_____ 3. Wald, Inc., has a June 30 year end. Its bank mails bank statements each Friday of every week and on the last business day of each month. For year end, Saturday, June 30, 19X3, the auditor should have the client ask the bank to mail directly to the auditor:
   a. Only the June 29 bank statement.
   b. Only the July 13 bank statement.
   c. Both the June 29 and July 6 bank statements.
   d. Both the July 6 and 13 bank statements.

_____ 4. The Jackson Company records checks as being issued on the day they are written; however, the checks are often held a number of days before being released. The audit procedure which is least likely to reveal this method of incorrect cash disbursements cutoff is to:
   a. Examine checks returned with cutoff bank statement for unreasonable time lag between date recorded in cash-disbursements book and date clearing bank.
   b. Reconcile vendors' invoices with accounts payable per books.
   c. Reconcile bank statement at year end.
   d. Reconcile exceptions to account-payable confirmations.

Questions 5, 6, and 7 are based on the following information:

Listed below are four interbank cash transfers of a client for late December 19X1 and early January 19X2. Your answer choice for items 5, 6, and 7 should be selected from this list.

	Bank Account 1 Disbursing Date (Month/Day)		Bank Account 2 Receiving Date (Month/Day)
	Per Bank	Per Books	Per Bank	Per Books
a.	12/31	12/30	12/31	12/30
b.	1/2	12/30	12/31	12/30
c.	1/3	12/31	1/2	1/2
d.	1/3	12/31	1/2	12/31

_____ 5. Which of the cash transfers indicates an error in cash cutoff at December 31, 19X1?

_____ 6. Which of the cash transfers would appear as a deposit in transit on December 31, 19X1, bank reconciliation?

_____ 7. Which of the cash transfers would not appear as an outstanding check on the December 31, 19X1, bank reconciliation?

_____ 8. On December 31, 19X1, a company erroneously prepared an account-payable voucher (Dr. Cash, Cr. Accounts Payable) for a transfer of funds between banks. A check for the transfer was drawn January 3, 19X2. This error resulted in overstatements of cash and accounts payable at December 31, 19X1. Of the following procedures, the least effective in disclosing this error is review of the:
   a. December 31, 19X1, bank reconciliations for the two banks.
   b. December 19X1 check register.
   c. Support for accounts payable at December 31, 19X1.
   d. Schedule of interbank transfers.

_____ 9. A CPA obtains a January 10 cut-off bank statement for the client directly from the bank. Very few of the outstanding checks listed on the client's December 31 bank reconciliation cleared during the cut-off period. A probable cause for this is that the client:
   a. Is engaged in kiting.
   b. Is engaged in lapping.
   c. Transmitted the checks to the payees after year-end.
   d. Has overstated its year-end bank balance.

_____ 10. When counting cash on hand the auditor must exercise control over all cash and other negotiable assets to prevent:
   a. Theft.
   b. Irregular endorsement.
   c. Substitution.
   d. Deposits-in-transit.

_____ 11. Which one of the following would be conducive to lapping if the cashier receives remittances from the mailroom?
   a. The cashier prepares the daily deposit.
   b. The cashier makes the daily deposit at a local bank.
   c. The cashier posts the receipts to the accounts receivable subsidiary ledger cards.
   d. The cashier endorses the checks.

_____ 12. A $80,000 sinking fund exists at 12/31/X0 to repay serial bonds maturing $10,000 per year in years X1-X9. How should the fund be shown on the 12/31/X0 balance sheet?
   a. $80,000 current
   b. $80,000 noncurrent
   c. $70,000 current, $10,000 noncurrent
   d. $10,000 current, $70,000 noncurrent

_____ 13. On the last day of the fiscal year, the cash disbursements clerk drew a company check on bank A and deposited the check in the company account bank B to cover a previous theft of cash. The disbursement has not been recorded. The auditor will best detect this form of kiting by:
   a. Comparing the detail of cash as shown by the cash receipts records with the detail on the confirmed duplicate deposit tickets for three days prior to and subsequent to year end.
   b. Preparing from the cash disbursements book a summary of bank transfers for one week prior to and subsequent to year end.
   c. Examining the composition of deposits in both bank A and B subsequent to year end.
   d. Examining paid checks returned with the bank statement of the next accounting period after year end.

_____ 14. Which of the following audit procedures is the most appropriate when internal control over cash is weak or when a client requests an investigation of cash transactions?
   a. Proof of cash.
   b. Bank reconciliation.
   c. Cash confirmation.
   d. Evaluate ratio of cash to current liabilities.

_____ 15. A responsibility that should be assigned to a specific employee and not shared jointly is that of:
   a. Access to the company's safe deposit box.
   b. Placing orders and maintaining relationships with a prime supplier.
   c. Attempting to collect a particular delinquent account.
   d. Custodianship of the cash working fund.

_____ 16. The use of fidelity bonds protects a company from embezzlement losses and also:
   a. Protects employees who make unintentional errors from possible monetary damages resulting from such errors.
   b. Allows the company to substitute the fidelity bonds for various parts of internal accounting control.
   c. Reduces the company's need to obtain expensive business interruption insurance.
   d. Minimizes the possibility of employing persons with dubious records in positions of trust.

_____ 17. Vos, Inc., which has a December 31 year end, closed an out-of-town division on April 21, 19X2. The checking account used by the division at a local bank was closed out as of April 21, 19X2. The bank, however, has continued to mail bank statements, with zero balances, as of the fifth of each month. Vos has requested the bank to mail the January 5, 19X3, bank statement directly to its independent auditor. For this closed checking account during the audit for 19X2, the auditor should ordinarily:
   a. Review only the January 5, 19X3, bank statement.
   b. Review only the bank statements for 19X2.
   c. Review only the bank statements for 19X2 and the January 5, 19X3 statement.

d. Send a bank confirmation as of December 31, 19X2, in addition to reviewing the bank statements for 19X2 and the January 5, 19X3 statement.

_____ 18. On receiving the bank cutoff statement, the auditor should trace:
   a. Deposits in transit on the year-end bank reconciliation to deposits in the cash receipts journal.
   b. Checks dated prior to year-end to the outstanding checks listed on the year-end bank reconciliation.
   c. Deposits listed on the cutoff statement to deposits in the cash receipts journal.
   d. Checks dated subsequent to year-end to the outstanding checks listed on the year-end bank reconciliation.

_____ 19. To gather evidence regarding the balance per bank in a bank reconciliation, an auditor would examine all of the following *except*:
   a. Cutoff bank statement.
   b. Year-end bank statement.
   c. Bank confirmation.
   d. General ledger.

_____ 20. A "proof of cash" used by an auditor:
   a. Proves that the client's year-end balance of cash is fairly stated.
   b. Confirms that the client has properly separated the custody function from the recording function with respect to cash.
   c. Validates that the client's bank did not make an error during the period being examined.
   d. Attests that the auditor has complied with generally accepted auditing standards.
   e. Determines if there were any unauthorized disbursements or unrecorded deposits for the given time period.*

*This question is from the ICMA examination.

SOLUTIONS

TRUE OR FALSE STATEMENTS

1. False	10. False	18. False
2. True	11. False	19. True
3. True	12. True	20. True
4. False	13. True	21. True
5. True	14. False	22. False
6. False	15. False	23. True
7. True	16. False	24. True
8. True	17. True	25. False
9. False		

COMPLETION STATEMENTS

1. transaction cycles, production
2. exist, balance sheet
3. deposit balances, loan balances, other deposit and loan accounts
4. restrictions, current, noncurrent
5. cash and negotiable instruments, custodian
6. personally mailed, return address
7. lines of credit, compensating balances, contingent liabilities
8. deposits in transit, outstanding checks
9. client, auditor
10. segregation of duties, bank transfers
11. transactions and balances, books
12. accounts receivable, surprise cash count
13. disbursing petty cash, replenishing
14. imprest level, one individual
15. confirming, bank cutoff statement.

MULTIPLE CHOICE QUESTIONS

1. b	5. c	9. c	13. d	17. d
2. b	6. d	10. c	14. a	18. b
3. d	7. a	11. c	15. d	19. d
4. c	8. b	12. c	16. d	20. e

Chapter 19

Completing the Audit/ Postaudit Responsibilities

A. CHAPTER OUTLINE

I. Completing the Field Work

  A. Making Subsequent Events Review

   1. Types of Events

   2. Auditing Procedures in the Subsequent Period

   3. Effects on Auditor's Report

  B. Reading Minutes of Meetings

  C. Obtaining Evidence Concerning Litigation, Claims, and Assessments

   1. Audit Considerations

   2. Letter of Audit Inquiry

   3. Effects of Responses on Auditor's Report

  D. Obtaining Client Representation Letter

   1. Content of Representation Letter

   2. Effects on the Auditor's Report

  E. Performing Analytical Procedures

II. Evaluating the Findings

  A. Making Final Assessment of Materiality and Audit Risk

  B. Making Technical Review of Financial Statements

  C. Formulating Opinion and Drafting Audit Report

  D. Making Final Review(s) of Working Papers

B. CHAPTER HIGHLIGHTS

1. The procedures performed in completing the audit have several **distinctive characteristics**; they:
    a. Do not pertain to specific transaction cycles or accounts.
    b. Are performed after the balance sheet date.
    c. Involve many subjective judgements by the auditor.
    d. Are usually performed by audit managers or other senior members of the **audit** team.

2. The auditor's responsibilities in **completing the audit** involve (a) completing the field work, (b) evaluating the findings, and (c) communicating with the client.

3. **Completing the field work** involves performing the following procedures to obtain additional audit evidence:
    a. Making subsequent events review.
    b. Reading minutes of meetings.
    c. Obtaining evidence concerning litigation, claims, and assessments.
    d. Obtaining client representation letter.
    e. Performing analytical procedures.

4. **Subsequent events** are events and transactions that occur after the balance sheet date but prior to the issuance of the financial statements and auditor's report.
    a. The **subsequent events period extends from the balance sheet date to the end of field work.**
    b. During this period, the auditor is required by GAAS to discover the occurrence of any subsequent event that has a material effect on the financial statements.
    c. The auditor has no responsibility to discover subsequent events that occur between the end of field work and the issuance of the audit report.

5. There are two types of **subsequent events:**
    a. **Type 1** consists of those events that provide additional evidence with respect to conditions that existed at the date of the balance sheet and affect the estimates inherent in the process of preparing financial statements.
    b. **Type 2** consists of those events that provide evidence with respect to conditions that did not exist at the date of the balance sheet but arose subsequent to that date.

    Type 1 events require **adjustment** of the financial statements; Type 2 events require **disclosure** in the statements.

6. The auditor is required to identify and evaluate subsequent events up to the **date of the auditor's report,** which should be as of the end of the field work.

7. The auditor's **responsibility for subsequent events is discharged** by (a) being alert for such events in performing year-end substantive tests and (b) performing specific auditing procedures at or near the completion of field work.

8. The **reading of minutes** of meetings of stockholders, the board of directors, and its subcommittees may reveal information about matters that have audit significance. The auditor should read the minutes as soon as they are available.

9. In making an audit in accordance with GAAS, the auditor must determine whether **litigation, claims and assessments** (LCA) are reported in conformity with GAAP.

10. With respect to LCA, the auditor should obtain **evidential matter** as to:
    a. The existence of a condition, situation, or set of circumstances indicating an uncertainty as to the possible loss to an entity arising from litigation, claims, and assessments.
    b. The period in which the underlying cause for legal action occurred.
    c. The degree of probability of an unfavorable outcome.
    d. The amount of range of potential loss.

11. Management represents the primary source of information about LCA, whereas a **letter of audit inquiry to the client's outside legal counsel** is the auditor's primary means of obtaining corroborating information as to LCA.

12. **Audit letter responses** will have no affect on the auditor's report when (1) there is a high probability of a favorable outcome or (2) the matters at issue are immaterial.
    a. When an uncertainty is not susceptible to reasonable estimation but is adequately disclosed in the financial statements, the auditor may issue an unqualified opinion with explanatory language.
    b. The refusal of a lawyer to respond is a scope limitation that should result in either a qualified opinion or a disclaimer of opinion, depending on materiality.

13. The auditor must obtain **written representations from management** as to matters that are either individually or collectively material to the financial statements. The objectives of a rep letter are to:
    a. Confirm oral representations given to the auditor.
    b. Document the continuing appropriateness of such representations.
    c. Reduce the possibility of misunderstandings concerning management's representations.

14. A **rep letter complements other auditing procedures** and may reveal matters not otherwise discovered by the auditor. The refusal of management to furnish a rep letter constitutes a limitation on the scope of the audit, which may preclude the issuance of a standard audit report.

15. Performing **analytical procedures** at the conclusion of the field work is a required part of an overall review.
    a. The objectives of the review are to assist the auditor in (1) assessing conclusions reached in the audit and (2) evaluating the overall financial statement presentation.
    b. The procedures should be performed by an individual having comprehensive knowledge of the client's business and history.
    c. The procedures should be (1) applied to critical audit areas identified in the audit and (2) based on financial statement data after all audit adjustments and reclassifications have been recognized.

16. The auditor has **two objectives in evaluating the findings: (1)** determining the opinion to be expressed and (2) determining whether GAAS have been met in the audit. These objectives are met by the following steps:
    a. Making final assessment of materiality and audit risk.
    b. Making technical review of financial statements.
    c. Formulating opinion and drafting audit report.
    d. Making final review(s) of working papers.

17. In **making a final assessment of materiality,** the auditor determines **likely misstatements** for an account from the following components:
    a. Uncollected misstatements specifically identified through substantive tests of details of transactions and balances (referred to as **known misstatements).**
    b. **Projected uncorrected misstatements** estimated through audit **sampling** techniques.
    c. Estimated misstatements detected through analytical procedures and quantified by other auditing procedures.

    The sum of likely misstatements in all accounts is referred to as **aggregate likely misstatement.**

18. Financial statement checklists may be used in **making a technical review of the financial statements.**

19. When the auditor concludes that audit risk is at an acceptable level, he or she can proceed with **formulating the opinion** supported by the findings. However, when audit risk is not acceptable, he or she should either (a) perform additional substantive tests or (b) convince the client to make the corrections necessary to reduce audit risk to an acceptable level.

20. The **ultimate responsibility** for summarizing the findings and formulating an opinion rests with the **partner in charge** of the engagement.

21. In completing the audit, **reviews of working papers** are usually made by the audit manager and the partner in charge of the engagement. Some firms require an **independent "cold" review** by a partner who did not participate in the audit. The rationale for this review is based on the objectivity of the reviewer, who may challenge matters approved by earlier reviews.

22. At the conclusion of the audit, the auditor's **communications to the audit committee** should include:
    a. Matters pertaining to the internal control structure.
    b. Matters pertaining to the conduct of the audit.

    The communication to management is made in a **management letter.**

23. In **communicating internal control structure matters,** the auditor is required to report **reportable conditions** which are defined as significant deficiencies in the design or operation of the internal control structure that could adversely affect the organization's ability to record, process, summarize, and report financial data consistent with the assertions of management in the financial statements.

24. The **report on internal control matters should be in writing** and the **distribution of the report should ordinarily be restricted** to the audit committee, management, and others within the organization. The report should:
    a. Indicate that the purpose of the audit is to report on the financial statements and not to provide assurance on the internal control structure.
    b. Include the definition of reportable conditions.
    c. Include the restriction on distribution.

25. A reportable condition may be of such magnitude as to be a **material weakness.** A material weakness is defined as a reportable condition in which the design or operation of the specific internal control structure elements do not reduce to a relatively low level the risk that misstatements in amounts that would be material in relation to the financial statements being audited may occur and not be detected within a timely period by employees in the normal course of performing their assigned functions.
    a. The auditor is not required by GAAS to separately identify and communicate material weaknesses to the audit committee.
    b. However, the client may request this information or the auditor may elect to report the information.

26. The auditor is required to **communicate to the audit committee** certain matters pertaining to the conduct of the audit. The communication may be oral or written, and it may occur during or shortly after the audit. Matters to be communicated to the audit committee include:
    a. Auditor's responsibility under GAAS.
    b. Significant accounting policies.
    c. Management judgments and accounting estimates.
    d. Significant audit adjustments.
    e. Disagreements with management.
    f. Consultation with other accountants.
    g. Major issues discussed with management prior to retention.
    h. Difficulties encountered in performing the audit.
    i. Reportable conditions pertaining to the internal control structure.

27. The issuance of a **management letter** is an integral, but voluntary, part of the services rendered by an auditor to a client. The letter may include comments on:
    a. Internal control structure matters that are not considered to be reportable conditions.
    b. Management of resources such as cash, inventories, and investments.
    c. Tax-related matters.

28. The auditor has **no responsibility** to make inquiry or to perform any auditing procedures concerning **subsequent events between the end of field work and the issuance of the audit report.** When such events come to the auditor's attention, it may be necessary to **redate** or **dual date** the report, provided management makes the necessary adjustments or disclosures.

29. The auditor has **no responsibility for the postaudit discovery of facts** existing (but unknown) at the date of the audit report. However, if (a) the **auditor becomes aware** of such facts and (b) the facts may have affected the report that was issued, the auditor is required to ascertain the reliability of the information, and when appropriate, take steps to prevent further reliance on the report.

30. Auditing standards do not require the auditor to conduct any **postaudit reviews of his or her work**. However, on discovery of an omitted procedure, the auditor should assess its importance to his or her ability to currently support the opinion expressed on the financial statements.

C. TRUE OR FALSE STATEMENTS.

Indicate in the space provided whether each of the following statements is true or false.

_____   1. The procedures performed in completing the audit are performed after the balance sheet date.

_____   2. Subsequent events are events and transactions that occur after the balance sheet date but prior to the date of the auditor's report.

_____   3. Type 1 subsequent events provide evidence as to conditions existing at the balance sheet date that require supplementary disclosure in the statements.

_____   4. The auditor is required to identify and evaluate subsequent events up to the date of issuance of the audit report.

_____   5. The reading of minutes is a required step in evaluating the findings.

_____   6. A letter of audit inquiry to the client's outside legal counsel is the auditor's primary means of verifying management's assertions concerning litigation, claims, and assessments (LCA).

_____   7. In lieu of a response from outside legal counsel concerning LCA, the auditor usually can rely on a client representation letter.

_____   8. A client representation letter is not a substitute for any auditing procedures considered necessary in the circumstances.

_____   9. One objective in evaluating the findings is to determine whether GAAS have been met in the audit.

_____   10. An overall review involves the use of analytical procedures at the time the audit report is issued.

_____   11. In making a final assessment of materiality and audit risk, the auditor determines the likely misstatement for an account.

_____   12. Uncorrected misstatements specifically identified through substantive tests of details of transactions and balances are referred to as known misstatements.

_____ 13. When audit risk is at an acceptable level, the auditor can proceed to issue an unqualified opinion on the financial statements.

_____ 14. The ultimate responsibility for summarizing audit findings and formulating an opinion on the financial statements rests with the partner in charge of the engagement.

_____ 15. Auditing standards require an independent "cold" review of working papers.

_____ 16. Financial statement checklists may be used by the auditor in making a technical review of the working papers.

_____ 17. In communicating internal control matters, the auditor is required to report reportable conditions and material weaknesses.

_____ 18. A reportable condition is a significant deficiency in the design or operation of the internal control structure.

_____ 19. Distribution of the report on internal control matters should be restricted to the audit committee, management, and others within the organization.

_____ 20. The auditor is required to communicate certain matters pertaining to the conduct of the audit to the audit committee.

_____ 21. The issuance of a management letter is required by GAAS in a financial statement audit.

_____ 22. Dual dating of an audit report refers to the balance sheet date and to the audit report date.

_____ 23. The auditor has no responsibility for the postaudit discovery of facts existing (but unknown) at the date of the audit report.

_____ 24. To prevent further reliance on a previously issued audit report, the auditor is required to notify both the client and any regulatory agencies having jurisdiction over the client.

_____ 25. The auditor is required by GAAS to make a post audit review for auditing procedures considered necessary in the circumstances that may have been omitted during the audit.

D. COMPLETION STATEMENTS

Fill in the blanks with the word or words that correctly complete the following statements.

1. The auditor's responsibilities in completing the audit involve _____ , _____ , and _____ .

2. Subsequent events occur after the date of the _____ but prior to issuance of the financial statements and the _____ .

3. The auditor has a responsibility for subsequent events from the balance sheet date to the end of _____ ; he or she has no responsibility for subsequent events from the date of the auditor's report to the _____ .

4. The primary means of obtaining corroborating information about litigation, claims, and assessments (LCA) is through a letter of _____ sent to the client's _____ .

5. The auditor is required to obtain certain _____ from management in meeting the _____ of field work.

6. An overall review involves the use of _____ at the conclusion of _____ .

7. The objectives in evaluating the findings are to determine the _____ to be expressed and whether _____ have been met in the audit.

8. In making a final assessment of materiality and audit risk, the component of misstatements found through _____ of details is referred to as _____ .

9. In completing the audit, reviews of the working papers are made by the _____ and the _____ .

10. Reportable conditions are _____ in the _____ or _____ of the internal control structure.

11. The issuance of a _____ is an integral but _____ part of the services rendered by an auditor to a client.

12. The auditor is required to communicate certain matters pertaining to the conduct of the _____ to the _____ or group that oversees the financial reporting process.

13. When knowledge of subsequent events occurring after the date of the auditor's report comes to the auditor's attention prior to issuance of the report, he or she may either _____ or _____ date the report.

14. The preferred treatment for the postaudit discovery of facts existing at the date of the audit report is to prepare revised _____ and to issue a revised _____.

15. Auditing standards do not require the auditor to conduct any _____ to discover _____ omitted from the audit.

E. MULTIPLE CHOICE

Choose the best answer for each of the following questions and enter the identifying letter in the space provided.

_____ 1. A major customer of an audit client suffers a fire just prior to completion of year end field work. The audit client believes that this event could have a significant direct effect on the financial statements. The auditor should:
   a. Advise management to disclose the event in notes to the financial statements.
   b. Disclose the event in the auditor's report.
   c. Withhold submission of the auditor's report until the extent of the direct effects on the financial statement is known.
   d. Advise management to adjust the financial statements.

_____ 2. The statement that best expresses the auditor's responsibility with respect to events occurring between the balance sheet date and the end of field work is that:
   a. The auditor has no responsibility for events occurring in the subsequent period unless these events affect transactions recorded on or before the balance sheet date.
   b. The auditor's responsibility is to determine that a proper cutoff has been made and that transactions recorded on or before the balance sheet date actually occurred.
   c. The auditor is fully responsible for events occurring in the subsequent period and should extend all detailed procedures through the last day of field work.
   d. The auditor is responsible for determining that a proper cutoff has been made and performing a general review of events occurring in the subsequent period.

_____ 3. "Subsequent events" for reporting purposes are defined as events which occur subsequent to the:
   a. Balance sheet date.
   b. Date of the auditor's report.
   c. Balance sheet date but prior to the issuance of the auditor's report.
   d. Date of the auditor's report and concern contingencies which are not reflected in the financial statements.

_____ 4. Which of the following material events occurring subsequent to the December 31, 19X3 balance sheet would not ordinarily result in an adjustment to the financial statements before they are issued on March 2, 19X4?
   a. Write-off of a receivable from a debtor who had suffered from deteriorating financial condition for the past six years. The debtor filed for bankruptcy on January 23, 19X4.
   b. Acquisition of a subsidiary on January 23, 19X4. Negotiations had begun in December of 19X3.
   c. Settlement of extended litigation on January 23, 19X4 in excess of the recorded year-end liability.
   d. A 3 for 5 reverse stock split consummated on January 23, 19X4.

_____ 5. An auditor should obtain evidential matter relevant to all the following factors concerning third-party litigation against a client except the:
   a. Period in which the underlying cause for legal action occurred.
   b. Probability of an unfavorable outcome.
   c. Jurisdiction in which the matter will be resolved.
   d. Existence of a situation indicating an uncertainty as to the possible loss.

_____ 6. The auditor's primary means of obtaining corroboration of management's information concerning litigation is a:
   a. Letter of audit inquiry to the client's lawyer.
   b. Letter of corroboration from the auditor's lawyer upon review of the legal documentation.
   c. Confirmation of claims and assessments from the other parties to the litigation.
   d. Confirmation of claims and assessments from an officer of the court presiding over the litigation.

_____ 7. The primary objective of analytical procedures used in the final review stage of an audit is to:
   a. Obtain evidence from details tested to corroborate particular assertions.
   b. Identify areas that represent specific risks relevant to the audit.
   c. Assist the auditor in assessing the validity of the conclusions reached.
   d. Satisfy doubts when questions arise about a client's ability to continue in existence.

_____ 8. An auditor's communication of internal control structure related matters noted in an audit usually should be addressed to the:
   a. Audit committee.
   b. Director of internal auditing.
   c. Chief financial officer.
   d. Chief accounting officer.

_____ 9. When reporting on conditions relating to an entity's internal control structure observed during an audit of the financial statements, the auditor should include a:
   a. Description of tests performed to search for material weaknesses.
   b. Statement of positive assurance on the structure.
   c. Paragraph describing the inherent limitations of the structure.
   d. Restriction on the distribution of the report.

_____ 10. Which of the following statements concerning material weaknesses and reportable conditions is correct?
   a. An auditor should identify and communicate material weaknesses separately from reportable conditions.
   b. All material weaknesses are reportable conditions.
   c. An auditor should report immediately material weaknesses and reportable conditions discovered during an audit.
   d. All reportable conditions are material weaknesses.

_____ 11. Which of the following auditing procedures is ordinarily performed last?
   a. Obtaining a management representation letter.
   b. Testing the purchasing function.
   c. Reading the minutes of director's meetings.
   d. Confirming accounts payable.

_____ 12. A written client representation letter most likely would be an auditor's best source of corroborative information of a client's plans to:
   a. Terminate an employee pension plan.
   b. Make a public offering of its common stock.
   c. Settle an outstanding lawsuit for an amount less than the accrued loss contingency.
   d. Discontinue a line of business.

_____ 13. A limitation on the scope of an auditor's examination sufficient to preclude an unqualified opinion will always result when management:
   a. Engages the auditor after the year-end physical inventory count is completed.
   b. Fails to correct a material internal control weakness that had been identified during the prior year's audit.
   c. Refuses to furnish a management representation letter to the auditor.
   d. Prevents the auditor from reviewing the working papers of the predecessor auditor.

_____ 14. "Provision has been made for any material loss that might be sustained as a result of purchase commitments for inventory quantities in excess of normal requirements or at prices in excess of the prevailing market prices." The foregoing passage is most likely from:
   a. A management representation letter.
   b. The explanatory paragraph of a qualified auditor's report.
   c. A vendor representation letter.
   d. The explanatory paragraph of an adverse auditor's report.

_____ 15. Although there is no professional requirement to do so on audit engagements, CPAs normally issue a formal "management" letter to their clients. The primary purpose of this letter is to provide:
   a. Evidence indicating whether the auditor is reasonably certain that the internal control structure is operating as prescribed.

    b. A permanent record of the internal control work performed by the auditor during the course of the engagement.

    c. A written record of discussions between auditor and client concerning the auditor's observations and suggestions for improvements.

    d. A summary of the auditor's observations that resulted from the auditor's special study of the internal control structure.

_____ 16. After issuance of the auditor's report, the auditor has no obligation to make any further inquiries with respect to audited financial statements covered by that report unless:

    a. A final resolution of a contingency that had resulted in a qualification of the auditor's report is made.

    b. A development occurs that may affect the client's ability to continue as a going concern.

    c. An investigation of the auditor's practice by a peer review committee ensues.

    d. New information is discovered concerning undisclosed related party transactions of the previously-audited period.

_____ 17. Ajax Company's auditor concludes that the omission of an audit procedure considered necessary at the time of the prior audit impairs the auditor's present ability to support the previously-expressed unqualified opinion. If the auditor believes there are stockholders currently relying on the opinion, the auditor should promptly:

    a. Notify the stockholders currently relying on the previously expressed unqualified opinion that they should not rely on it.

    b. Advise management to disclose this development in its next interim report to the stockholders.

    c. Advise management to revise the financial statements with full disclosure of the auditor's inability to support the unqualified opinion.

    d. Undertake to apply the omitted procedure or alternate procedures that would provide a satisfactory basis for the opinion.

_____ 18. An auditor concludes that an audit procedure considered necessary at the time of the audit has been omitted. The auditor should assess the importance of the omitted procedure to the ability to support the previously expressed opinion. Which of the following would be least helpful in making that assessment?

    a. A discussion with the client about whether there are persons relying on the auditor's report.

    b. A reevaluation of the overall scope of the audit.

    c. A discussion of the circumstances with engagement personnel.

    d. A review of the other audit procedures that were applied that might compensate for the one omitted.

_____ 19. If an auditor dates the auditor's report on financial statements for the year ended December 31, 19X4, as of February 10, 19X5, except for Note J, as to which the date is March 3, 19X5, the auditor is taking responsibility for:

    a. All subsequent events occurring through March 3, 19X5.

    b. All subsequent events occurring through February 10, 19X5 only.

c. All subsequent events occurring through February 10, 19X5, and the specific subsequent event referred to in Note J through March 3, 19X5.

d. Only the specific subsequent event referred to in Note J through March 3, 19X5.

_____ 20. Three months subsequent to the date of the audit report, a CPA becomes aware of facts which existed at the date of the report and which affect the reliability of the financial statements of a client whose securities are widely held. If the client refuses to make appropriate disclosure, the CPA should notify:

a. Regulatory agencies having jurisdiction over the client.

b. All stockholders.

c. All present and potential investors in the company.

d. Stockbrokers and the financial press.

SOLUTIONS

TRUE OR FALSE STATEMENTS

1. True	10. False	18. True
2. False	11. True	19. True
3. False	12. True	20. True
4. False	13. False	21. False
5. False	14. True	22. False
6. True	15. False	23. True
7. False	16. False	24. True
8. True	17. False	25. False
9. True		

COMPLETION STATEMENTS

1. completing the field work, evaluating the findings, communicating with the client.
2. balance sheet, auditor's report
3. field work, issuance of the auditor's report
4. audit inquiry, outside legal counsel
5. written representations, third standard
6. analytical procedures, field work
7. opinion, GAAS
8. substantive tests, known misstatements
9. audit manager, partner in charge of the engagement
10. significant deficiencies, design, operation
11. management letter, voluntary
12. audit, audit committee
13. redate, dual
14. financial statements, audit report
15. postaudit reviews, auditing procedures

MULTIPLE CHOICE QUESTIONS

1. a	5. c	9. d	13. c	17. b
2. d	6. a	10. b	14. a	18. a
3. c	7. c	11. a	15. c	19. c
4. b	8. a	12. d	16. d	20. a

Chapter 20

Reporting on Audited Financial Statements

A. CHAPTER OUTLINE

I. Standards of Reporting

    A. First Standard of Reporting

        1. Sources of GAAP

        2. Promulgated GAAP

    B. Second Standard of Reporting

        1. Accounting Changes Affecting Consistency

        2. Changes not Affecting Consistency

    C. Third Standard of Reporting

    D. Fourth Standard of Reporting

        1. Expressing an Opinion

        2. Financial Statements

        3. Character of the Audit

        4. Association with Financial Statements

        5. Degree of Responsibility

II. The Auditor's Report

    A. Standard Report

    B. Departures from Standard Report

        1. Explanatory Language with Unqualified Opinion

        2. Other Types of Opinions

III. Effects of Circumstances Causing Departures from the Standard Report

    A. Scope Limitation

        1. Limited Reporting Engagements

        2. Other Types of Opinions

    B. Nonconformity with GAAP

1. Explanatory Language with Unqualified Opinion

2. Other Types of Opinions

C. Inconsistency in Accounting Principles

1. Explanatory Language with Unqualified Opinion

2. Other Types of Opinions

D. Inadequate Disclosure

E. Uncertainty

1. Explanatory Language with Unqualified Opinion

2. Other Types of Opinions

F. Substantial Doubt About Going Concern Status

1. Explanatory Language with Unqualified Opinion

2. Other Types of Opinions

G. Emphasis of a Matter

H. Opinion Based in Part on Report of Another Auditor

1. Decision Not to Make Reference

2. Decision to Make Reference

3. Explanatory Language with Unqualified Opinion

4. Other Types of Opinions

I. Summary of Effects of Circumstances on Auditors' Reports

IV. **Other Reporting Considerations**

A. Reporting When the CPA is Not Independent

B. Circumstances Concerning Comparative Financial Statements

1. Different Opinions

2. Updating an Opinion

3. Change of Auditors

C. Information Accompanying Audited Financial Statements

1. Required Supplementary Information

2. Voluntary Information Provided by Management

3. Additional Information Provided by the Auditor

D. Financial Statements Prepared for Use in Other Countries

V. **Summary**

B. CHAPTER HIGHLIGHTS

1. The **first standard of reporting** states:
   The report shall state whether the financial statements are presented in accordance with **generally accepted accounting principles**.
   a. This standard requires an explicit assertion by the auditor.
   b. It is an expression of an opinion rather than a statement of fact.

2. In **meeting the first reporting standard**, the auditor must obtain **evidence** concerning whether:
   a. The accounting principles selected and applied have general acceptance.
   b. The accounting principles are appropriate in the circumstances.
   c. The financial statements, including the related notes, are informative of matters that may affect their use, understanding and interpretation.
   d. The information presented in the financial statements is classified and summarized in a reasonable manner.
   e. The statements reflect the underlying events and transactions in a manner that presents the financial position, results of operations, and cash flows within reasonable and practicable limits.

3. The **sources of established accounting principles** are generally the following:
   a. Accounting principles promulgated by a body designated by the AICPA Council to establish such principles, pursuant to Rule 203 of the AICPA Code of Professional Conduct. **Promulgated accounting principles** consist of:
      • FASB Statements of Financial Accounting Standards and FASB interpretations.
      • Accounting Principles Board (APB) Opinions and AICPA Accounting Research Bulletins issued by bodies prior to the FASB.
      • GASB Statements of Governmental Accounting Standards and GASB Interpretations.
   b. Pronouncements of bodies composed of expert accountants that follow a due process procedure, including broad distribution of proposed accounting principles for public comment, for the intended purpose of establishing accounting principles or describing existing practices that are generally accepted.
   c. Practices or pronouncements that are widely recognized as being generally accepted because they represent prevalent practice in a particular industry or the knowledgeable application to specific circumstances of pronouncements that are generally accepted.
   d. Other accounting literature.

4. The **second standard of reporting** states:
   The report shall identify those circumstances in which such principles have not been **consistently observed** in the current period in relation to the preceding period.
   a. Unless the report contains specific language to the contrary, the reader can conclude that accounting principles have been consistently applied.
   b. The **objectives** of this standard are to (1) give assurance as to the comparability of financial statements between accounting periods and (2) require appropriate reporting when comparability has been materially affected by changes in the application of accounting principles.

5. As used in the consistency standard, **changes in an accounting principle include**:
    a. A change in the principle itself, such as a change from a sales basis to a production basis in recording farm revenue.
    b. A change in the method of applying a principle, such as a change from the straight-line method of depreciation to the sum-of-the-years'-digits method.
    c. A change in the reporting entity, such as presenting consolidated statements in place of individual company statements or changes in specific subsidiaries constituting the consolidated group.
    d. The correction of an error in principle, as, for example, a change from a principle not generally accepted to one that is generally accepted.
    e. A change in principle inseparable from a change in estimate, such as a change from capitalizing and amortizing a cost to recording it as an expense when incurred because future benefits are now doubtful.

6. The **third standard of reporting** states:
    Informative disclosures in the financial statements are to be regarded as reasonably adequate unless otherwise stated in the report.
    a. Unless there is explicit wording in the report to the contrary, the reader can conclude that the disclosure reporting standard has been met.
    b. Informative disclosures involve **material matters** relating to the form, arrangement, and content of the financial statements and the accompanying notes.

7. The **fourth standard of reporting** states:
    The report shall either contain an **expression of opinion** regarding the financial statements, taken as a whole, or an assertion to the effect that an opinion cannot be expressed. When an overall opinion cannot be expressed, the reasons therefor should be stated. In all cases where an auditor's name is associated with financial statements, the report should contain a clear-cut indication of the character of the audit, if any, and the degree of responsibility the auditor is taking.
    a. The objective of this standard is to prevent misinterpretation of the degree of responsibility the auditor is assuming when his or her name is associated with financial statements.
    b. This standard directly influences the form, content, and language of the auditor's report.

8. The **fourth standard of reporting**:
    a. Requires the auditor to **express an opinion** or to give the reasons why an opinion cannot be expressed.
    b. Applies to reporting on the audit of a single statement as well as a complete set of basic financial statements.
    c. Indicates that whenever the auditor's name is associated with financial statements, the report should describe the **character of the auditor's work** and the **degree of responsibility** the auditor is taking.

9. The **auditor's standard report** consists of (a) three paragraphs, identified respectively as the introductory, scope, and opinion paragraphs and (b) standard language. The standard report is:
   a. Normally **addressed** to the individuals or groups that appointed the auditors.
   b. **Dated** as of the completion of field work.
   c. **Signed** in the name of the firm.

10. **Departures** from the standard report occur when the auditor concludes that:
   a. Explanatory language should be added to the report while still expressing an unqualified opinion, or
   b. An opinion other than an unqualified opinion should be expressed.

11. The following circumstances may result in **adding explanatory language** to a standard report with an unqualified opinion:
   a. Nonconformity with a promulgated accounting principle necessary for fair presentation in unusual circumstances.
   b. Inconsistency in accounting principles accounted for in conformity with GAAP.
   c. Uncertainty accounted for in conformity with GAAP.
   d. Substantial doubt about an entity's going concern status accounted for in conformity with GAAP.
   e. Emphasis of a matter by the auditor.
   f. Opinion based in part on report of another auditor.

12. When explanatory language is added, the:
   a. Explanatory information may be presented in an explanatory paragraph in most cases **following** the opinion paragraph, on in the introductory or scope paragraphs.
   b. Except for the last circumstance (item ll (f) above), **no reference** should be made to the explanatory information in the opinion paragraph.

13. In addition to an unqualified opinion, an auditor may express **a qualified, adverse, or disclaimer of opinion.** When other than an unqualified opinion is expressed, the report should contain:
   a. One or more explanatory paragraphs **before** the opinion paragraph that gives the substantive reason(s) for the opinion expressed, and
   b. A **reference** to the explanatory paragraph(s) in the opinion paragraph.

14. In deciding on the **appropriate opinion,** the auditor must answer the following questions:
   a. Was sufficient evidence obtained in the audit(s) to have **a reasonable basis** for an opinion on the financial statements?
   b. Do the financial statements **present fairly,** in all material respects, the financial position, results of operations, and cash flows in conformity with GAAP?

15. **Materiality** is important in answering the foregoing questions:
   a. Affirmative answers to both questions will result in an unqualified opinion.
   b. A negative answer to the first question means that there was **a scope limitation** which should result in a qualified opinion or a disclaimer of opinion.
   c. A negative answer to the second question means that there has been **nonconformity with GAAP** which should result in a qualified opinion or an adverse opinion.

16. The following **circumstances** will result in issuing **other than an unqualified opinion**:
    a. Scope limitation.
    b. Nonconformity with GAAP (other than required nonconformity with promulgated GAAP in unusual circumstances).
    c. Inconsistency in accounting principles not accounted for in conformity with GAAP.
    d. Inadequate disclosure.
    e. Uncertainty not accounted for in conformity with GAAP.
    f. Substantial doubt about an entity's going concern status not accounted for in conformity with GAAP.
    g. Circumstances pertaining to opinion based in part on report of another auditor.

17. A **scope limitation** may be imposed by the client or result from circumstances, such as appointment too late to perform procedures considered necessary in the circumstances, and inadequate client records.
    a. A **limited reporting engagement** occurs when the auditor is asked to audit one basic financial statement. This type of engagement does not result in a scope limitation, and a standard report is issued except that the language in each paragraph is modified to refer only to the statement audited.
    b. When a **qualified opinion** is expressed the auditor should:
        • Indicate the scope limitation in the scope paragraph.
        • Give the substantive reasons for the limitation in an explanatory paragraph.
        • Express a qualified opinion in the opinion paragraph with reference to the explanatory paragraph.
    c. When a **disclaimer of opinion** is expressed:
        • The introductory paragraph is modified.
        • The scope paragraph is omitted.
        • An explanatory paragraph is included after the introductory paragraph. The third and concluding paragraph contains a denial of opinion.

18. **Nonconformity with GAAP** may result in explanatory language with an unqualified opinion but generally it will result in another type of opinion.
    a. Explanatory language with an unqualified opinion occurs in connection with Ethics Rule 203 when, due to unusual circumstances, the auditor concludes that compliance with **promulgated principles** will result in misleading financial statements. In such case, the report should contain:
        • Standard introductory and scope paragraphs.
        • An explanatory paragraph preceding the opinion paragraph that explains the circumstances and states that the use of the alternative principle is justified.
        • An unqualified opinion in a standard opinion paragraph.
    b. When a **qualified opinion** is expressed, the auditor should:
        • Disclose in an explanatory paragraph(s) preceding the opinion paragraph all of the substantive reasons for the opinion.
        • Disclose in the explanatory paragraph(s) the principle effects of the subject matter of the qualification on financial position, results of operations, and cash flows, if practicable. If not practicable, the report should so state.
        • Express a qualified opinion in the opinion paragraph with reference to the explanatory paragraph(s).

c. The effects on the report of an **adverse opinion** are similar to the effects of a qualified opinion except that the opinion paragraph should state that because of the effects of the matter(s) described in the explanatory paragraph(s), the financial statements do not present fairly.

19. The effect on the audit report of **inconsistent application of accounting principles** depends on whether the change has been accounted for in conformity with GAAP. A change in conformity with GAAP occurs when:
    a. The new principle is a generally accepted accounting principle.
    b. The change is properly accounted for and disclosed in the financial statements, and
    c. Management can justify that the new principle is preferable.

20. When the change in accounting principles is **not made in conformity with GAAP**, the auditor should:
    a. Express either a qualified opinion or an adverse opinion depending on the materiality of the change.
    b. Add an explanatory paragraph immediately before the opinion paragraph to describe the nonconformity with GAAP.

21. When there is **inadequate disclosure** of essential information in the financial statements, the auditor should express either a qualified opinion or an adverse opinion because of nonconformity with GAAP.
    a. If practicable, the auditor should provide the essential information in one or more explanatory paragraphs of the audit report unless its omission is recognized by a Statement on Auditing Standards.
    b. If a statement of cash flows is omitted, the auditor (1) will normally conclude that a qualified opinion should be expressed and (2) is not required to present the statement.

22. The term **uncertainty** applies to the outcome of a financial statement item that is not susceptible to reasonable estimation prior to the balance sheet date.
    a. The existence of an uncertainty may result in adding explanatory language to the standard report when management properly discloses:
        • a probable material loss because a reasonable estimate cannot be made.
        • the reasonable possibility of a material loss.
    b. Uncertainties will result in expressing other than an unqualified opinion when there is either (1) a scope limitation or (2) nonconformity with GAAP.
    c. A **nonconformity with GAAP** generally is attributable to either (1) inadequate disclosure, (2) use of inappropriate accounting principles, or (3) unreasonable accounting estimates.

23. In an audit, the entity is normally assumed to be a **going concern** that will continue in existence. The auditor has a responsibility to evaluate whether in fact the entity has the ability to continue for a reasonable period of time, not to exceed one year beyond the date of the financial statements being audited. If the auditor has doubts about the entity's ability to continue, the audit report should:
    a. Be **standard with explanatory language** when the circumstances are **adequately disclosed in the notes** to the financial statements.
    b. Contain **other than an unqualified opinion** when the circumstances are **not adequately disclosed** in the financial statements.

24. When the auditor wishes to **emphasize a matter**, the report should (1) have standard wording in the introductory, scope, and opinion paragraphs, (b) describe the matter being emphasized in an explanatory paragraph, and (c) make no reference to the explanatory material in the opinion paragraph.

25. When **two or more auditing firms** are involved in an audit, one firm should be the principal auditor.
    a. When the principal auditor **assumes responsibility** for the work of the other auditor, **no reference** is made to the other auditor in the audit report. This decision occurs when:
       • The other auditors are associated or correspondent firms whose work is well known to the principal auditor.
       • The work is performed under the principal auditor's guidance and control.
       • The principal auditor reviews the audit programs and working papers of the other auditors.
    b. The principal auditor will **make reference to another auditor** when one or more of the foregoing factors are not present, and may also decide to make reference when the portion of the financial statements audited by another auditor is material to the financial statements taken as a whole.

26. When the principal auditor makes reference to another auditor, the report should contain **explanatory language and an unqualified opinion**. The language includes:
    • Indicating in the introductory paragraph the magnitude of the portion of the financial statements audited by the other auditor(s).
    • Stating in the scope paragraph that the reports of other auditors are part of the auditor's reasonable basis for an opinion.
    • Making reference to the other auditor's report in the opinion paragraph.

    When the principal auditor **cannot rely on the report of another auditor**, a scope limitation exists, and the principal auditor should express either a qualified opinion or a disclaimer of opinion.

27. When the auditor is **not independent**, he or she should issue a one paragraph report (a) stating that he or she is not independent and that an audit was not made and (b) expressing a disclaimer of opinion.

28. The auditor's report on the current period's financial statements should also cover the financial statements of prior years presented on a **comparative** basis.
    a. When the auditor wishes to express a **different opinion** on one or more of the statements, the circumstances should be explained in the report and there should be more than one opinion paragraph.
    b. When the auditor wishes to **update an opinion**, he or she should explain the circumstances in an explanatory paragraph preceding the opinion paragraph.
    c. When there has been a **change of auditors**, the change should be explained in the introductory paragraph.

29. **Information accompanying financial statements** consists of supplementary information required by the FASB and GASB and voluntary information provided by the management. The auditor is not required to audit any of the information because the data are outside the basic financial statements.

30. The auditor is required to:
    a. (1) Apply certain **limited procedures to supplementary information** required by the FASB and the GASB and (2) report any deficiencies in or omissions of such information, and
    b. Read **voluntary information provided by management** to determine whether the data or the manner of presentation are materially inconsistent with the financial statements.

31. An auditor may report on financial statements prepared for use in **other countries**.
    a. If the use is only outside the U.S., the report may either be (1) the U.S.-style auditor's report modified for the accounting principles of another country, or (2) the standard auditor's report of the other country.
    b. If the use will also be within the U.S., the U.S.-style report should be used with a qualified or adverse opinion depending on the materiality of departures from the U.S. GAAP.

C. TRUE OR FALSE STATEMENTS

Indicate in the space provided whether each of the following statements is true or false.

_____ 1. The first standard of reporting requires an explicit assertion by the auditor in the auditor's report.

_____ 2. In determining whether financial statements are prepared in conformity with GAAP, the auditor must obtain evidence that the accounting principles are appropriate in the circumstances.

_____ 3. The second standard of reporting requires the auditor to state in the auditor's report whether or not accounting principles have been consistently applied between accounting periods.

_____ 4. The third standard of reporting requires the auditor to explicitly state in the auditor's report whether informative disclosures in the financial statements are adequate.

_____ 5. The objective of the fourth standard of reporting is to prevent misinterpretation of the degree of responsibility assumed by the auditor.

_____ 6. The auditor's report is normally addressed to management and the board of directors.

_____ 7. The auditor's report is normally dated as of the balance sheet date and it is signed in the name of the auditing firm.

_____ 8. A departure from the standard report occurs when explanatory language is added to a report with an unqualified opinion.

_____ 9. Explanatory language can be added to the audit report with an unqualified opinion when there is a scope limitation.

_____ 10. The auditor should express other than an unqualified opinion when an uncertainty is accounted for in conformity with GAAP.

_____ 11. When a qualified opinion is expressed because of a scope limitation, the scope paragraph should be omitted.

_____ 12. When a disclaimer of opinion is expressed because of a scope opinion, the auditor should issue a four paragraph audit report.

_____ 13. When there is a justified departure from promulgated GAAP, the audit report should contain explanatory language with an unqualified opinion.

_____ 14. If a statement of cash flows is not presented, the auditor will normally express a qualified opinion.

_____ 15. The term uncertainty applies to the outcome of a financial statement item that is not susceptible to reasonable estimation prior to the balance sheet date.

_____ 16. The auditor has a responsibility to evaluate whether the entity has the ability to continue as a going concern for a reasonable period of time.

_____ 17. When the auditor concludes that there is doubt as to the entity's ability to continue as a going concern, the audit report should not contain an unqualified opinion.

_____ 18. When the auditor wishes to emphasize a matter, a four paragraph report and an unqualified opinion should result.

_____ 19. When reference is made to another auditor in the audit report, it is necessary to add one or more explanatory paragraphs.

_____ 20. Reference to the report of another auditor in the opinion paragraph does not result in a qualified opinion.

_____ 21. When the auditor is not independent, a one paragraph report should be issued with a disclaimer of opinion.

_____ 22. When the auditor expresses different opinions on comparative financial statements, the report should have two opinion paragraphs.

_____ 23. When there has been a change of auditors for comparative financial statements, the change should be indicated in the scope paragraph of the audit report.

_____ 24. The auditor is required to apply auditing procedures to supplemental information required by the FASB and GASB.

_____ 25. In reporting on financial statements prepared for use in the U.S. and other countries, the U.S. auditor must use the U.S.-style audit report.

D. COMPLETION STATEMENTS

Fill in the blanks with the word or words that correctly complete the following statements.

1. The sources of established accounting principles include those promulgated by a body designated by the _____ under Rule 203 of the AICPA _____.

2. The fourth reporting standard requires either the expression of an _____ on the financial statements taken as a _____ or an _____ to the effect that an overall opinion cannot be expressed.

3. The auditor's standard report contains three paragraphs identified, respectively, as the _____, _____, and _____ paragraphs.

4. When another type of opinion is expressed, the audit report should contain explanatory language _____ the opinion paragraph and _____ should be made to the language in the opinion paragraph.

5. When other than an unqualified opinion is expressed because of a scope limitation, the auditor may express either a _____ opinion or a _____ opinion.

6. Generally, when there is nonconformity with GAAP, the auditor is required to issue a _____ paragraph report and to express either a _____ or _____ opinion.

7. A change in accounting principles is in conformity with GAAP when the new principle is a _____, the change is properly _____ in the financial statements, and management can justify that the new principle is _____.

8. When there is inadequate disclosure, the auditor should express either a _____ or _____ opinion because of nonconformity with _____.

9. Uncertainties will result in expressing other than an unqualified opinion when there is either a _____ or _____.

10. When the principle auditor makes reference to another auditor in the audit report, the auditor should indicate the magnitude of the work done by the _____ in the _____ paragraph of the report.

11. When the auditor's current audit produces evidence requiring a change of opinion in a prior year's report, the different opinion should be indicated in an _____ paragraph of the current year's report positioned _____ the opinion paragraph.

12. When there has been a change in auditors during the periods covered by comparative statements and the predecessor's report is not presented, the _____ should state the change in the (an) _____ paragraph of the current audit report.

13. For required supplementary information, the auditor is required to apply certain _____ to the information and to report any deficiencies in such information in an (the) _____ paragraph in the audit report.

14. When an auditor is not independent, his or her report should contain a _____ opinion and should not describe any _____ performed.

15. In reporting on financial statements to be used only outside the U.S., the auditor may use either the _____ audit report modified for the accounting principles of the other country or the _____ of the other country.

E. MULTIPLE CHOICE

Choose the best answer for each of the following questions and enter the identifying letter in the space provided.

_____ 1. In which of the following situations would an auditor ordinarily issue an unqualified audit opinion without an explanatory paragraph?
a. The auditor wishes to emphasize that the entity had significant related party transactions.
b. The auditor decides to make reference to the report of another auditor as a basis, in part, for the auditor's opinion.
c. The entity issues financial statements that present financial position and results of operations, but omits the statement of cash flows.
d. The auditor has substantial doubt about the entity's ability to continue as a going concern, but the circumstances are fully disclosed in the financial statements.

_____ 2. When there has been a change in accounting principle that materially affects the comparability of the comparative financial statements presented and the auditor concurs with the change, the auditor should:

	Concur explicitly with the change	Issue an "expect for" qualified opinion	Refer to the change in an explanatory paragraph
a.	No	No	Yes
b.	Yes	No	Yes
c.	Yes	Yes	No
d.	No	Yes	No

_____ 3. An auditor most likely would issue a disclaimer of opinion because of:
   a. Inadequate disclosure of material information.
   b. The omission of the statement of cash flows.
   c. A material departure from generally accepted accounting principles.
   d. Management's refusal to furnish written representations.

_____ 4. The financial statements of KCP America, a U.S. entity, are prepared for inclusion in the consolidated financial statements of its non-U.S. parent. These financial statements are prepared in conformity with the accounting principles generally accepted in the parent's country, and are for use only in that country. How may KCP America's auditor report on these financial statements?
   I. A U.S.-style report (unmodified).
   II. A U.S.-style report modified to report on the accounting principes of the parent's country.
   III. The report form of the parent's country.

	I	II	III
a.	Yes	No	No
b.	No	Yes	No
c.	Yes	No	Yes
d.	No	Yes	Yes

_____ 5. When an auditor qualifies an opinion because of the inability to confirm accounts receivable by direct communication with debtors, the wording of the opinion paragraph of the auditor's report should indicate that the qualification pertains to the:
   a. Limitation on the auditor's scope.
   b. Possible effects on the financial statements.
   c. Lack of sufficient competent evidential matter.
   d. Departure from generally accepted auditing standards.

_____ 6. When an auditor qualifies an opinion because of inadequate disclosure, the auditor should describe the nature of the omission in a separate explanatory paragraph and modify the:

	Introductory Paragraph	Scope Paragraph	Opinion Paragraph
a.	Yes	No	No
b.	Yes	Yes	No
c.	No	Yes	Yes
d.	No	No	Yes

_____ 7. An auditor includes a separate paragraph in an otherwise unmodified report to emphasize that the entity being reported upon had significant transactions with related parties. The inclusion of this separate paragraph:
   a. Is appropriate and would not negate the unqualified opinion.
   b. Is considered an "except for" qualification of the opinion.
   c. Violates generally accepted auditing standards if this information is already disclosed in footnotes to the financial statements.
   d. Necessitates a revision of the opinion paragraph to include the phrase "With the foregoing explanation."

_____ 8. The adverse affects of events causing an auditor to believe there is substantial doubt about an entity's ability to continue as a going concern would most likely be mitigated by evidence relating to the:
a. Ability to expand operations into new product lines in the future.
b. Feasibility of plans to purchase leased equipment at less than market value.
c. Marketability of assets that management plans to sell.
d. Committed arrangements to convert preferred stock to long-term debt.

_____ 9. If an auditor is satisfied that there is only a remote likelihood of a loss resulting from the resolution of a matter involving an uncertainty, the auditor should express a(an):
a. Unqualified opinion.
b. Unqualified opinion with a separate explanatory paragraph.
c. Qualified opinion or disclaimer of opinion, depending upon the materiality of the loss.
d. Qualified opinion or disclaimer of opinion, depending on whether the uncertainty is adequately disclosed.

_____ 10. Tech Company has disclosed an uncertainty due to pending litigation. The auditor's decision to issue a qualified opinion rather than an unqualified opinion with an explanatory paragraph most likely would be determined by the:
a. Lack of sufficient evidence.
b. Inability to estimate the amount of loss
c. Entity's lack of experience with such litigation.
d. Lack of insurance coverage for possible losses from such litigation.

_____ 11. An auditor may not issue a qualified opinion when:
a. A scope limitation prevents the auditor from completing an important audit procedure.
b. The auditor's report refers to the work of a specialist.
c. An accounting principle at variance with generally accepted accounting principles is used.
d. The auditor lacks independence with respect to the audited entity.

_____ 12. An explanatory paragraph following the opinion paragraph of an auditor's report describes an uncertainty as follows:
As discussed in Note X to the financial statements, the Company is a defendant in a lawsuit alleging infringement of certain patent rights and claiming damages. Discovery proceedings are in progress. The ultimate outcome of the litigation cannot presently be determined. Accordingly, no provision for any liability that may result upon adjudication has been made in the accompanying financial statements.

What type of opinion should the auditor express under these circumstances?

a. Unqualified.
b. "Subject to" qualified.
c. "Except for" qualified.
d. Disclaimer.

_____ 13. When issuing the standard auditor's report on comparative financial statements, does an auditor make the following representations explicitly or implicitly?

	Consistent Application of Accounting Principles	Examination of Evidence on a Test Basis
a.	Explicitly	Explicitly
b.	Implicitly	Implicitly
c.	Implicitly	Explicitly
d.	Explicitly	Implicitly

_____ 14. An auditor who qualifies an opinion because of an insufficiency of evidential matter should describe the limitation in an explanatory paragraph. The auditor should also refer to the limitation in the:

	Scope Paragraph	Opinion Paragraph	Notes to the Financial Statements
a.	Yes	No	Yes
b.	No	Yes	No
c.	Yes	Yes	No
d.	Yes	Yes	Yes

_____ 15. Eagle Company's financial statements contain a departure from generally accepted accounting principles because, due to unusual circumstances, the statements would otherwise be misleading. The auditor should express an opinion that is
a. Unqualified but not mention the departure in the auditor's report.
b. Unqualified and describe the departure in a separate paragraph.
c. Qualified and describe the departure in a separate paragraph.
d. Qualified or adverse, depending on materiality, and describe the departure in a separate paragraph.

_____ 16. If a publicly-held entity declines to include in its financial report supplementary information required by the FASB, the auditor should issue:
a. An unqualified opinion with a separate explanatory paragraph.
b. Either a disclaimer of opinion or an adverse opinion.
c. Either a qualified opinion or a disclaimer of opinion.
d. Either an adverse opinion or a qualified opinion.

_____ 17. Comparative financial statements include the financial statements of a prior period that were examined by a predecessor auditor whose report is not presented. If the predecessor auditor's report was qualified, the successor auditor must:
a. Obtain written approval from the predecessor auditor to include the prior year's financial statements.
b. Issue a standard comparative audit report indicating the division of responsibility.
c. Express an opinion on the current year statements alone and make no reference to the prior year statements.
d. Disclose the reasons for any qualification in the predecessor auditor's opinion.

_____ 18. When the financial statements contain a departure from generally accepted accounting principles, the effect of which is material, the auditor should:
  a. Qualify the opinion and explain the effect of the departure from generally accepted accounting principles in an explanatory paragraph.
  b. Qualify the opinion and describe the departure from generally accepted accounting principles within the opinion paragraph.
  c. Disclaim an opinion and explain the effect of the departure from generally accepted accounting principles in an explanatory paragraph.
  d. Disclaim an opinion and describe the departure from generally accepted accounting principles within the opinion paragraph.

_____ 19. The principal auditor is satisfied with the independence and professional reputation of the other auditor who has audited a subsidiary but wants to indicate the division of responsibility. The principal auditor should modify:
  a. Only the scope paragraph of the report.
  b. Only the introductory and scope paragraphs.
  c. Only the scope and opinion paragraphs of the report.
  d. Each of the paragraphs of the standard report.

_____ 20. Which of the following statements is correct regarding the auditor's responsibilities for supplementary information required by the FASB?
  a. Because the supplementary information is a required part of the basic financial statements, the auditor should apply normal auditing procedures.
  b. The omission of, but not deficiencies in, supplementary information should be disclosed in the opinion paragraph of the auditor's report.
  c. Because the supplementary information is not a required part of the basic financial statements, the auditor should apply only certain limited procedures.
  d. The omission of supplementary information ordinarily requires the auditor to issue an adverse opinion, but mere deficiencies require a qualified opinion.

SOLUTIONS

TRUE OR FALSE STATEMENTS

1. True	10. False	18. True
2. True	11. False	19. False
3. False	12. False	20. True
4. False	13. True	21. True
5. True	14. True	22. True
6. False	15. True	23. False
7. False	16. True	24. False
8. True	17. False	25. True
9. False		

COMPLETION STATEMENTS

1. AICPA Council, Code of Professional Conduct
2. opinion, whole, assertion
3. introductory, scope, opinion
4. before, reference
5. qualified, disclaimer of
6. four, qualified, adverse
7. general accepted accounting principle, accounted for and disclosed, preferable
8. qualified, adverse, GAAP
9. scope limitation, nonconformity with GAAP
10. other auditor, introductory
11. explanatory, before
12. successor auditor, introductory
13. limited procedures, explanatory
14. disclaimer of, auditing procedures
15. U.S.-style, standard report

MULTIPLE CHOICE QUESTIONS

1. b	5. b	9. a	13. c	17. d
2. a	6. d	10. a	14. c	18. a
3. d	7. a	11. d	15. b	19. d
4. d	8. c	12. a	16. a	20. c

Chapter 21

Other Services and Reports

A. CHAPTER OUTLINE

  I. Accepting and Performing Attest Engagements

    A. Attestation Standards

    B. Types of Attest Engagements

    C. Levels of Assurance and Attestation Risk

    D. Report Distribution

  II. Special Reports

    A. Other Comprehensive Bases of Accounting

    B. Specified Elements, Accounts, or Items of a Financial Statement

      1. Audit

      2. Agreed-upon Procedures

    C. Compliance Reports Related to Audited Financial Statements

  III. Review Services

    A. SAS 71 Review of Interim Financial Information

      1. Additional Requirements in SAS 71 Reviews

      2. Accountant's Report on SAS 71 Review of IFI

    B. SSARS Review of Financial Statements

      1. Accountant's Report on SSARS Review of Financial Statements

  IV. Other Attest Services

    A. Reporting on Internal Control

      1. Reporting on Management's Written Assertion about the Effectiveness of an Entity's ICS over Financial Reporting

      2. Reporting on the ICS over the Processing of Transactions by Service Organizations

      B. Reporting on Prospective Financial Information

          1. Types of Prospective Financial Information

          2. Examination of Prospective Financial Statements

          3. Applying Agreed-upon Procedures

      C. Compliance Attestation

          1. Agreed-upon Procedures Engagements

          2. Examination Engagements

      D. Summary of Attest Services

  V. Nonattest Accounting Services

      A. Unaudited Financial Statements of a Public Entity

      B. Compilation of Financial Statements of a Nonpublic Entity

          1. Objective and Nature

          2. Accountant's Report on Compilation

      C. Compilation of Prospective Financial Statements

      D. Reporting on the Application of Accounting Principles

      E. Change of Engagement

VI. Summary

B. CHAPTER HIGHLIGHTS

1. An **attest engagement** is one in which a practitioner (CPA) is engaged to issue or does issue a **written communication** that expresses a **conclusion** about the reliability of a **written assertion** that is the responsibility of another party.

2. There are eleven **attestation standards** grouped into three categories: general, field work, and reporting. There are three significant conceptual differences between these standards and GAAS. Attestation standards:
   a. Extend the attest function beyond historical financial statements.
   b. Allow the CPA to give assurances on assertions below the level expressed in the traditional financial statement audit.
   c. Provide for attest services tailored to the needs of specific users and for "limited-use" reports.

3. **Four types of attest engagements** are recognized in the professional standards, i.e., Statements on Standards for Attestation Engagements **(SSAE's)**:
   a. Audit
   b. Examination
   c. Review
   d. Agreed-upon procedures

4. A CPA may express **three types of assurance** in attest engagements:
   a. Positive assurance on the basis of an audit or examination of an assertion.
   b. Negative assurance on the basis of a review of an assertion.
   c. A summary of findings on the basis of applying agreed-upon procedures to an assertion.

5. The effect of the type of assurance on the **distribution of the report** is:
   a. Positive assurance - unrestricted distribution.
   b. Negative assurance - restricted or unrestricted distribution.
   c. Summary of findings - restricted distribution.

6. The term **special reports** applies to auditor's reports issued in connection with:
   a. Financial statements that are prepared in conformity with a comprehensive basis of accounting other than generally accepted accounting principles.
   b. Specified elements, accounts, or items of a financial statement.
   c. Compliance with aspects of contractual agreements or regulatory requirements related to audited financial statements.
   d. Financial presentations to comply with contractual agreements or regulatory provisions.
   e. Financial information presented in prescribed forms or schedules that require a prescribed form of auditor's report.

7. The CPA's **responsibilities for engagements** resulting in the issuance of special reports are currently contained in Statements on Auditing Standards since they are either based on an audit or pertain to services for which a SAS was issued prior to the SSARSs.

8. Besides GAAP, each of the following is recognized as an **other comprehensive basis of accounting (OCBOA)**:
   a. A basis used to comply with the requirements or financial reporting provisions of a governmental regulatory agency.
   b. A basis used to file the entity's income tax return.
   c. The cash receipts and disbursements basis of accounting and modifications of the cash basis having substantial support.
   d. A basis that uses a definite set of criteria that has substantial support such as the price-level basis of accounting.

9. **All GAAS apply** whenever the auditor examines and reports on any financial statement prepared on an OCBOA. The auditor's report should include four paragraphs:
   a. An introductory paragraph that is the same as in the auditor's standard report except that more distinctive titles should be used for the financial statements, such as statement of assets and liabilities arising from cash transactions.
   b. A scope paragraph that is the same as in the auditor's standard report.
   c. An explanatory paragraph following the scope paragraph that states the basis of presentation and refers to the note to the financial statements that describes the comprehensive basis of accounting other than GAAP.
   d. An opinion paragraph that expresses the auditor's opinion (or disclaims an opinion) on whether the financial statements are presented fairly, in all material respects, in conformity with the basis of accounting described.

10. An auditor may report on **specified elements, accounts, or items of a financial statement** when he or she has been engaged to **audit** the data or to apply **agreed-upon procedures** to the data.
    a. All GAAS are applicable when the specified data are presented in conformity with GAAP or an OCBOA- otherwise, the first reporting standard is not applicable.
    b. An engagement to express an opinion on specified data may be made in conjunction with a financial statement audit or in a separate engagement.
    c. Distinctive wording is required in the auditor's report on specific items because the auditor is not reporting on financial statements taken as a whole.
    d. The report based on applying agreed-upon procedures should include (1) a summary of findings, (2) a disclaimer of opinion on the specified data, and (3) a limitation on the distribution of the report.

11. **Compliance reports related to audited financial statements** may be issued either as a separate report or in one or more explanatory paragraphs added to the auditor's report on the financial statements. In either case, the auditor expresses negative assurance on compliance and distribution of the report is limited. Examples of this type of engagement include debt covenant compliance, and regulatory compliance.

12. A **review service** involves the application of **limited procedures** to financial information or statements to provide **limited assurance** that no material modifications to the information are needed to comply with GAAP. The term **independent accountant**, rather than independent auditor, is used to describe the CPA's association. **Two types of review services exist:**
    a. **SAS 71**- Reviews of interim financial information (IFI) that is (1) for a public entity, either presented alone or in conjunction with audited financial statements, or (2) included in a note to audited financial statements for either a public or nonpublic entity.
    b. **SSARS** - Reviews of financial statements of nonpublic entities as well as annual or interim statements for public entities whose statements are not audited.

13. A review service differs significantly from an audit. It is generally **limited to inquiry and analytical procedures.** In this type of service, the accountant is expected to:
    a. Possess (or acquire) an adequate level of knowledge of the accounting principles and practices of the industry in which the entity operates, and
    b. Have (or obtain) an understanding of the entity's business (i.e., organization, operating characteristics, nature of assets, liabilities, revenues and expenses).

14. **Limited procedures** common to both types of review engagements are:
    a. Certain prescribed inquiries of management about the entity's accounting principles and practices (and any changes thereto).
    b. Performing analytical procedures to identify relationships and items appearing unusual.
    c. Obtaining information about actions taken at stockholders' or board of directors' meetings.
    d. Reading the information for compliance with GAAP.
    e. Obtaining written representations from management.

15. SAS 71 reviews deal with IFI for less than a year or for a twelve-month period that ends on other than the entity's fiscal year end. The **major impetus** for these reviews is the **SEC's requirement for footnote disclosure** (in conjunction with a 10-K filing) of two years of IFI. While the information is labeled "unaudited," it must be subjected to a SAS 71 review. The review may be done **timely** (in conjunction with 10-Q filings) **or concurrently** with the year end audit.

16. **Additional requirements** of SAS 71 reviews include:
    a. Developing an understanding of the internal control structure, since these reviews are only done in conjunction with audits.
    b. Reading (rather than inquiring about) the minutes of stockholder or board of directors meetings.

17. Should the accountant conclude that the **IFI is materially misstated** due to a departure from GAAP, the accountant should communicate with the audit committee. If the audit committee does not respond appropriately within a reasonable time, the accountant should consider withdrawing from the IFI engagement, the audit, or both.

18. The **accountant's report on a SAS 71 review of IFI** should contain the following elements:
    a. A statement that the review was made in accordance with the standards for such reviews.
    b. An identification of the IFI reviewed.
    c. A description of the procedures for a review of IFI.
    d. A statement that a review is significantly less in scope than an audit in accordance with GAAS and, accordingly, no opinion (i.e., a disclaimer) is expressed.
    e. A statement as to whether the accountant is aware of any material modifications that should be made to the information to make it conform with GAAP (negative assurance).

19. **A SSARS review** was developed as a lower cost and lower assurance alternative to an audit. These services differ from SAS 71 reviews in that they do not require an understanding of the ICS to develop review procedures and to identify potential misstatements. The accountant's report is essentially identical to a SAS 71 report, except the reference to standards (i.e., SSARS) is included in the introductory paragraph rather than the scope paragraph. To avoid confusion about the level of accountant involvement, each page of the reviewed statements should be labeled "see accountant's review report."

20. In **reporting on an entity's internal control**, a CPA may accept an attest engagement to:
    a. Report on management's written assertion about the effectiveness of the entity's internal control structure (ICS) over financial reporting, or
    b. Report on the ICS over the processing of transactions for service organizations.

21. With regard to the effectiveness of the ICS over financial reporting, the **following aspects of the ICS** should be considered:
    a. Design and operating effectiveness of the overall ICS.
    b. Design and operating effectiveness of a segment of the ICS.
    c. Suitability of the design of the ICS only.
    d. Design and operating effectiveness of the ICS based on regulatory criteria.

22. In addition to performing examinations of the ICS, the **accountant may perform more limited agreed-upon procedures**, but SSAE 2 **prohibits review** or other negative assurance engagements.

23. An independent accountant **should perform ICS engagements only when management**:
    a. Accepts responsibility for the effectiveness of the ICS.
    b. Evaluates the effectiveness of the ICS using reasonable criteria established by a recognized body.
    c. Refers to those criteria in a report containing its written assertion.

24. When engaged to express an opinion on the ICS, the **methodologies are similar to those in performing a financial statement audit**. However **tests of controls must be performed on all significant assertions** (not just those relied upon in a lower assessed control risk approach). In addition, the CPA should obtain a written representation from management concerning its responsibility for the ICS.

25. The **CPA's report** on an engagement to express an opinion on the ICS should include (a) a description of the scope of the engagement, (b) the date to which the opinion relates, (c) a statement about management's responsibility for establishing and maintaining the ICS, (d) a brief explanation of the broad objectives and inherent limitations of the ICS, and (e) the CPA's opinion on whether the ICS taken as a whole meets the criteria of internal control as established in COSO's *Internal Control-Integrated Framework.*

26. A **report on the ICS of a data processing service organization** may extend to (a) a report on just the policies and procedures placed in operation, or to (b) a report on the policies and procedures placed in operation and tests of operating effectiveness. This report is then provided to the service organization's customers who use the service organization as part of their own ICS.

27. **Prospective financial statements** may be based on a financial forecast or a financial projection. A financial forecast is based on conditions expected to exist (i.e., the most likely assumption) and the course of action expected to be taken. A financial projection involves one or more hypothetical assumptions and courses of action.

28. A CPA may perform **three types of services** pertaining to prospective financial statements when third party use is anticipated:
    a. Compilation (preparation - no assurance given),
    b. Examination (positive assurance given on conformance with AICPA guidelines),
    c. Application of agreed-upon procedures (negative assurance or summary of findings given).

29. An engagement to perform services in regard to **compliance with specified requirements** (i.e., laws, regulations, contracts, or grants) may be financial or nonfinancial in nature and may take the form of (a) agreed-upon procedures, or (b) examinations (i.e., positive assurance opinion on compliance in accordance with SSAE 3's guidelines for such engagements).

30. **Agreed-upon procedure engagements** may focus on management's written assertions about (a) compliance with the requirements, (b) the effectiveness of internal controls over compliance, or (c) both.

31. **Nonattest accounting services** include engagements to (a) prepare a working trial balance, (b) assist in adjusting the books of account, (c) prepare tax returns, and (d) provide manual or automated bookkeeping or data processing services.

32. An accountant is **associated with financial statements** when he or she (a) consents to the use of his or her name in a report, document, or written communication containing the statements, or (b) submits to clients or others financial statements that he or she has prepared or assisted in preparing.

33. When **associated with the unaudited financial statements of a public entity**, accountants are not required to perform any auditing procedures. However, the report must state that an audit was not made and include a disclaimer of opinion. Also, each page of the financial statements should be marked "unaudited". However if the CPA knows from experience or through the work done that the statements are not in conformity with GAAP, the accountant should request the client to make the necessary revisions. If the client refuses, the CPA

should describe the known departures in the report in addition to the disclaimer, (i.e., a "modified disclaimer"), or, if necessary, withdraw from the engagement.

34. Preparing, or assisting in preparing, financial statements for a nonpublic entity is referred to as a **compilation engagement.** In this type of engagement, a clear engagement letter stating the limited nature of the engagement is imperative. The accountant is expected to be knowledgeable about the client and the accounting principles and practices of the industry in which it operates. The CPA is not required to verify information furnished by the client.

35. Upon reading the compiled statements to determine that they are appropriate in form and free from obvious material errors, the accountant should issue a **report** that states:
    a. A compilation has been performed in accordance with standards established by the AICPA.
    b. A compilation is limited to presenting in the form of financial statements information that is the representation of management (owners).
    c. The statements have not been audited or reviewed, and, accordingly, no opinion or any other form of assurance on them is expressed.

    In addition, to avoid confusion over the scope of services, each page of the financial statements should include a reference such as "See Accountant's Compilation Report."

36. **Modifications of the standard report** on a compilation are required when (a) the financial statements are not in conformity with GAAP, (b) the statements omit substantially all disclosures, or (c) the CPA is not independent of the client. The modifications in (a) and (b) take the form of an explanatory paragraph following the disclaimer paragraph stating the departure and that such items may be useful to informed readers of the statements.

37. **Compilations of prospective financial statements** involve:
    a. Assembling the statements based on management's assumptions.
    b. Performing required compilation procedures, including reading the statements and accompanying summaries to ensure that the statements are (a) in conformity with AICPA Guidelines and (b) not obviously inappropriate.
    c. Issuing a report that:
       • Identifies the statements presented.
       • States that the compiled statements comply with the AICPA standards.
       • States the limitation in scope of the compilation.
       • Gives the caveat that prospective results may not be achieved.
       • States that the accountant assumes no responsibility for updating the report.

38. A CPA may issue an oral or written report on the **application of accounting principles** when consulted about (a) the proper application of accounting principles to completed or proposed transactions and (b) the type of opinion that may be rendered on any entity's financial statements in connection with the application of accounting principles.

39. A **change of engagement** is a "step up" when it results in a higher level or assurance than originally agreed to (e.g., a change from a compilation to a review or a review to an audit). It is a "step down" when a lower level of assurance is requested. The latter is precluded when the client has imposed restrictions on the CPA's work at a higher level of assurance.

C. TRUE OR FALSE STATEMENTS

Indicate in the space provided whether each of the following statements is true or false.

_____ 1. Statements on Standards for Attestation Engagements (SSAEs) are the joint responsibility of the Auditing Standards Board and the Accounting and Review Services Committee.

_____ 2. The categories of attestation standards are general, field work, and reporting.

_____ 3. Positive assurance results in a conclusion by the CPA that nothing came to his or her attention that the assertions were not presented in conformity with the criteria.

_____ 4. A negative assurance or a summary of findings should only be given when attestation risk as at a low level.

_____ 5. When negative assurance is given on the basis of a review service, the distribution of the report may be general or limited depending on the nature of the assertions.

_____ 6. A CPA's association with special reports may involve two types of attest service: audit or review.

_____ 7. A standard report on financial statements prepared on a comprehensive basis of accounting other than GAAP contains three paragraphs.

_____ 8. All GAAS apply when the auditor audits and reports on financial statements prepared on an OCBOA.

_____ 9. An engagement to express an opinion on specified elements, accounts, or items of a financial statement may involve an audit or the application of agreed-upon procedures.

_____ 10. Compliance reports related to audited financial statements may be given in a separate report or in one or more explanatory paragraphs following the opinion paragraph of the auditor's report on the audited financial statements.

_____ 11. To express an opinion on an entity's internal control structure, it generally will be necessary for the auditor to expand the scope of the study beyond that involved in complying with the second standard of field work in a financial statement audit.

_____ 12. In an engagement based on preestablished requirements, the CPA's report may express positive assurance but it must also indicate it is intended for limited distribution.

_____ 13. A report on the internal control structure of a service organization may contain either a report on the policies and procedures placed in operation or on the effectiveness of these procedures, or both.

_____ 14. A financial forecast differs from a financial projection in terms of assumptions and the expected course of action.

_____ 15. A CPA may not express positive assurance based on an examination of prospective financial statements.

_____ 16. In a SAS 71 review of interim financial information (IFI) of a public entity, the report provides positive assurance on whether the information conforms with GAAP.

_____ 17. The accountant's report on a SSARS review of financial statements should contain a statement that a review is significantly less in scope than an audit in accordance with GAAS.

_____ 18. A review of the financial statements of a nonpublic entity consists principally of analytical procedures applied to financial data and obtaining a management representation letter.

_____ 19. An accounting service does not result in expressing any kind of assurance but the accountant does have to be independent in performing such services.

_____ 20. When the CPA is associated with the unaudited financial statements of a public company that are not in conformity with GAAP, he or she should express either a qualified opinion or an adverse opinion.

_____ 21. In performing a compilation service the CPA is not required to verify the information furnished by the client.

_____ 22. When a CPA is not independent of a client, the report on compiled financial statements need not mention the CPA's lack of independence.

_____ 23. When there has been no misunderstanding concerning the original engagement, a CPA may accept a request from the client to "step up" to a higher level of assurance or "step down" to a lower level of assurance.

_____ 24. A CPA's report on a compilation of prospective financial statements should include a caveat that the prospective results may not be achieved.

_____ 25. When a client consults a CPA about the proper application of accounting principles to hypothetical transactions, the CPA's conclusions must be expressed in writing.

D. COMPLETION STATEMENTS

Fill in the blanks with the word or words that correctly complete the following statements.

1. There are eleven attestation standards consisting of _____ standards, _____ standards, and _____ standards.

2. The three levels of assurance that may be expressed in attestation engagements are _____, _____, and _____.

3. A special report on financial statements prepared on an OCBOA should contain _____ paragraphs and an opinion as to whether the financial statements are fairly presented in conformity with the _____.

4. An auditor may report on specified elements, accounts, or items of a financial statement when he or she has been engaged to _____ the data or to apply _____.

5. The accountant's report on an engagement to express an opinion on an entity's internal control structure (ICS) for financial statements should contain an opinion on whether the ICS taken was sufficient to meet the _____ of internal control established by _____.

6. A CPA's report on an internal control engagement based on preestablished criteria should indicate whether the study included _____ on the procedures covered by the study, and describe the _____ of internal control.

7. Reports on the ICS of service organizations are used as a part of the _____ control systems and are relied upon by _____, but no _____ should be made to the service auditor's report.

8. Two types of prospective financial information are _____ and _____.

9. SAS 71 reviews of interim financial information for a public entity may be done on a _____ basis or done _____ with the year end audit.

10. The report on a review of the financial statements of a nonpublic entity should state that the review is substantially less in _____ than an audit in accordance with _____.

11. A report on the unaudited financial statements of a public company should include a _____ of opinion, and each page of the financial statements should be marked _____ .

12. The report on a compilation of historical financial statements should conclude with a statement that the accountant does not _____ or any other form of _____ on the compiled statements.

13. Departures from the standard report in a compilation engagement are required when the financial statements either are not in _____ or omit substantially _____ , or the CPA is not _____ .

14. A CPA is prohibited from agreeing to a "step-down" change when the client has _____ on the CPA's work at the _____ .

15. An accountant's report on the application of accounting principles should include a statement that the responsibility for the proper accounting treatment rests with the _____ of the financial statements, who should consult with their _____ .

E. MULTIPLE CHOICE

Choose the best answer for each of the following questions and enter the identifying letter in the space provided.

_____ 1. Which of the following professional services would be considered an attest engagement?
a. A management consulting engagement to provide EDP advice to a client.
b. An engagement to report on compliance with statutory requirements.
c. An income tax engagement to prepare federal and state tax returns.
d. The compilation of financial statements from a client's accounting records.

_____ 2. An auditor's report issued in connection with which of the following is generally not considered to be a special report?
a. Compliance with aspects of contractual agreements unrelated to audited financial statements.
b. Specified elements, accounts, or items of a financial statement presented in a document.
c. Financial statements prepared in accordance with an entity's income tax basis.
d. Financial information presented in a prescribed schedule that require a prescribed form of auditor's report.

_____ 3. When an auditor conducts an audit in accordance with generally accepted auditing standards and concludes that the financial statements are fairly presented in accordance with a comprehensive basis of accounting other than generally accepted accounting principles such as the cash basis of accounting, the auditor should issue a:
a. Disclaimer of opinion.
b. Review report.
c. Qualified opinion.
d. Special report.

_____ 4. If the auditor believes that financial statements prepared on the entity's income tax basis are not suitably titled, the auditor should:
a. Issue a disclaimer of opinion.
b. Explain in the notes to the financial statements the terminology used.
c. Issue a compilation report.
d. Modify the auditor's report to disclose any reservations.

_____ 5. An accountant may accept an engagement to apply agreed-upon procedures that are not sufficient to express an opinion on one or more specified accounts or items of a financial statement provided that:
a. The accountant's report does not enumerate the procedures performed.

b. The financial statements are prepared in accordance with a comprehensive basis of accounting other than generally accepted accounting principles.

c. Distribution of the accountant's report is restricted.

d. The accountant is also the entity's continuing auditor.

_____ 6. The accountant's report expressing an opinion on an entity's internal control structure should state that the:

a. Establishment and maintenance of the internal control structure are the responsibility of management.

b. Objectives of the client's internal control structure are being met.

c. Study and evaluation of the internal control structure was conducted in accordance with generally accepted auditing standards.

d. Inherent limitations of the client's internal control structure were examined.

_____ 7. When an independent auditor reports on internal control based on criteria established by governmental agencies, the report should:

a. Not include the agency's name in the report.

b. Indicate matters covered by the study and whether the auditor's study included tests of controls with the procedures covered by the study.

c. Not express a conclusion based on the agency's criteria.

d. Assume responsibility for the comprehensiveness of the criteria established by the agency and include recommendations for corrective action.

_____ 8. When providing limited assurance that the financial statements of a nonpublic entity require no material modifications to be in accordance with generally accepted accounting principles, the accountant should:

a. Understand the internal control structure that the entity uses.

b. Test the accounting records that identify inconsistencies with the prior year's financial statements.

c. Understand the accounting principles of the industry in which the entity operates.

d. Develop audit programs to determine whether the entity's financial statements are fairly presented.

_____ 9. Which of the following procedures is not usually performed by the accountant in a review engagement of a nonpublic entity?

a. Communicating any material weaknesses discovered during the study and evaluation of internal control.

b. Reading the financial statements to consider whether they conform with generally accepted accounting principles.

c. Writing an engagement letter to establish an understanding regarding the services to be performed.

d. Issuing a report stating that the review was performed in accordance with standards established by the AICPA.

_____ 10. Performing inquiry and analytical procedures is the primary basis for an accountant to issue a:

a. Report on compliance with requirements governing major federal assistance programs in accordance with the Single Audit Act.

b. Review report on prospective financial statements that present an entity's expected financial position.
c. Management advisory report prepared at the request of a client's audit committee.
d. Review report on comparative financial statements for a nonpublic entity in its second year of operation.

_____ 11. Each page of a nonpublic entity's financial statements reviewed by an accountant should include the following reference:
a. See Accountant's Review Report.
b. Reviewed. No Accountant's Assurance Expressed.
c. See Accountant's Footnotes.
d. Reviewed. No Material Modifications Required.

_____ 12. Given one or more hypothetical assumptions, a responsible party may prepare, to the best of its knowledge and belief, an entity's expected financial position, results of operations, and cash flows. Such prospective financial statements are known as:
a. Pro forma financial statements.
b. Financial projections.
c. Partial presentations.
d. Financial forecasts.

_____ 13. Prospective financial information presented in the format of historical financial statements that omit either gross profit or net income is deemed to be a:
a. Partial presentation.
b. Projected balance sheet.
c. Financial forecast.
d. Financial projection.

_____ 14. An accountant should not submit unaudited financial statements to the management of a nonpublic company unless, at a minimum, the accountant:
a. Assists in adjusting the books of account and prepares the trial balance.
b. Types or reproduces the financial statements on plain paper.
c. Complies with the standards applicable to compilation engagements.
d. Applies analytical procedures to the financial statements.

_____ 15. Financial statements compiled without audit or review by an accountant should be accompanied by a report stating that:
a. The financial statements have not been audited or reviewed and, accordingly, the accountant expresses only limited assurance on them.
b. A compilation is limited to presenting in the form of financial statements information that is the representation of management.
c. The accountant is not aware of any material modifications that should be made to the financial statements for them to conform with generally accepted accounting principles.
d. A compilation is less in scope than a review, and substantially less in scope than an audit in accordance with generally accepted auditing standards.

_____ 16. When compiling a nonpublic entity's financial statements, an accountant would be least likely to:
   a. Perform analytical procedures designed to identify relationships that appear to be unusual.
   b. Read the compiled financial statements and consider whether they appear to include adequate disclosure.
   c. Omit substantially all of the disclosures required by generally accepted accounting principles.
   d. Issue a compilation report on one or more, but not all, of the basic financial statements.

_____ 17. Prior to commencing the compilation of financial statements of a nonpublic entity, the accountant should:
   a. Perform analytical procedures sufficient to determine whether fluctuations among account balances appear reasonable.
   b. Complete the study and evaluation of the entity's internal control structure.
   c. Verify that the financial information supplied by the entity agrees with the books of original entry.
   d. Acquire a knowledge of any specialized accounting principles and practices used in the entity's industry.

_____ 18. When an independent CPA is associated with the financial statements of a publicly held entity but has not audited or reviewed such statements, the appropriate form of report to be issued must include a(an):
   a. Disclaimer of opinion.
   b. Compilation report.
   c. Adverse opinion.
   d. Unaudited association report.

_____ 19. A report based on a SAS 71 review of interim financial information would include all of the following elements except:
   a. A statement that an audit was performed in accordance with generally accepted auditing standards.
   b. A description of the procedures performed or a reference to the procedures described in an engagement letter.
   c. A statement that a limited review would not necessarily disclose all matters of significance.
   d. An identification of the interim financial information reviewed.

_____ 20. An accountant's standard report on a compilation of a projection should not include a:
   a. Statement that the accountant expresses only limited assurance that the results may be achieved.
   b. Separate paragraph that describes the limitations on the presentation's usefulness.
   c. Statement that a compilation of a projection is limited in scope.
   d. Disclaimer of responsibility to update the report for events occurring after the report's date.

SOLUTIONS

TRUE OR FALSE STATEMENTS

1. True		10. True		18. False
2. True		11. True		19. False
3. False		12. True		20. False
4. True		13. True		21. True
5. True		14. True		22. False
6. False		15. False		23. True
7. False		16. False		24. True
8. True		17. True		25. False
9. True				

COMPLETION STATEMENTS

1. general, field work, reporting
2. positive assurance, negative assurance, summary of findings
3. four, basis of accounting described
4. audit, agreed-upon procedures
5. criteria, COSO
6. tests of controls, objectives and limitations
7. customer's, customer auditor's, reference
8. financial forecasts, financial projections
9. timely, concurrently
10. scope, GAAS
11. disclaimer, unaudited
12. express an opinion, assurance
13. conformity with GAAP, all disclosures, independent
14. imposed restrictions, higher level of assurance
15. preparers, continuing accountant

MULTIPLE CHOICE QUESTIONS

1. b	5. c	9. a	13. a	17. d
2. a	6. a	10. d	14. c	18. a
3. d	7. b	11. a	15. b	19. a
4. d	8. c	12. b	16. d	20. c

Chapter 22

Internal, Operational, and Governmental Auditing

A. CHAPTER OUTLINE

I. Internal Auditing

    A. Internal Auditing Defined

    B. Evolution of Internal Auditing

    C. Objectives and Scope

    D. Practice Standards

        1. Independence

        2. Professional Proficiency

        3. Scope of Work

        4. Performance of Audit Work

        5. Management of the Internal Auditing Department

    E. Relationship with External Auditors

II. Operational Auditing

    A. Operational Auditing Defined

    B. Phases of an Operational Audit

        1. Select Auditee

        2. Plan Audit

        3. Perform Audit

        4. Report Findings

        5. Perform Follow-Up

    C. Independent Public Accountant Involvement and Standards

III. Governmental Auditing

    A. Types of Government Audits

    B. Generally Accepted Government Auditing Standards (GAGAS)

        1. General Standards

B. CHAPTER HIGHLIGHTS

1. Internal auditing is an independent appraisal function established within an organization to examine and evaluate its activities as a service to the organization. It has evolved into a **highly professional activity** with a reporting responsibility directly to the board of directors or its audit committee.

2. The national association of internal auditors is the **Institute of Internal Auditing (IIA)**. Its functions include (a) administering the Certificate of Internal Auditor's Examination, (b) establishing practice standards, and (c) establishing a code of ethics.

3. The **scope** of internal auditing includes:
    a. Reviewing the reliability and integrity of financial and operating information and the means used to identify, measure, classify, and report such information.
    b. Reviewing the systems established to ensure compliance with those policies, plans, procedures, laws, and regulations which could have a significant impact on operations and reports, and determining whether the organization is in compliance.
    c. Reviewing the means of safeguarding assets and, as appropriate, verifying the existence of such assets.
    d. Appraising the economy and efficiency with which resources are employed.
    e. Reviewing operations or programs to ascertain whether results are consistent with established objectives and goals and whether the operations or programs are being carried out as planned.

4. The IIA has established **practice standards** for the professional practice of internal auditing. There are five general standards:
    a. **Independence**. Internal auditors should be independent of the activities they audit.
    b. **Professional Proficiency**. Internal audits should be performed with proficiency and due professional care.
    c. **Scope of Work.** The scope of the internal audit should encompass the examination and evaluation of the adequacy and effectiveness of the organization's system of internal control and the quality of performance in carrying out assigned responsibilities.
    d. **Performance of Audit Work**. Audit work should include planning the audit, examining and evaluating information, communicating results, and following up.
    e. **Management of the Internal Auditing Department**. The director of internal auditing should properly manage the internal auditing department.

5. Each general standard is supported by two or more specific standards, and the specific standards are accompanied by **guidelines**. There are similarities between the general and specific IIA standards and AICPA GAAS.

6. The IIA's concept of **independence differs from the AICPA's** concept. The internal auditor achieves independence through organizational status and objectivity.

7. The **specific standards** pertain to:
    a. Professional proficiency applies to both the internal auditing department and to the internal auditor.

b. Scope of work includes compliance and operational audits as well as financial audits.
c. Following up requires the internal auditor to assess the appropriateness of the action taken on reported audit findings and recommendations.

8. There is usually a **close relationship** between internal auditors and the entity's independent auditors. However, the following differences exist between the two types of auditors:

	Internal Auditors	**External Auditors**
Employer	Companies and governmental units	CPA firms
National Organization	Institute of Internal Auditors (IIA)	American Institute of Certified Public Accountants (AICPA)
Certifying designation	Certified Internal Auditor (CIA)	Certified Public Accountant (CPA)
License to practice	No	Yes
Primary responsibility	To board of directors	To third parties
Scope of audits	All activities of an organization	Primarily financial statements

9. **Operational auditing** is a systematic process of evaluating an organization's effectiveness, efficiency, and economy of operations under management's control and reporting to appropriate persons the results of the evaluation along with recommendations for improvement.

10. The **phases of an operational audit** are (a) select auditee, (b) plan audit, (c) perform the audit, (d) report findings to management, and (e) perform follow-up.

11. In **selecting the auditee** an understanding of potential auditees is obtained by:
a. Reviewing background file data on each auditee.
b. Touring the auditee's facilities to ascertain how it accomplishes its objectives.
c. Studying relevant documentation about the auditee's operations such as policies and procedures manuals, flowcharts, performance and quality control standards, and job descriptions.
d. Interviewing the manager of the activity about specific problem areas (often called the entry interview).

  e. Applying analytical procedures to identify trends and unusual relationships.

  f. Conducting mini audit probes (or tests) to confirm or clarify the auditor's understanding of potential problems.

12. **Audit planning** is critical because of the diversity of operational audits. Planning includes (a) developing an audit program, (b) selecting the audit team, and (c) scheduling the work.

13. In **performing the audit**, the auditor searches for facts pertaining to the problems identified in the auditee. The auditor relies primarily on inquiry and observation in making the audit, but may also use analysis.

14. The auditor does not use standard language in **reporting the findings**. The report should contain:

  a. A statement of the objectives and scope of the audit.

  b. A general description of the work done in the audit.

  c. A summary of the findings.

  d. Recommendations for improvement.

  e. Comments of the auditee.

15. **Performing follow-up** is an important phase of an operational audit. The failure of the auditor to receive an appropriate response should be communicated to senior management.

16. When independent public accountants perform operational audits they should follow the **practice standards for MAS engagements established by the AICPA** and the standards specified in Rule 201 - General Standards in the AICPA's Code of Professional Conduct.

17. Government audits are classified into two types:

  a. **Financial statement audits** which include financial statement audits and financial related audits.

  b. **Performance audits** which include economy and efficiency and program audits.

18. The U.S. **General Accounting Office (GAO)** establishes audit standards, called **generally accepted government auditing standards (GAGAS).**

  a. GAGAS are classified into five categories: (1) general, (2) field work-financial audits, (3) reporting-financial audits, (4) field work-performance audits, and (5) reporting-performance audits.

  b. GAGAS specifically include the GAAS of field work and reporting, and the general category of GAGAS is similar to the general category of GAAS.

19. The **general category of GAGAS** pertains primarily to the **qualifications of the auditor**. There are four specific standards: (a) qualifications, (b) independence, (c) due professional care, and (d) quality control.

20. The **field work standards for financial audits** consist of:

  a. The AICPA field work standards by incorporation but without restating them, and

  b. Supplemental standards pertaining to planning and evidence (working papers).

21. The **reporting standards for financial audits** include supplemental standards pertaining to:
    a. Statement on auditing standards.
    b. Report on compliance.
    c. Report on internal controls.
    d. Reporting on financial related audits.
    e. Privileged and confidential information.
    f. Report distribution.

22. Independent public accountants must **state in their report** that they have **followed both GAGAS and GAAS** in performing the audit.

23. The **third additional reporting standard** requires that either the auditors' reports on financial statements or a separate report referred to therein include the **same information on irregularities and illegal acts that is reported to audit committees under AICPA** standards. The standard also requires auditors to report irregularities or illegal acts to external parties when (1) the auditee is required to report such events by law or regulation, and (2) an auditee who receives assistance from a governmental agency fails to report an irregularity or illegal act involving the assistance.

24. The third additional reporting standard also requires that auditors' reports on financial statements to either **include a report on internal control** or refer to a separate report thereon. In the report, the auditor (1) identifies categories of controls, (2) describes the scope of work, and (3) reports deficiencies that represent *reportable conditions* under AICPA standards.

25. The **objectives of the Single Audit Act** are to:
    a. Improve the financial management of state and local governments with respect to federal financial assistance programs.
    b. Establish uniform requirements for audits of federal financial assistance provided to state and local governments.
    c. Promote the efficient and effective use of audit resources.
    d. Ensure that federal departments and agencies, to the maximum extent practicable, rely on and use audit work done pursuant to the requirements of the Single Audit Act.

26. The Single Audit Act provides that any state or local government receiving **$100,000 or more in federal financial assistance**, either directly from a federal agency or indirectly through another state or local government in any fiscal year, **must have an annual single audit pursuant to the Act**. **Major programs** and **nonmajor programs** are delineated by expenditure thresholds, and a **cognizant (federal) agency** is designated to monitor compliance with the Act.

27. The **auditor's responsibilities under the Act** requires the auditor to determine whether:
    a. The financial statements of the government, department, agency, or establishment present fairly its financial position and the results of its financial operations in accordance with GAAS and GAGAS.
    b. The organization has internal controls to provide reasonable assurance that it is in compliance with applicable laws and regulations that may have a material impact on the financial statements.

    c. The organization has internal controls to provide reasonable assurance that it is managing federal financial assistance programs in compliance with applicable laws and regulations.

    d. The organization has complied with laws, regulations and specific requirements applicable to each major and nonmajor federal financial assistance program.

28. There are **nine general requirements** with which all federal financial recipients must comply. They involve significant national policies and include prohibitions against partisan political activity, civil rights violations, violating work conditions and wage requirements, drug-free work environment requirements, violation of federal cost principles, violation of federal reporting requirements.

29. In **testing compliance with general requirements**, the auditor should:
    a. Follow guidance contained in the *OMB Compliance Supplement*.
    b. Report in the form of procedures and findings, rather than an opinion.

30. **Testing compliance with specific requirements** pertains to such matters as the types of service allowed, the eligibility of recipients, and matching contributions by recipients, and other special tests and provisions.
    a. The auditor should use the previously described risk concepts in evaluating compliance with requirements applicable to each program.
    c. The auditor's report on compliance with specific requirements is similar to the auditor's opinion (i.e., standard report, qualified, adverse, or disclaimer). Any instances of noncompliance are reported in a schedule of findings and questioned costs.

31. **Compliance auditing of nonmajor programs** is limited to transactions selected by the auditor.
    a. Each selected transaction should be tested for compliance with the specific requirements applicable to the individual transaction.
    b. The auditor's report on compliance may be issued separately or be combined with the report on major programs.

C. TRUE OR FALSE STATEMENTS

Indicate in the space provided whether each of the following statements is true or false.

_____   1. Internal auditing is an independent appraisal function established within an organization as a service to the organization.

_____   2. The national association of internal auditors is the Institute of Certified Internal Auditors (ICIA).

_____   3. The scope of internal auditing includes reviewing the means of safeguarding assets.

_____   4. The Institute of Internal Auditors has established practice standards for the professional practice of internal auditing.

_____ 5. The independence standard for internal auditing states that internal auditors should be independent of the companies they audit.

_____ 6. The general standards include both scope of work and performance of work standards.

_____ 7. The specific standards pertaining to professional proficiency apply only to the director of internal auditing.

_____ 8. In meeting the specific standard of following up, the auditor is expected to assess the action taken by the auditee.

_____ 9. The relationship between internal auditors and the entity's external auditors is usually remote.

_____ 10. The reporting responsibility of internal auditors is basically the same as for external auditors.

_____ 11. Operational auditing consists of a systematic process of evaluating an organization's effectiveness, efficiency, and economy of operations.

_____ 12. The phases of an operational audit are the same as in a financial statement audit.

_____ 13. The objective in selecting the auditee is to identify the activities that have the highest audit potential.

_____ 14. The operational audit report may include comments by the auditee.

_____ 15. The U.S. General Accounting Office establishes generally accepted government auditing standards (GAGAS).

_____ 16. GAGAS are classified into four categories.

_____ 17. The general category of GAGAS pertains primarily to the independence of the auditor.

_____ 18. The AICPA field work standards are included in the field work standards for governmental financial audits by incorporation.

_____ 19. Independent public accountants must state in their report that they have followed both GAGAS and GAAS in performing a governmental audit.

_____ 20. The Single Audit Act requires that each state or local government should have an annual audit.

_____ 21. In compliance auditing of major federal assistance programs, the auditor must only test specific requirements.

_____ 22. Specific requirements pertain to significant national policy matters.

_____ 23. The failure of an organization to comply with general requirements will result in a qualified or adverse opinion.

_____ 24. Compliance auditing of nonmajor programs is limited to transactions selected by the auditor.

_____ 25. Any instances of noncompliance with specific requirements of federal financial assistance programs are noted in a schedule of findings and questioned costs accompanying the auditor's opinion.

D. COMPLETION STATEMENTS

Fill in the blanks with the word or words that correctly complete the following statements.

1. Internal auditing is an _____ function established within an organization to _____ and _____ its activities as a service to the organization.

2. The IIA's practice standards consist of _____ standards, _____ standards, and _____.

3. There are similarities between the IIA's _____ and the AICPA's _____.

4. The internal auditor achieves independence by meeting the specific standards of _____ and _____.

5. The general standard of professional proficiency states that internal audits should be performed with _____ and with _____ care.

6. The general standard of performance of audit work includes planning the audit, _____ information, _____ results, and _____.

7. The specific standards pertaining to scope of audit work include standards that apply to _____ audits, _____ audits, and _____ audits.

8. There usually is a close working relationship between an entity's _____ and its _____.

9. The phases of an operational audit that differ conceptually from a financial statement audit are _____ and _____.

10. The preliminary study made in selecting the auditee is a _____ process that results in a ranking of _____.

11. When independent public accountants perform operational audits, they should follow the AICPA's practice standards for _____ and applicable standards required in the AICPA's _____.

12. Government audits are classified into two types:_____ audits and _____ audits.

13. GAGAS for financial audits consist of _____ standards, _____ standards, and _____ standards.

14. One objective of the Single Audit Act includes improving the _____ management of state and local governments with respect to _____ programs.

15. In addition to reports required under GAGAS, the Single Audit Act requires the auditor to issue reports on a _____ of the entity's federal assistance programs, compliance with _____ and _____.

E. MULTIPLE CHOICE (All five-part questions are from the ICMA Examination)

Choose the best answer for each of the following questions and enter the identifying letter in the space provided.

_____   1. Because of the pervasive effects of laws and regulations on the financial statements of governmental units, an auditor should obtain written management representations acknowledging that management has:
a. Implemented internal control policies and procedures designed to detect all illegal acts.
b. Documented the procedures performed to evaluate the governmental unit's compliance with laws and regulations.
c. Identified and disclosed all laws and regulations that have a direct and material effect on its financial statements.
d. Reported all known illegal acts and material weaknesses in internal control structure to the funding agency or regulatory body.

_____   2. Kent is auditing an entity's compliance with requirements governing a major federal financial assistance program in accordance with the Single Audit Act. Kent detected noncompliance with requirements that have a material effect on that program. Kent's report on compliance should express a(an):
a. Unqualified opinion with a separate explanatory paragraph.
b. Qualified opinion or an adverse opinion.
c. Adverse opinion or a disclaimer of opinion.
d. Limited assurance on the items tested.

_____ 3. The GAO standards of reporting for governmental financial audits incorporate the AICPA standards of reporting and prescribe supplemental standards to satisfy the unique needs of governmental audits. Which of the following is a supplemental reporting standard for government financial audits?
    a. A written report on the auditor's understanding of the entity's internal control structure and assessment of control risk should be prepared.
    b. Material indications of illegal acts should be reported in a document with distribution restricted to senior officials of the entity audited.
    c. Instances of abuse, fraud, mismanagement, and waste should be reported to the organization with legal oversight authority over the entity audited.
    d. All privileged and confidential information discovered should be reported to the senior officials of the organization that arranged for the audit.

_____ 4. To provide for the greatest degree of independence in performing internal auditing functions, an internal auditor most likely should report to the:
    a. Financial vice president.
    b. Corporate controller.
    c. Board of directors.
    d. Corporate stockholders.

_____ 5. The Institute of Internal Auditors classifies its general practice standards pertaining to the competency and work of an internal auditor as:
    a. Professional proficiency, scope of work, and reporting.
    b. Scope of work, performance of audit work, and due professional care.
    c. Professional proficiency, scope of work, and performance of audit work.
    d. Performance of audit work, professional proficiency, and independence.

_____ 6. The circumstance which has had the most extensive impact on the internal audit function in terms of promoting its status within business organizations is the:
    a. Passage of the Securities Act of 1933.
    b. Codification of auditing standards and procedures issued by the American Institute of Certified Public Accountants.
    c. Passage of the Securities Exchange Act of 1934.
    d. Yale Express case.
    e. Passage of the Foreign Corrupt Practices Act of 1977.

_____ 7. The best description of the scope of internal auditing is that it encompasses:
    a. Primarily financial auditing.
    b. Primarily operational auditing.
    c. Primarily the safeguarding of assets and verifying the existence of such assets.
    d. Both financial and operational auditing.

_____ 8. According to the Standards, who is responsible for coordinating the internal and external audits of a company?
    a. Chairman of the audit committee of the board.
    b. Director of internal auditing.
    c. Senior management to whom the auditing department reports.
    d. Vice-president of finance.

_____ 9. A Certified Internal Auditor is in violation of the Code of Ethics when accepting a gift from a company employee unless the gift is:
   a. Small in dollar value.
   b. Approved by senior management.
   c. Reciprocated by the auditor.
   d. Reported as income.

_____ 10. When an internal auditor has completed an assignment but has discovered no deficiencies and can offer no substantial recommendations, a written report:
   a. Should be prepared and sent to the auditee.
   b. Should be prepared only if the auditee requests it.
   c. Should be prepared only for the internal auditor's supervisor.
   d. Should be prepared only for the internal auditor's files.
   e. Should not be prepared; an oral report should be made to the auditee.

_____ 11. A corporation maintains an internal audit department, the head of which reports directly to the president. Which of the following statements best describes the relationship between the internal auditors and an independent auditor?
   a. The independent auditor may not make use of internal auditors to provide direct assistance in performing any substantive tests or tests of controls.
   b. The independent auditor should consider the work performed by the internal auditors in determining the nature, timing and extent of his or her own auditing procedures.
   c. The independent auditor should coordinate work with that of the internal auditors to make certain that there is no duplication of tests or procedures.
   d. The independent auditor should avoid inspecting the work papers and reports of the internal auditors in order to avoid bias in the external audit.
   e. The independent auditor should give no consideration to the work performed by the internal auditors since their audit objectives are likely to differ considerably from those of the external audit.

_____ 12. To ensure adequate reporting status and effective lines of communication, it is appropriate for the head of internal auditing to report to an officer:
   a. Who has budgetary responsibility for the functions that will be audited.
   b. Who has experience as an internal auditor.
   c. Who has the responsibility for issuing written policies, procedures, and guidelines.
   d. Whose status is such that he or she can command prompt and proper consideration of the auditor's reports and recommendations.

_____ 13. From a modern internal auditing perspective, which of the following statements represents the most important benefit of an internal audit department to management?
   a. Assurance that published financial statements are correct.
   b. Assurance that fraudulent activities will be detected.
   c. Assurance that the organization is complying with legal requirements.
   d. Assurance that there is reasonable control over day-to-day operations.
   e. A reduction of external audit activities could be accomplished.

_____ 14. Which of the following contains the most distinct statement of internal auditing's obligation to serve the organization?
a. Standards for the Professional Practice of Internal Auditing.
b. Institute of Internal Auditors' Code of Ethics.
c. Certified Internal Auditor Code of Ethics.
d. Statement of Responsibilities of Internal Auditing.

_____ 15. An operational audit normally would be:
a. Performed by the external auditor.
b. Performed by a team consisting of equal numbers of external and internal auditors.
c. Initiated only when an operating division is experiencing an operating loss.
d. Initiated by internal auditors at the request of top management or the audit committee.
e. Avoided if a company is not experiencing operating problems.

_____ 16. The internal audit department of Slager Industries is performing an operational audit of the firm's electronic data processing (EDP) function. Which one of the following areas of investigation would be most appropriate in its operational audit?
a. A review of the EDP system owner's manual issued by the manufacturer.
b. A review of the EDP department's organization structure.
c. An examination of a random sample of work performed by keypunch operators.
d. A review of entries on the tape librarian's log.
e. A test to determine if the computer's processing controls are working properly.

_____ 17. Operational audits are directed at many activities within an organization. The primary purpose of an operational audit is usually to:
a. Resolve conflicts between management and first-level supervisors.
b. Render an opinion on the fairness of financial statements.
c. Foster independence from the external auditor.
d. Detect management fraud.
e. Assess performance.

_____ 18. A governmental audit may extend beyond an examination leading to the expression of an opinion on the fairness of financial presentation to include:

	Program results	Compliance	Economy & efficiency
a.	Yes	Yes	No
b.	Yes	Yes	Yes
c.	No	Yes	Yes
d.	Yes	No	Yes

_____ 19. A program-results audit of a government-sponsored assistance program would place emphasis on the:
a. Acquisition and utilization of materials, facilities, and personnel for the program.
b. Accuracy of financial statements and reporting requirements for the program.
c. Ability of the responsible department or agency to measure program effectiveness.
d. Identification of potential cost savings for the program.

_____ 20. A CPA has performed an audit of the general purpose financial statements of Big City. The audit scope included the additional requirements of the Single Audit Act. When reporting on Big City's internal controls used in administering a federal financial assistance program, the CPA should:

    a. Communicate those weaknesses that are material in relation to the general purpose financial statements.

    b. Express an opinion on the systems used to administer major federal financial assistance programs and express negative assurance on the systems used to administer nonmajor federal financial assistance programs.

    c. Communicate those weaknesses that are material in relation to the federal financial assistance program.

    d. Express negative assurance on the systems used to administer major federal financial assistance programs and express no opinion on the systems used to administer nonmajor federal financial assistance programs.

SOLUTIONS

TRUE OR FALSE STATEMENTS

1. True	10. False	18. True
2. False	11. True	19. True
3. True	12. False	20. False
4. True	13. True	21. False
5. False	14. True	22. False
6. True	15. True	23. False
7. False	16 True	24. True
8. True	17. False	25. False
9. False		

COMPLETION STATEMENTS

1. independent appraisal, examine, evaluate
2. general, specific, guidelines
3. general standards, GAAS
4. organizational status, objectivity
5. proficiency, due professional
6. examining and evaluating, communicating, following up
7. financial statement, compliance, operational
8. internal auditors, external auditors
9. selecting the auditee, performing follow up
10. screening, potential auditees
11. MAS engagements, Code of Professional Conduct
12. financial statement, performance
13. general, field work, reporting
14. financial, federal financial assistance
15. supplementary schedule, laws and regulations, internal control

MULTIPLE CHOICE QUESTIONS

1. c	5. c	9. a	13. d	17. e
2. b	6. e	10. a	14. d	18. b
3. a	7. d	11. b	15. d	19. c
4. c	8. b	12. d	16. b	20. c

Chapter 23

The Independent Accountant and the Securities and Exchange Commission

A. CHAPTER OUTLINE

I. Securities and Exchange Commission

    A. Authority of the SEC

    B. Organization of the SEC

        1. Division of Corporation Finance

        2. Office of the Chief Accountant

II. Reporting and Registration Requirements

    A. Integrated Disclosure System

    B. Electronic Data Gathering, Analysis, and Retrieval System

    C. Types of Accounting Pronouncements

        1. Regulation S-X

        2. Regulation S-K

        3. Regulation S-T

        4. Financial Reporting Releases (FRRs)

        5. Staff Accounting Bulletins (SABs)

    D. Qualifications of Independent Accountants

    E. Requirements for Accountants' Reports

    F. Registration of Securities

        1. Review of Registration Statements

        2. Registration Process

III. Securities Act of 1933

    A. Registration Under the 1933 Act

        1. Business Disclosures

        2. Financial Statements

        3. Selected Financial Data

B. CHAPTER HIGHLIGHTS

1. The authority of the **Securities and Exchange Commission (SEC)** extends to the **offer and initial sale of securities** to the public and to the **subsequent trading** of such securities on national exchange and over-the-counter markets.

2. The SEC is headed by a **five-person commission** and its professional staff is organized into five divisions and numerous offices. Those that relate most directly to the independent accountant include (a) the Division of Corporation Finance, and (b) the Office of the Chief Accountant.

3. **The Division of Corporation Finance** is responsible for preventing (a) fraudulent offerings of securities to the public and (b) the distribution of incomplete, false, or misleading information pertaining to security offerings. This division:
    a. Assists the Commission in the establishment of standards of economic and financial information to be included in documents filed with the SEC.
    b. Enforces adherence to such standards by issuers, underwriters, and others with respect to securities or in over-the-counter markets by reviewing and processing registration statements and periodic reports under the applicable securities acts.
    c. Prescribes and enforces the information to be included in proxy solicitations.
    d. Administers the disclosure requirements of the federal securities laws.
    e. Prepares Staff Accounting Bulletins (SABs) in conjunction with the Office of the Chief Accountant.

4. The **chief accountant** is the SEC's principal expert adviser on accounting and auditing matters. The chief accountant's duties include:
    a. Carrying out SEC policy on accounting principles and the form and content of financial statements filed with it.
    b. Participating in administrative and court proceedings involving accounting and auditing matters.
    c. Recommending the taking of disciplinary action against accountants under the SEC's Rules of Practice.
    d. Preparing Financial Reporting Releases (FRRs).
    e. Issuing Accounting and Auditing Enforcement Releases (AAERs). Issuing SABs in conjunction with the Division of Corporation Finance.

5. The SEC has the authority to **prescribe accounting and reporting requirements** for companies under its jurisdiction. Throughout its history, however, the SEC has cooperated with the private sector in the development of GAAP, and it has indicated that it intends to continue this policy.

6. The **integrated disclosure system** requires the following standard package of information for all SEC forms:
    a. Audited consolidated financial statements.
    b. A five-year summary of selected financial data.

    c. A management discussion and analysis of the company's financial condition and results of operations.

    d. Market price and dividend information on the company's common stock and related security holder matters.

7. The SEC issues **five types of accounting-related pronouncements** for the guidance of registrants and independent accountants: Regulation S-X, Regulation S-K, Regulation S-T FRR, and SABs.

    a. Regulation S-X is the principal accounting regulation.

    b. Regulation S-K is the principal disclosure regulation for nonfinancial statement or text information.

    c. Regulation S-T governs the phased-in mandated electronic filing of documents under EDGAR.

    d.. FRRs contain amendments to the rules and regulations.

    e. SABs are interpretations of rules and regulations.

8. **Financial Reporting Releases (FRR)** include:

    a. New disclosure requirements or specified accounting treatment for certain types of transactions.

    b. Opinions of the Commission on major accounting issues.

    c. Clarification of existing rules and regulations, such as the rule on independence.

9. **Regulation S-X** prescribes the **qualifications of accountants**, which include requirements concerning independence. The rules on independence are practically identical with the AICPA's Rules of Professional Conduct on independence.

10. Regulation S-X also sets forth **standards of reporting for accountant's reports**. These requirements consist of (a) technical requirements, (b) representations as to the audit, (c) opinion to be expressed, and (d) exceptions. These requirements are in substance essentially the same as the reporting standards described in Chapters 20 and 21.

11. The **review of a registration statement** is made in the Division of Corporation Finance. If a registration is selected for review, the review may be complete or limited. A complete review involves an examination of the statement by a team consisting of a financial analyst, an attorney, and an accountant.

12. The **Securities Act of 1933** has two basic objectives:

    a. To provide investors with material financial and other information concerning securities offered for public sale.

    b. To prohibit misrepresentation, deceit, and other fraudulent acts and practices in the sale of securities generally (whether or not required to be registered).

13. A registration statement under the 1933 Act consists of two parts: **a prospectus and other detailed information**. A prospectus is a separate booklet or pamphlet given to prospective purchasers of the security that describes the company and the securities offered. This part of the registration statement includes the prescribed financial statements. The prospectus includes the information that is to be presented to all prospective investors. Other detailed information pertains to ancillary data that are only filed with the SEC.

14. The **primary registration forms under the 1933 Act** are Forms S-1, S-2, S-3, and S-4. Form S1 is the most commonly used form.

15. The **principal financial information required under Form S-1** consists of (a) business disclosures, (b) financial statements, (c) selected financial data, and (d) management's discussion and analysis of financial condition and results of operations.

16. The **financial statements in Form S-1** must be presented for the issuing company in one of the following forms:
    a. Financial statements for the company itself, if it has no subsidiaries which must be consolidated.
    b. Consolidated financial statements only, unless it is necessary to include "separate parent company" statements on a supplemental schedule.

17. The **financial statements required for a registration statement** include: (a) audited balance sheets as of the end of each of the two preceding fiscal years, (b) audited statements of income, retained earnings, and cash flows for three years, (c) interim financial data from the date of the balance sheet to within 135 days of the date of filing if the most recent audited financial statements do not fall within this period.

18. The **accountants major responsibilities** under the 1933 Act are to:
    a. Make an audit of the financial statements in accordance with GAAS.
    b. Read any unaudited financial statements included therein for matters that might require disclosure in the audited financial statements.
    c. Read the entire registration statement for data that may be materially inconsistent with the financial statements or be a material misstatement of fact.
    d. Perform a subsequent events review up to the effective date of the registration statement.
    e. Issue a comfort letter to underwriters.

19. The **subsequent events review** consists of a reasonable investigation up to the effective date of the registration statement. The **S-1 review** consists of performing the subsequent events procedures described in Chapter 19. In addition, the accountant should:
    a. Read the entire prospectus and other pertinent parts of the registration statement.
    b. Inquire of and obtain written confirmation from officers and other executives having responsibility for financial and accounting matters as to whether there have occurred any events other than those reflected or disclosed in the registration statement which, in the officers' or other executives' opinions, have a material effect on the audited financial statements included therein or which should be disclosed in order to keep those statements from being misleading.

20. **Letters for underwriters** are designed to give comfort (assurance) to underwriters that the financial and accounting data not covered by the independent accountant's opinion on the audited financial statements included in a prospectus are (a) in compliance with the Securities Act of 1933 and (b) in conformity with GAAP, consistently applied.

21. A **comfort letter** generally will refer to one or more of the following:
    a. The independence of the accountants.
    b. Compliance as to form in all material respects of the audited financial statements and schedules with the applicable accounting requirements of the Act and the published rules and regulations thereunder.
    c. Unaudited financial statements or condensed financial statements in the registration statement.
    d. Changes in selected financial statement items during a period subsequent to the date and period of the latest financial statements in the registration statement.
    e. Tables, statistics, and other financial information in the registration statements.

22. **Accountant's reports** under the 1933 Act consist of (a) a report on the audited financial statements and (b) the accountant's consent to the use of his or her name as an expert.

23. The **Securities Exchange Act of 1934** provides for both the registration of securities and the filing of annual and other periodic reports to keep current the data in the original filing.

24. **Form 10**, which is the most common registration form under the 1934 Act, requires the same financial information as Form S-1, except that no interim financial data are required.

25. **Form 10-K** is the general report form used in annual reporting. The requirements under this form for audited financial statements, selected financial data, and management's discussion and analysis are the same as under 1933 Act filings.

26. **Form 10-Q** requires quarterly reporting to the SEC on (a) interim financial information and (b) the preferability of changes in GAAP.

27. **Form 8-K**, which is a special reporting form, requires disclosure of certain material corporate events, such as a change in the company's independent accountants.

28. The SEC may **initiate legal action and impose sanctions against independent accountants** through administrative proceedings for violations of the securities laws.

29. **Enforcement actions taken by the SEC** against accountants are published in Accounting and Auditing Enforcement Releases (**AAERs**).

30. Under **Rule 2(e)**, the SEC may disqualify and deny, temporarily or permanently, an accountant's privilege of appearing or practicing before it.

C. TRUE OR FALSE STATEMENTS

Indicate in the space provided whether each of the following statements is true or false.

_____ 1. The SEC is an independent federal regulatory agency which administers the federal securities acts and reports directly to the President of the United States.

_____ 2. The authority of the SEC extends to the offer and initial sale, but not to the subsequent trading, of securities on national and over-the-counter markets.

_____ 3. The SEC is headed by a five-person commission that does not include the chief accountant.

_____ 4. The SEC evaluates the merit of a security in a registration statement.

_____ 5. The Division of Corporation Finance is responsible for preventing fraudulent offerings of securities to the public.

_____ 6. One of the specific responsibilities of the Division of Corporation Finance is to assist in the preparation of Staff Accounting Bulletins (SABs).

_____ 7. The chief accountant is not the SEC's principal expert advisor on accounting and auditing matters.

_____ 8. The integrated disclosure system requires a standard package of information which includes audited consolidated financial statements and a five-year summary of selected financial data.

_____ 9. The accounting provisions of Regulation S-X usually parallel generally accepted accounting principles.

_____ 10. Regulation S-K prescribes disclosure requirements for nonfinancial statement information.

_____ 11. Financial Reporting Releases (FRR) include opinions of the Commission on SEC accounting rules and on disciplinary actions against accountants.

_____ 12. The SEC's rules on independence are essentially the same as the AICPA's Rules of Professional Conduct on independence.

_____ 13. Reviews of registration statements are made by the Office of the Chief Accountant.

_____ 14. The prospectus of a registration statement does not contain prescribed financial statements.

_____ 15. In a registration statement, a company may include forecasts or other forward looking financial information.

_____ 16. A subsequent events review (S-1) consists of a reasonable investigation of events up to the effective date of the registration statement.

_____ 17. The procedures performed in a comfort letter engagement are established by the independent accountant.

_____ 18. The comfort letter generally will not include a statement on the independence of the accountant.

_____ 19. The accountant's consent requires a reasonable investigation which cannot be accomplished short of an audit.

_____ 20. The financial information required in a registration under the 1934 Act differs significantly from the information required in a 1933 Act registration.

_____ 21. Interim information filed quarterly with the SEC must either be audited or reviewed by an independent accountant.

_____ 22. The special reporting requirements of the SEC do not require the accountant to indicate approval of changes in the registrant's independent accountant.

_____ 23. The SEC has the authority to impose sanctions against independent accountants through injunctive proceedings.

_____ 24. The SEC does not believe that ordinary negligence is sufficient to support an injunctive action in a court of law.

_____ 25. Under Administrative Rule 2(e), the SEC may disqualify and deny an accountant's privilege of practicing before it.

D. COMPLETION STATEMENTS

Fill in the blanks with the word or words that correctly complete the following statements.

1. The SEC is headed by a _____ appointed by the _____.

2. The SEC has the authority to prescribe the _____ requirements for companies under its _____.

3. The independent accountant's involvement with the SEC is usually through the Division of _____ and the Office of the _____.

4. In addition to audited financial statements the SEC's integrated disclosure system requires a _____ of selected financial data and a _____ by management.

5. Features of the integrated disclosure system include incorporation of information by _____ and _____ reporting.

6. Regulation S-X is the principal _____ regulation, and amendments to Regulation S-X are made through the issuance of _____.

7. Regulation S-K prescribes the _____ requirements for _____ or text information.

8. In addition to Regulations S-X and S-K the major accounting pronouncements of the SEC are _____, _____, and _____.

9. To amend existing rules and to issue new regulations pertaining to accounting and auditing matters, the _____ issues _____.

10. Regulation S-X prescribes the _____ for accountants and the reporting standards for the _____.

11. The Securities Act of 1933 is known as the _____ law; the Securities Exchange Act of 1934 is known as the _____ act.

12. A registration statement consists of two parts: (a) a _____ and (b) _____.

13. The form most widely used in a 1934 Act registration is _____ ; the form used in annual reporting is _____.

14. Quarterly reporting Form 10-Q contains two major accounting requirements: (a) _____ and (b) _____.

15. Enforcement of the securities acts is made through either _____ or _____ proceedings.

E. MULTIPLE CHOICE (All five part questions are from the ICMA Examination)

Choose the best answer for each of the following questions and enter the identifying letter in the space provided.

_____ 1. The registration of a security under the Securities Act of 1933 provides an investor with:
   a. A guarantee by the SEC that the facts contained in the registration statement are accurate.
   b. An assurance against loss resulting from purchasing the security.
   c. Information on the principal purpose for which the offering's proceeds will be used.
   d. Information on the issuing corporation's trade secrets.

_____ 2. The Securities and Exchange Commission has authority to:
   a. Prescribe specific auditing procedures to detect fraud concerning inventories and accounts receivable of companies engaged in interstate commerce.
   b. Deny lack of privity as a defense in third-party actions for gross negligence against the auditors of public companies.

    c. Determine accounting principles for the purpose of financial reporting by companies offering securities to the public.

    d. Require a change of auditors of governmental entities after a given period of years as a means of ensuring auditor independence.

_____ 3. When an independent audit report is incorporated by reference in an SEC registration statement, a prospectus that includes a statement about the independent accountant's involvement should refer to the independent accountant as:

    a. Auditor of the financial reports.

    b. Management's designate before the SEC.

    c. Certified preparer of the report.

    d. Expert in auditing and accounting.

_____ 4. The form and content for financial statements filed with the Securities and Exchange Commission are specified in:

    a. SEC Financial Reporting Releases.

    b. SEC Regulation S-X.

    c. The statements of the Financial Accounting Standards Board.

    d. The Securities Acts of 1933 and 1934.

    e. The Securities Acts Amendments of 1964.

_____ 5. The SEC prescribes certain qualifications for accountants before it will accept their certification of financial reports. Which one of the following qualifications has been prescribed by the SEC?

    a. The CPA must be from a regional or national firm of CPAs.

    b. The CPA must be independent of the management of the filing company.

    c. The CPA must be in practice a minimum of five years.

    d. The CPA must have audited the filing company for each of the preceding two years.

    e. The CPA must have legal counsel.

_____ 6. Financial Reporting Releases (FRR) and Staff Accounting Bulletins (SABs) are two pronouncements issued by the Securities and Exchange Commission. FRRs and SABs differ in that:

    a. FRRs are part of the 1934 Securities Exchange Act while SABs are not part of that Act.

    b. SABs represent official rules of the Commission while FRRs do not.

    c. SABs pertain to the 1933 Securities Act while FRRs pertain to the 1934 Securities Exchange Act.

    d. SABs represent amendments to Regulation S-X while FRRs do not represent such amendments.

    e. FRRs represent requirements applicable to the form and content of financial statements filed with the SEC while SABs represent accounting interpretations followed by the SEC.

_____ 7. Two interesting and important topics concerning the Securities and Exchange Commission are the role the commission plays in the development of accounting principles and the impact the SEC has had and will continue to have on the accounting profession and business in general. Which of the following statements concerning the SEC's authority relative to accounting practice is false?

a. The SEC has the statutory authority to regulate and to prescribe the form and content of financial statements and other reports it receives.

b. Regulation S-X of the SEC is the principal source relating to the form and content of financial statements to be included in registration statements and financial reports filed with the Commission.

c. The SEC does not regard FASB Statements on Accounting Standards as GAAP.

d. If the Commission disagrees with some presentation in the registrant's financial statements but the principles used by the registrant have substantial authoritative support, the SEC often will accept footnotes to the statements in lieu of correcting the statements to the SEC view, provided the SEC has not previously expressed its opinion on the matter in published material.

e. The SEC has reserved the right to rule against a registrant even if the registrant follows principles having substantial authoritative support, as well as to determine which accounting principles have substantial authoritative support.

_____ 8. The following statements pertain to letters for underwriters. Which of the following statements is false?

a. Obtaining a comfort letter from the independent accountants is one action taken by underwriters in establishing a due diligence defense against possible legal claims under the Act.

b. A comfort letter engagement involves a limited review rather than an audit.

c. In a comfort letter engagement, the underwriter specifies the limited review procedures to be performed.

d. The accountant's conclusions are expressed in the form of negative assurance.

e. A comfort letter is required under securities acts.

_____ 9. Regulations S-X and S-K are two pronouncements issued by the SEC. These publications differ in that:

a. Regulation S-X relates to interpretations of accounting rules and Regulation SK relates to disclosure rules.

b. Regulation S-X represents the official accounting rules and Regulation S-K represents the official disclosure rules of the SEC for nonfinancial accounting data.

c. Regulation S-X represents the official disclosure rules and Regulation S-K is the interpretation of such rules.

d. Regulation S-X is issued by the chief accountant whereas Regulation S-K is issued by the office of the legal counsel.

e. Regulation S-X represents the official accounting rules of the SEC and Regulation S-K represents amendments of such rules.

_____ 10. Sanctions under administrative proceedings by the SEC may include all but one of the following:
   a. Disqualify an accountant from practicing before the Commission.
   b. Deny, temporarily or permanently, an accountant the privilege of practicing before the Commission.
   c. Suspend an accountant from appearing or practicing before it.
   d. Impose a mandatory continuing education program on an accountant.
   e. Enjoin an accountant from future violations of the securities acts.

_____ 11. An accountant's involvement in a 1933 Act registration includes all of the following except:
   a. Reading unaudited financial statements included therein.
   b. Reading the entire registration statement.
   c. Making an audit of financial statements in accordance with GAAS.
   d. Making a subsequent events review following the effective date of the registration statement.
   e. Issuing a comfort letter to underwriters.

_____ 12. All but one of the following statements concerning the chief accountant is true.
   a. Carries out SEC policy on accounting principles.
   b. Has a fixed term of office.
   c. Prepares Financial Reporting Releases (FRRs).
   d. Directs administrative policy pertaining to accounting and auditing matters.
   e. Consults and rules on accounting questions from registrants and independent accountants.

_____ 13. The underlying concept of the Securities and Exchange Commissions's integrated disclosure program, which took effect for fiscal years ending after December 15, 1980, recognizes:
   a. The need for more detailed regulatory requirements to maintain separate generally accepted accounting principles and SEC disclosures.
   b. That no basic information can be described as common to the annual report and the 10-K
   c. The efficient capital markets concept (i.e., widely followed companies produce information for the public in various forms resulting in less need for a specific disclosure format).
   d. Recent actions to provide oversight of the SEC by the senior technical committees of professional organizations.
   e. The elimination of the need for an unqualified auditor's opinion on financial statements filed with the SEC.

_____ 14. Consolidated financial statements filed by ongoing companies with the SEC under the integrated disclosure requirements should include an:
   a. Audited balance sheet for the three most recent fiscal years.
   b. Audited balance sheet, income statement and statement of changes in cash flows for each of the two most recent fiscal years.

c. Audited current year-end balance sheet only.

d. Audited balance sheet for the two most recent fiscal years and statements of income and cash flows for the three most recent fiscal years.

e. External auditor's opinion on current fiscal year financial statements only.

_____ 15. The SEC integrated disclosure of financial information sets forth criteria for conditions for "Management Discussion and Analysis of Financial Conditions and Results of Operations." One of these criteria is that:

a. Forward looking information is encouraged but not required to be disclosed.

b. A discussion of financial conditions for the most recent seven fiscal years be included.

c. Information on the effects of inflation is to be provided only when it has a significant effect on the financial statements.

d. An analysis of income from foreign operations be included even if such operations are not material to the results of the firm.

e. Identification of all equity security investments in defense contracts and oil and gas subsidiaries be included whether or not such investments are material to the overall financial statements and operations.

_____ 16. Under the integrated reporting rules of the SEC, "Selected Financial Data" are required in Form 10-K, the annual shareholders' report, and many 1933 Act filings. These data should be for the period of at least the:

a. Current year and preceding year, or life of the registrant and predecessors if the company has been in existence less than two years.

b. Current year only.

c. Current year and two preceding years, or life of the registrant and predecessors if the company has been in existence less than three years.

d. Current year and four preceding years, or life of the registrant and predecessors if the company has been in existence less than five years.

e. Current year and three preceding years, or life of the registrant and predecessors if the company has been in existence less than four years.

_____ 17. The form required by the SEC in annual reporting under the 1934 Act is:

a. Form 10.

b. Form 10-K

c. Form 8-K

d. Form 10-Q.

e. None of the above.

_____ 18. Comfort letters are ordinarily signed by the:

a. Independent auditor.

b. Client.

c. Client's lawyer.

d. Internal auditor.

_____ 19. A significant event affecting a company registered under the Securities and Exchange Act of 1934 should be reported on:
   a. Form 10-K
   b. Form 10-Q.
   c. Form S-1.
   d. Form 8-K
   e. Form 11-K

_____ 20. Nonfinancial statement disclosures are specified in:
   a. Regulation S-K
   b. Financial Reporting Releases.
   c. Staff Accounting Bulletins.
   d. Accounting and Auditing Enforcement Releases.
   e. Regulation S-X.

SOLUTIONS

TRUE OR FALSE STATEMENTS

1. False	10. True	18. False
2. False	11. False	19. True
3. True	12. True	20. False
4. False	13. False	21. False
5. True	14. False	22. True
6. True	15. True	23. False
7. False	16 True	24. False
8. True	17. False	25. True
9. True		

COMPLETION STATEMENTS

1. five-person commission, President of the United States
2. accounting and reporting, jurisdiction
3. Corporation Finance, Chief Accountant
4. five-year summary, discussion and analysis
5. reference, continuous
6. accounting, Financial Reporting Releases (FRRs)
7. disclosure, nonfinancial
8. Regulation S-T, Financial Reporting Releases (FRRs), Staff Accounting Bulletins (SABs)
9. Commission, Financial Reporting Releases (FRRs)
10. qualifications, accountant's report
11. truth in securities, continuous disclosure
12. prospectus, ancillary information
13. Form 10, Form 10-K
14. interim financial information, changes in accounting principles
15. injunctive, administrative

MULTIPLE CHOICE QUESTIONS

1. c	5. b	9. b	13. c	17. b
2. c	6. e	10. e	14. d	18. a
3. d	7. c	11. d	15. a	19. d
4. b	8. e	12. b	16. d	20. a

NOTES

NOTES

NOTES

NOTES

NOTES

NOTES

NOTES

NOTES

NOTES